Welsh Painters Talking

Welsh Painters Talking

to Tony Curtis

Foreword by
David Alston

Portraits by
Bernard Mitchell

seren

seren is the book imprint of
Poetry Wales Press Ltd
Wyndham Street, Bridgend,
CF31 1EF, Wales

A CIP record for this book is available at the British Library

ISBN 1-85411-200-7

The publisher works with the financial support of the Arts Council of Wales

The support of the Regional Research Fund Committee at the University of Glamorgan is gratefully acknowledged

Jacket Illustration:
'Running Away with the Hairdresser' by Kevin Sinnott
(oil on canvas, 160 x 216 cm, coll: National Museums & Galleries of Wales)

Welsh Painters Talking, an exhibition to coincide with this book took place at the National Museum & Gallery, Cardiff from 20 September to 26 October 1997

Printed in Plantin by WBC Book Manufacturers, Bridgend

CONTENTS

Acknowledgments

Thanks are due to Dr David Alston, Keeper of Art at the National Museums & Galleries of Wales, Cardiff, and curator of the accompanying exhibition; Bernard Mitchell for the photographs of the artists; Rachael Thomas for compiling the reference material on the artists; the Regional Research Fund Committee at the University of Glamorgan, under the Chairmanship of Dr David Adamson for supporting the research and production of this book; and those collectors who have generously allowed the reproduction of paintings. Martin Tinney, who represents many Welsh artists, deserves especial thianks for his continued help in the production of this book and the organisation of the accompanying exhibition.

The conversations with Charles Burton, Shani Rhys James and Arthur Giardelli have appeared in abbreviated form in *Planet*.

Foreword

There are few survey histories of art in Wales, let alone Welsh art, embracing its course over time or even its immediate past. The premises and viewpoints on to the culture adopted by such surveys as do exist have been called into question, whilst at the same time the paucity of such books, and the material they cover has been seen as symptomatic of an essentially non-visual culture. The present work does not pretend to be a survey – but it is a contribution of raw materials towards the manufacture of a more apposite cultural history and appears at a time of growing interest in both the contemporary scene and its roots in this closing century of discontinuities and ruptures.

Over several years a poet gets into conversation with a number of painters. A tape recorder is not an inhibit to their talk. The realisation that with several conversations 'in the bag', others shaping up and still others prompted by the thought of whom it might be important to get into conversation with, the idea of a book of collected conversations begins to form. The casual genesis of the present book belies the growing sense of purpose and conviction on the part of the interviewer and the sense of moment which the publication both creates and confirms. The resulting book documents how several succeeding generations of artists see themselves in a variously defined cultural context which in turn they both respond to and influence.

The interview is essentially a twentieth century presentational form. Spurred on by the advancing technologies of sound and visual recording, it has largely supplanted the memoir. As with many aspects of our century it replaces reflection with ostensible immediacy. It appears to guarantee matters of meaning and intentionality. A journal has recently been founded in Scotland – *Transcript* – whose chief editorial approach is recorded interviews with artists. Back in the nineteenth century the form the interview took was more often than not a set piece questionnaire as opposed to a discursive conversation. As such it was a sort of Salon game where personalities of the day gave their responses in a form which encouraged pithy formulations – a sort of shadow-boxing around the demand for honesty and the need for reserve. Proust, when quizzed "What is your ideal of happiness?" in one such questionnaire replied "Not, I am afraid, a very elevated one – I dare not say for I should be afraid of destroying it by putting it into words".

Of course, words are not a natural medium for painters. They are preoccupied with an articulacy which has little to do with putting into words. Indeed for their art, putting into words is the last thing they would want to do . . . for fear of destroying it. There are great contributions to critical discourse by artists in our century, often to some theoretical framework for what they are engaged in – but such pronouncements are rarely hypotheses to be tested in practice, they are more often an attempted distillation of thought stemming from practice. These rationalisations, manifestoes, proclamations by artists have helped class and categorise artistic production. The cultural historian in the modernist period could construct traditions, progressions, tendencies. Our present time is facing up to a more fragmentary sense of artistic activities and where they fit in. Idiosyncrasy, locality, individuality are reasserting themselves in the face of the homogenisation of cultures as a whole. The interview with the artist usefully puts the creator back into their activity, it can reassert the critical area of the preoccupations of any given painter. The reader gets an insight into the artist's divulged beliefs about what art is for them, what their aspirations for their own art might be. Understanding what somebody wanted or wants from their work, this mapping of the whole area of desire attached to the art work is crucial and not easily adduced. It might not be telling us what any resulting object in the world is, but it is informing us of the area which each artist's intentionality might see the work as occupying. Crucially too, the interview with the artist strongly conveys to us the position of the artist as the first viewer of their work in both its making and completion. A book of interviews with painters is a good contribution to art history by and from artists themselves as opposed to one formed by social historians, aesthetic philosophers, cultural critics and the like. At the same time in the varying and complex personalities of the artists in this book we discover a fair measure of social history, philosophy and cultural commentary within each artistic persona.

Tony Curtis, in instigating these recorded conversations, is the first to signal that the choice of artists here could have been other, that there could have been, could be, other books to do, embracing other figures, and that historical significance has not necessarily determined choice – but a more subjective process of acquaintance and enthusiasm. I think this book is nonetheless (allowing for these disclaimers) a contribution to our historic understanding of art in Wales in the second half of our century. Firstly, because of its focus on painters – a focus made not through any polemical decision on the interviewer's part, but nonetheless one of significance. Painting is alive and well and continues in Wales – might be one of the messages of this book. Painting as an artistic practice – and one can perhaps understand the puzzlement of the lay reader at this point – is a questioned activity. The French painter Delaroche in the nineteenth century with the advent of photography may have been the first to announce the death of painting – but its demise has been proclaimed at regular intervals since. We could say the rumours of its death have been grossly exaggerated. True, in the intervening period and particularly in recent times, the idea of painting only being possible if accomplished as a *tabula rasa*, or so questionable as a form to carry meaning that it has to be envisaged as a compilation of empty referential signs, has all served to torture the still animate body. As these interviews implicitly convey, the activity persists. A Iwan Bala can find his practice as a painter inflected, pushed and pulled by the practice of sculptors and installation artists, whilst a Charles Burton draws attention to the apparently inexhaustible, almost philosophic challenge of realisation through the medium of paint.

A second contribution to our understanding of history coming through this miscellany stems from the span of the book. There are artists here only ten years or so younger than the century; there are others whose exhibition careers began during the last ten years. The circumstances of artists trained and coming into their careers around the Second World War, the Fifties and early Sixties, and in a later period around the Eighties is given a piecemeal plotting. As elements in a jigsaw picture, they lead to other reflections.

If there are histories here, their common denominators are secreted through these lives lived through differing times. This collection of interviews clearly is not a survey history. Such a survey needs a reappraisal of the context of art in Wales – the task Peter Lord and his team at the Centre for Advanced Welsh and Celtic Studies are currently embarked upon – an approach to cultural grounding that views culture fundamentally from the inside. Certain themes do emerge from these individual narratives. Firstly, obliquely or explicitly, these artists define themselves in relation to place – that place being Wales, in almost all instances their workplace.

The artists making up this book are a mixture of Welsh born and bred, some just bred, and some neither Welsh born nor bred, but settled in, or pulled towards Wales in some way. The analogy might be that of a family. Like a family, this book is made up of stay at homes – still in the family home – not seeing a reason to have moved, yet not entirely comfortable. If they have moved away it was only better to move back, eventually or immediately, unable at the same time to be precise about how their ties could not be broken. Then there are the prodigals – whose time away has been defining, vital, but for whom the pull back has been strong. Finally there are the foster children – who have their own particular crises of identity especially in a land of literal and metaphorical redoubts.

For Welsh artists, training has almost always involved London – and has not been as self-sufficient in Wales as maybe Scottish artists could claim through Scotland's art school tradition developed in the late nineteenth century and in the early part of the twentieth as a marker of cultural confidence. An interesting sub-text or shared theme for several of the interviewees is the affection and respect for early inspirational teachers and significant emigré figures – most notably from eastern

Europe – Herman perhaps but even more so in this, the people connected with Cedric Morris and the Industrial Valleys settlements – admired and influential if difficult figures like Heinz Koppel. These teachers at some level imparted the view, indeed gave artists the confidence to do work out of their own situation rather than deny it and escape it.

As a consequence there is a stratum of argument coursing through this book which like a seam in a rock appears and disappears from interview to interview – and that is the relevance or irrelevance of certain artistic movements of the last forty years. How could the ephemeral, essentially metropolitan cultures, increasingly expressed with means which forcibly denied the relevance of the practice of painting, have an impact here – other than perhaps in fashionably transforming the art colleges and the way they formed students, some would say, in a counter-productive way. It has taken some time for the dust of forceful dogmas to settle and be evaluated. A lot of artists in this book have appeared sidelined as a result. For some, this suited them and they reconciled themselves to the fact that they could not be other than they were as artists. Their vindication has been often a prolonged personal one – before it has become a public one – and still is one which travels too infrequently beyond Wales.

Turning from interviewees to interviewer gives us further reasons to warmly welcome this book. As a writer and poet, Tony Curtis is becoming more familiarly present to us in slim paperbacks – perfect bound, with content word perfect. Indeed, his recent poetry has been acclaimed. Over the years as editor and compiler he has been involved in a number of culturally defining anthologies, but this is a first anthology for him of artists. With the interviewer a poet – and a poet with an enthusiasm for the visual – the resultant interviews go beyond being informative both biographically and in drawing out his subjects on key concerns in their art. As a fellow artist interested in the creative process, there are also moments in several of the interviews where the possible analogies between writing a poem and creating a painting are essayed. Indeed some of the artists offer this terrain of analogy back to the interviewer: "I suppose writing is a bit like that. . ." or words to that effect. What is also interesting here are what emerge as as critical differences. Some of these hinge on notions of artistic intentionality, what consciously or subconsciously is at work in making a work of art. The processes of the visual and the verbal offer as many differences as similarities. One is put in mind of John Berger's essay 'Who is an artist?' where he subjects the experience of looking at a tree and its branches cut out and interwoven against a sky to a systematic analysis and writes of how a writer might see this, a philosopher, and finally a painter. The physical properties of things pre-occupy the painter in order for him or her to find the metaphoric. The metaphoric is more instantly grasped by the poet who might then tie it back to a physical object. The painter's raw materials remain raw materials throughout the creative process. Not knowing whether something is quite right has to be tested by experiment for the visual artist – who can probably only aspire to achieving the state of something being better than it was before by revision or wholesale setting aside. The poem may be triggered by its end image, the painting perhaps rarely, even where the artist is methodical and where an element of the work is heavily weighted towards the planned composition of any piece as is the case of some of the artists in this book. This intermittent dialogue, about the nature of art and the nature of writing pursued with all of these artists, only occurs because of this interlocutor's way into painting – but it is an underlying theme which produces one of the riches of this book.

* * *

I am pleased that the appearance of this book can be linked to a launch exhibition at the National Museum & Gallery, Cardiff where we can also show the photographic documentation of artists in their studios by Bernard Mitchell, part of a much larger valuable photographic compilation he has made of artists and their studios in Wales. It is gratifying that the National Museum was clearly an important formative resource to a number of the artists in this book – and part of the challenge, for what is now the National Museum & Gallery, is to remain a source of stimulus for successive generations of artists.

David Alston
Keeper of Art, National Museums & Galleries of Wales
July 1997

Introduction

These twelve interviews with painters in Wales concern their paintings, their beliefs, their lives and struggles, as well as outlining the social and historical circumstances of their working lives. The post-war years have seen a progressively varied and vibrant development in the visual arts in a small country too often marginalised in surveys of modern art. Some of the contributors have strong views about this neglect; some are critical of the arts administrations and the teaching institutions whose role, it is strongly argued, should have been and should continue to be at the centre of support for the visual arts in Wales. Almost without exception, however, these painters are enthusiastic about other artists, from the old masters to their contemporaries.

Wales and its landscape have, of course, attracted notable figures such as Wilson, Sandby, Turner, Sisley, Piper and Sutherland, but such men came and saw and left. In this century Augustus and Gwen John, David Jones and Ceri Richards have received international critical attention. But too little has been made of those other artists who have committed themselves to Wales in the post-war years. I hope this book goes some way towards encouraging attention.

I began work on this book in 1992 when visiting John Knapp-Fisher in his Pembrokeshire house that functions as both gallery and studio. I have some strong roots in Pembrokeshire and John's place a few miles north of St David's, together with Arthur and Bim Giardelli's The Golden Plover in Warren, are among the ports of call on our regular itinerary through that most beautiful and threatened county. I have two of John's watercolours, the first bought in the early 1980s after John Tripp and I had given a poetry reading in Trevigan Cottage in Croesgoch. I thought that it would be interesting to visit John and this time interview him in the year when he was celebrating twenty-five years of living as a painter and selling his work from that house. Talking to the artist in his workplace and surrounded by his paintings was a fascinating experience for me. I can appreciate the theatricality of an exhibition opening, the buzzing social energy of such an event; and there is too the quiet pleasure of being in an empty gallery space, moving from picture to picture at leisure; and most of all the constant pleasure of living with others' work, others' visions of the world as we move about our houses. But few of us have the chance to experience the art in the presence of the artist. What happened that day in October 1992 was to convince me that such a book was possible and to set the practice for this book. In each case I have visited the painter in both studio and house, making one or more visits. I have tape recorded an interview which I later transcribed and sent to them for revision and approval.

This book, and the exhibition in the National Museums & Gallery in

Cardiff in September 1997, owes everything to the painters themselves. I am indebted to them, and to David Alston, the Keeper of Art, whose support for the project has been crucial. In every case, the painters have been welcoming and co-operative, generous with their time and hospitality. Some of the interviews have been made immediately before or after a solo exhibition of the painter's work; some of these artists have been away from the public eye for too long, others are centrally associated with the public's perception of art in Wales. Some are old friends of mine, others new. The twelve painters I've talked to are all committed artists and engaging personalities. Of course, the selection is necessarily based on my judgement and my prejudices. There could have been another twelve rewarding painters in this book: they should be in the next book.

This is the first book on contemporary art in Wales for a decade and I have dealt with painters and painters alone. Of course there are notable artists working in other media – one thinks of David Nash, Philip Jones Griffiths, David Hurn, Lois Williams, David Petersen, Robert Harding, Michael Casson, Colin See-Paynton, Anna Adam, Christine Jones and others – but painting gives this book its focus and there are other books to be produced which will, no doubt, deal with these other media and other artists. I look forward to them; Wales needs to explore, record and celebrate its visual arts. Peter Lord's extensive work at Aberystwyth in historical art is providing us with the sense of a tradition, purpose and context for our art. I offer *Welsh Painters Talking* as a contribution to what I hope will be a more concerted appreciation in the next century of the fine art work from Wales which, just as much as our literature, underpins our sense of a distinct identity.

Tony Curtis

ARTHUR GIARDELLI

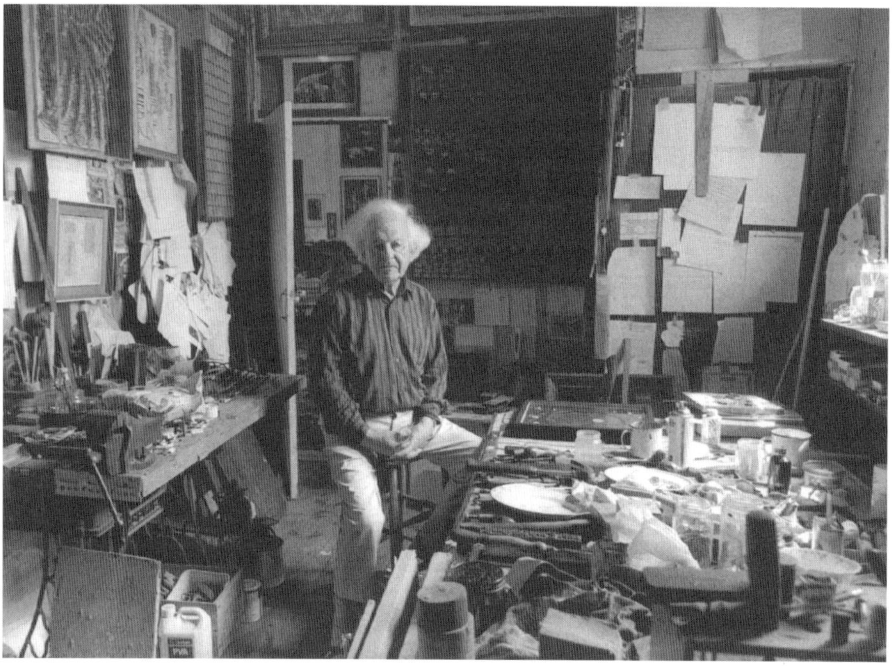

I interviewed Arthur Giardelli in the summer of 1994. I call regularly, if infrequently, on Arthur and Bim in their house The Golden Plover in Warren, near Pembroke when visiting my mother in Lydstep. Theirs is a converted school house and they use the school hall to exhibit their work to visitors and holidaymakers who are welcome to call in. There are examples of both Arthur's and Bim's watercolours for sale. In the main body of the house are their studios, and living rooms with remarkable works forming their collection.

Wales is very important to you; you've lived here a long time and when in your constructions you use shells and flotsam, they are Pembrokeshire shells and the gifts of the beach. You have used watercolours often to respond to the coast here. But your being in Wales is accidental, isn't it?

I came to Dowlais with an evacuated school in the war. But we had visited an uncle in Amroth when I was a boy, so I knew something of Wales. And I never felt altogether English – I felt that at school, having an Italian name and not being tall.

But you went from school to Oxford.

I spent so much time in school in the art room that my father got worried about this and had the idea with my headmaster that I should go to Oxford. So my life changed at eighteen and I studied English, French and Italian in the sixth form. I went up to Oxford in 1930 and as soon as I got there I went to the Ruskin School of Art. When I had the chance to do a 'special subject' I said that I wanted to do Botticelli's illustrations to *The Divine Comedy*, and they let me. Kenneth Clark lent me a book to study those illustrations. I just wasn't going to get away from paintings, one way or another.

I went to the Ruskin one day a week. The first time I saw a naked woman was in the art studio there. And I was astounded because when I was a boy of fourteen my father would take me to the British Museum and arrange for me to draw the statues. I thought that naked women were like the statues. So at nineteen when I saw the real thing I was flabbergasted

There were some fine teachers at the Ruskin – Barnett Freedman was there, and Gilbert Spencer and, of course, Rutherston, brother of Rothenstein. I became fascinated by this problem of drawing, and never let go of it. When I began teaching in Folkestone I went to art school at night and made drawings. At Oxford we were taught the Florentine tradition of drawing the nude figure.

My father had always taken us at weekends to the National Gallery or the Tate Gallery. That's why I feel so critical of the National Museum of Wales – they actually charge you to go in. It's outrageous. In my time a little boy could wander into the museum and listen to a lecture.

Your father was a patent agent for a German company who lost his position when the Great War broke out. So he became a teacher; is that why you went into the profession?
I became a teacher because that was the only thing I had any competence in.

And you still teach, even now in your eighties, for the Extra-Mural Department at UCW Aberystwyth. It's a nice balancing act which several artists have achieved, isn't it?
Yes. But I would hate to have to teach painting. I teach people about Michelangelo and Raphael. I believe that we work as artists in a great tradition and art is bound to suffer if we don't know that tradition. Reynolds said: "Never copy your contemporaries. Seek to emulate those who have gone before, those whose art has stood the test of time". I think that if you don't know about that, then you don't know a damn thing about art. Unless you know really deeply about the art of the great masters, you aren't really an artist at all, in the European tradition. Emulating one's successful contemporaries is bound to be disastrous; one may become fashionable. One is surrounded by it in our culture, which has lost touch with the visual arts. Things are too much related to the value, or rather the cost, of a painting.

You mean the international company which buys a van Gogh and keeps it in a vault?
Exactly. That's stupid, isn't it? As a teacher I could give people an entry into European culture,Velasquez and Breughel and Rubens; whereas the language barrier would prevent them from experiencing great European works of literature. You can't understand Turner unless you know something about Claude; you can't understand Claude unless you know something about Cranach and Altdorfer; you can't understand Dürer unless you know something about Giovanni Bellini. It is a coherent whole: it's not a language, nevertheless it is a means of communication, a means of entering into the wisdom of centuries of time.

Several artists have told me that in the art schools of the Sixties they felt that drawing was out of fashion. Do you agree that over the last thirty years art education has at times lost its way?
I don't know much about that. I do understand that drawing is the basic skill; it's the way in which you explain how you see something. One earns the appreciation of a work of art by experience. One comes to understand a tradition to which every artist makes some sort of contribution.

I suppose that in the viewer, the purchaser and the artist what resonates is something to do with the line, the texture and the colours. Those basics must in some way be pleasing, must be promising more on the twentieth view than they did on the first viewing. A work of art must be something that you can live with.

ARTHUR GIARDELLI

I think a work of art is transitive. A work of art takes you beyond itself to something other. It may take you through itself into a dream world of which formerly you had no understanding. It may take you to see a thorn tree in such a way as you had never seen it before. A Turner landscape isn't painted so that you can enjoy the colour of his picture, or the structure of his picture. it makes you say, "I have never seen a sunset before! I must look again". Nature is a mystery, the human mind is a mystery. When I look at a Velasquez picture of a glass of water I am in awe of glass and I'll look at water again. And that is true of every good work of art. Any work which stops at itself isn't worth having. A work of art takes you beyond itself into other realms, into life itself.

Living as you do surrounded by great works, David Jones, Ceri Richards, Léger and so on, you must have sustenance any time that you want it.

Yes, but the time has got to come when you must see the world through your own eyes. You learn about the world through drawing and painting.

I was at an exhibition of Jonathan Cramp's watercolours recently in Fishguard. Now they are paintings of great skill, an almost photographic accuracy. But looking at that large work of yours on the wall, I feel that by using brass, sacking, paint and shells you are conveying a deeper sense of the power of wave and the presence of beach.

We don't see the world in the way in which a camera does. A camera does not let open a door to us. It produces prisons. It closes the world to us. Most people are in that kind of prison these days. Even before the invention of the photograph Chardin said, "The eye needs to be taught how to look at nature. How many have never seen and will never see her – that is the anguish of the artist's life", the artist's job is to help us see the world.

But a lot of people who come to Pembrokeshire want to take away an image, whether it's a postcard or a watercolour, and they are satisfied by a photographic representation of where they've been.

And so what they can no longer see is Pembrokeshire. What they will see is the photograph. The camera sees with one eye, it's absolutely still: and the camera hasn't got a mind. When I look at a photograph of where I have been my memory becomes restricted to just that.

Yet there are some great photographers, aren't there?

I have known one great photographer – his name was Raymond Moore. I first met him on Skomer and admired him greatly.

What visitors may not take away from here is the feel of the sand under their feet. The wonderful sound of the sea. There is a sustenance to be found on the coast.

When you live in a city, you never see the night sky, you never get too hot or too cold or wet through.

You have a desire to come to terms with landscape that leads you to use materials from that landscape.

In my watercolours I work on the spot from nature. I expect to go into the essence of it to the extent that when someone looks at it they say, "Well, I don't see it like that". If I get that response, then my drawing may be a good one. It is common for someone to come into my gallery and say, "The colours are gorgeous, but you don't really see them like that, do you?" And my answer is, "What the hell do you think I put them down for?"

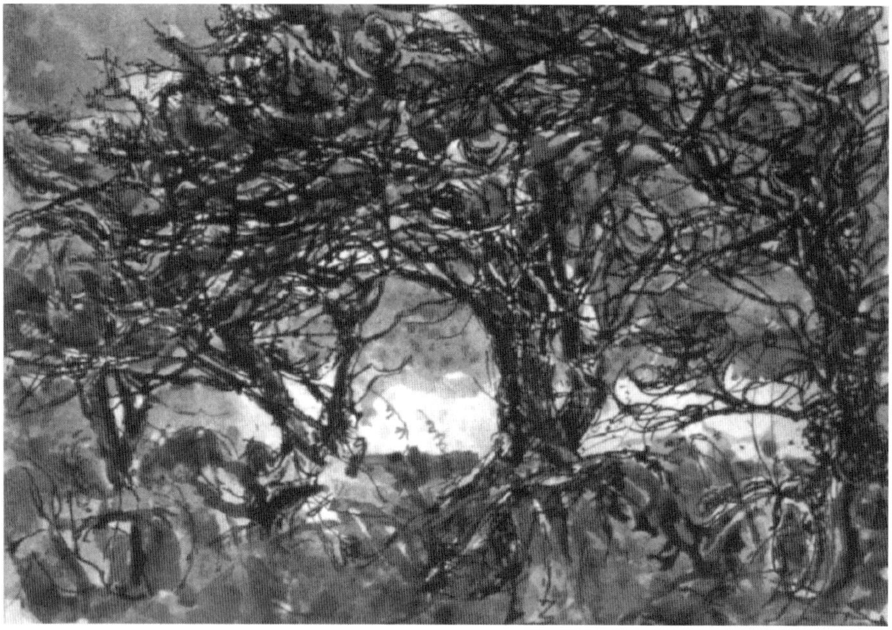

Winter Thorn Trees watercolour, 51 x 68.5 cm, 1995, coll: the artist

I have painted thorn trees so many times because they are the very character of Pembrokeshire – the thorn, the violence of the wind which makes the thorn tree hiss, and the fact that the thorn tree can live in any weather. And it's very slow growing, there's a slow splendour about it. An extraordinary richness. And, of course there's a religious significance to it as well. So I've really studied thorn trees. They come alive, if possible, under my pen. When I work in my studio on a relief construction I try to put down the forms, textures, tones and colours which remain in my mind after my work out of doors on thorn trees, fields and the sea or a flight of birds. But there is more to it than that. You can't imagine the beginning of the sea; it's beyond any thinkable period of time. It struck me one day that a watch without hands conveyed something of that notion. So I used watch faces in my construction. They also stand for one of the whites of the sea. Moreover, the shape and white enamel of the watch face with its Roman or Arabic numbers is beautiful in itself. If one can make a woman's body out of marble, why not the sea out of torn paper, shell and watch parts. I like giving discarded things a new life.

There are more than one black, more than one white?

That's right. I am trying to discover for myself and to bring to the attention of other people the miracle of variety in nature and man-made things.

When you say "miracle" it brings me to the thorn trees and the fact that several of the versions I've seen are very obviously a crucifixion scene.

How very odd, I've never thought of that before. You're quite right. Of course, I thought of the crown of thorns. But we've got the three in our garden at the back of the house.

Is your art then some sort of sacrament?

I don't think that nature is a machine which will one day altogether be understood. In that sense it's a miracle, it is beyond human comprehension. One of the fascinations of the arts is that each artist will take you a bit further into that infinite mystery of nature.

"Nature" to include human experience as well?

Our limitations are one of the reasons why we can't understand it.

Some artists and writers do keep nature at a distance. Wales has been visited by artists since the Romantic period almost as if they were visiting a studio which God had arranged for them. They took bits of it back with them. There is a landscape tradition which works in that way, isn't there? But what I'm seeing here with your work is a desire to get into that mystery by using the found object as a key to open the experience.

There is a sense in which the shell is a key to the sea. The shell has been made by a sea creature, and the inside of the shell is the colour of the sea, and the shape of the shell is the shape of the waves.

Yes, at Kettle's Yard in Cambridge the juxtaposition of the found object with art object is fascinating. The Gaudier-Brzeska and Moore sculptures and the the pebbles.

I am reminded that when we had the Czech artist Ota Janecek to stay with us a few years ago and went to the beach at Freshwater West he picked up one pebble, then another, and simply gazed at them and filled his pockets with these pebbles. He'd evidently never seen such things before. We take them for granted.

Who has influenced you?

When I was trying to find my way, although I was interested in school teaching, I did want to become a painter and Cedric Morris helped greatly. I was teaching at Dowlais when I met him and he encouraged me to go over later and work in his studios in Suffolk. Then he told me to take my work to the Redfern Gallery in London and they showed my work for a number of years. It was Cedric who said, "I think that you could become an artist". And not only that, he encouraged me to sit beside him and watch him work. He actually knelt on the ground and he had the canvas on the ground with his pigments and I watched this man look at nature. It was so easy, I felt that I could do it.

So that was an insight into the direct involvement with nature, but also an insight into the way that the world of galleries and exhibiting worked. Cedric Morris was the principal of an art school, wasn't he?

He founded an art school with a great friend of his called Arthur Lett Haines. It was not like any other kind of art school. He would point out what was good in what one was doing. He was positive and encouraging.

It seems to me that the way in which you are responding to the forces of nature reminds me very much of Vernon Watkins in a poem such as 'The Feather': "How could a blind rock satisfy the hungers of the sea?" Have there been occasions when literature, poetry, has led you to do things?

Well I was reading Dante at Oxford and I've been reading him ever since. I'm currently reading Byron's letters. And I'm always reading a French book. My favourite French poet is Villon. My reading in European literature helps me to understand the paintings of Europe. My favourite novel is *Moby Dick* – that's the sea again, of course. And I've used 'The Dry Salvages' often to choose titles for the paintings. I bought the first editions of *The Four Quartets.*

The wave, the curve, seems to figure so importantly in your work. Is there a musicality to that?

I'm sure there is. Music has always fed my understanding. When I was at Dowlais during the war I taught music at Cyfarthfa Castle.

Can you talk about the circumstances which brought you to Dowlais? You left the employ of the Folkestone school on declaring yourself a conscientious objector, didn't you?

When the war began, the school where I taught in Folkestone was evacuated to the Merthyr area. Soon after I became front page news in the Merthyr Tydfil newspaper. But a few months after, the local education authority asked me if I would teach the violin in their schools. So I became violin master in Cyfarthfa, the host school of the Folkestone school that had sacked me! I understood something about Wales then – they do dislike the English! There was a profound antipathy between the two schools – chalk and cheese. I got to know the Dowlais people: the men were steel-workers or coal-workers and I talked with them while we did fire-service duties at night when the air-raid alarm sounded.

I had become friendly with the Quaker, John Denithorne, who ran a settlement in Dowlais, and I had served already on their committee advising conscientious objectors. He organised concerts for my wife, who was a professional pianist, and for me in the Dowlais area, which helped us to get by after my sacking. I lectured on classical music for the WEA and Cardiff University. We used to give lecture-recitals – the music of Bach, the Beethoven Sonatas and so on. I loved playing, but I soon discovered I'm not a composer, and I wanted to be a maker. Incidentally, my job at Aberystwyth was originally to lecture on Music and Art.

Do you still play?

I play the viola at Christmas carols at our local church. Do you go to the Church of Wales?

No, I suppose I'm a reluctant atheist. There's a poem about scattering my father's ashes on the headland at Lydstep – "The dead go where we send them". I can take a sense of mystery from R.S. Thomas and Dylan and Vernon Watkins – I feel strongly about things, but I can't believe in an after-life or the personification of a god. I think that when Peter Prendergast goes to the mountains and Will Roberts to the country, and when we go to the sea, we are certainly involving ourselves with the life-force, whether you can call that God or not, I don't know. But I can't take that next step and call that life-force "God".

Byron says that the essence of life is doubt. I couldn't be an atheist, because that implies a certainty. We are too weak altogether intellectually or spiritually to dare to deny. I think doubt is a proper state of mind: it implies some sort of humility which is part of us.

I can see the attraction of embracing a system of belief.

In some ways I wish my grandfather had preserved his Catholic faith. My father went to war, my mother took us to the country and I was brought up as a little country boy in the Church choir. My father was more English than the English; he never learned Italian. My grandfather fought with Garibaldi and then there was nothing left for him and he came to London. He spent most of his life in Soho, and was secretary of various Italian clubs. The reason my father carted me off to the National Gallery was that it was part of my Italian heritage.

None of your work has been specifically religious – there's no Deposition like Ceri Richards, no Stations of the Cross like Will Roberts.

But I am a Christian and I think Christianity has to do with doubt. Faith implies that you don't know.

Our great contemporary poet, R.S. Thomas, certainly has huge anguish about doubt.

I used to go to his church when I was in Aberystwyth and found out he was there. He used to invite me to tea afterwards. But the absurd thing was that it was a very small congregation. No members of the university would go, as I recall.

Of course, the University of Wales has a poor record of honouring literary and artistic figures. And Wales in general has lacked an art history, a system of critical appreciation, of contextualisation, hasn't it?
That's partly the fault of Non-conformity and partly poverty. If the artist had been employed by the Church, then a tradition could have continued. Too many art teachers and even artists know too little about the European tradition in art.

You were very active and remain so in the 56 Group Wales. What part has that organisation played in invigorating the visual arts in Wales?
It is run for art by artists. The Arts Council began by supporting us, but they prefer now to support art galleries. The number of invitations we get from overseas is overwhelming, but we simply aren't sufficiently well funded to respond to enough of them. The British Council can be very supportive though.

The 56 Group, which later became the 56 Group Wales, was founded by Eric Malthouse, John Edmunds and David Tinker. After three years I was made Chairman. We have exhibited in all sorts of places, Tenby and Aberystwyth as well as Holland, Italy and Germany. Some of our best artists are and have been members. Membership is by proposal, then invitation and the whole group decides on the basis of slides and examples of work. Some artists have become so successful that they don't need us; if artists leave Wales for more than two years they must resign. If the group decides that an artist's work is not really progressing or being produced, then he is asked to resign.

You live with some fine work by David Jones. How do you regard him, and

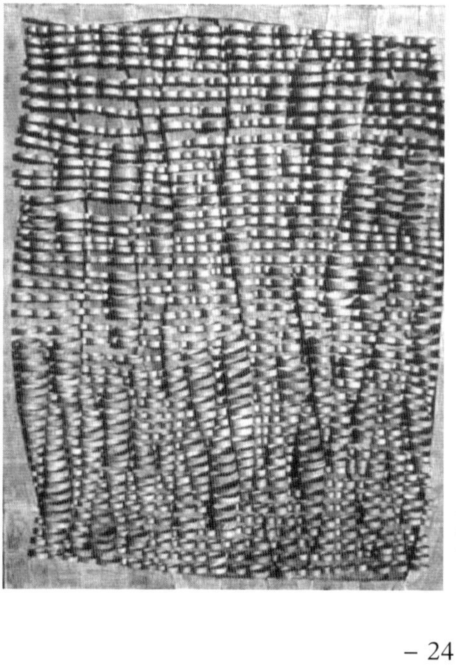

Jack Sound,
torn paper, 82 x 68 cms,
1975, coll: Lewis & Eileen Allen

how did you meet him?

In 1939 I bought a watercolour at an exhibition in Somerset, a David Jones painting of a beach seen from the verandah of his parents' seaside villa at Hove. When I got back to Merthyr I wrote to C.E.M.A. asking them to send exhibitions by Cedric Morris and David Jones to Wales. They did. In the show was a drawing of a ram with a spear through its side; it was owned by the artist. I wrote to C.E.M.A. asking whether he would sell it. He wouldn't. But the owner of 'Manawydan's Glass Door' wanted to sell hers, so I bought that. I wrote to David Jones about my purchase and my interest in his work and got no reply. Years later I met by chance Ray Howard Jones on Skomer. She took me to Harrow to see David Jones, who took me up to his room overlooking trees and fields. When I asked him why he hadn't answered my letters he replied, "I thought you would be some mid-European".

After that when I had to go up to London I would telephone him, asking whether it would be convenient for me to call on my way back to Wales. It always was because he never went out. When he had to leave his room with a view because Harrow School needed it, he moved down the hill to a small room in a house called Monksdene. When I asked to see his work he would take up his portfolios from against the wall. I had read mediaeval French and Italian literature at Oxford and so wanted to hear from him why he had retold these stories in the 'Matter of Britain'. He told me of his life in the trenches, of living with the Gill family, of his journey to Jerusalem. In this one room he had his memories of when he moved about in the world of Eliot and Sickert, his Roman Catholic faith, his books; his reading of Coleridge and Malory bore fruit in his poetry and paintings.

In later years, when Bim and I went to see him we used to draw him as he talked. David and I exchanged letters and I began to write articles and lecture about his work.

But doesn't Jones have a clear agenda to argue for a pan-Catholic Europe?
In Parenthesis *is wonderful, but too densely allusive for most readers.*

I think he is a better painter than a poet. He's a natural painter. But his message is incomplete without his essays and great and difficult poetry. As for religion, I feel more and more sympathy with the Catholic faith. I must have faith so as to understand.

You and Bim still travel regularly to the continent to paint, don't you?

Bim and I paint mostly in or not too far from our home, but we also travel to paint and to see what others have done in other times and places: carpet makers in Turkey, workers in brass in Nepal, sculptors in China. We have drawn the Acropolis, the Ca da Mosto in Venice, the Charles Bridge in Prague, the Treasury in Petra, domes in the Kremlin, skyscrapers in Singapore, temples in India, from Cape Wrath to the banks of the Seine. Someone said, "Go west, young man". No, go east.

And you exhibit widely?

Since the 1960s my work has been available at the Grosvenor Gallery, now at Albemarle Street in London. Eric Estorick got me going at his gallery by commissioning me to make a relief construction, three feet by four feet, for his wife's birthday present. Throughout the sixties my work was shown at their gallery in Dover Street and later when they had a dealer's gallery in South Molton Street. My work was acquired from that gallery by the Tate, the National Museum of Wales, the Contemporary Art Society of Great Britain, the Saidenberg Gallery in New York and the Contemporary Art Society for Wales.

The Estoricks commissioned me to make the street door to their gallery in South Molton Street and from that I got a similar commission from the Brook Street Gallery. I made both in brass and wood. From the early seventies Estorick centred his attention on his world-wide responsibilities for the work of Erté. After the death of Erté he decided, in 1993, to have again a streetside public gallery in Mayfair and he opened in Albemarle Street, where he invited me to have an exhibition of my watercolours and relief constructions. It ran throughout March 1994. But, by then, alas, that great art lover and collector had died, leaving most of his astounding collection in charitable trust in London.

I can see that we need patrons and enthusiasts in the arts, as well as well-managed public collections. How do you react to Peter Lord's arguments regarding the visual arts in Wales?

I've read articles in *Planet*, but haven't read his book yet. He's done great service in stirring things up at the National Museum.

I wrote a letter to the *Western Mail* earlier this year to say that the National Museum in Cardiff should show Welsh art in its own right. Their argument is that they show it in the context of European. When Matisse and Vlaminck and Picasso looked at African masks, they didn't see them in the European context, but their whole lives as artists were refreshed by that contact. The responsibility of the National Museum of Wales is to show the art of Wales. If we hadn't included the word "Wales" in the 56 Group, we certainly wouldn't have created much interest abroad. Of course, you can't just throw out the Monets and Cézannes. You have to have a basis of judgement; you shouldn't include things simply because they are Welsh.

I suppose Peter Lord is right to remind us of our tradition, which hasn't been studied sufficiently before.

I myself pressed the Picton Gallery before it closed to show Pembrokeshire painters. I felt that it should represent work done in the area. Also, I was glad to be asked to write the Introduction to a recent book on Pembrokeshire painters.

There is something very special about Pembrokeshire, isn't there – Piper and

Sutherland came down. What is it about the place?
We look into the setting sun. And when you look into the setting sun across the sea you are looking into a magic and a mystery – your eyes are dazzled by it. It's in the *Mabinogion* isn't it? Grassholm becomes Gwales. Only an island which you look at through the setting sun could become an island with a palace on it. In Pembrokeshire we watch the sea swallow that ball of fire, the sun.

You are looking into the end of things, and that's a sobering thing to do.
Yes, the artist paints against the light in order to simplify the structures.

I can see in the constructions which you have on your walls – the sun and moon and the watch faces – this conjunction is an attempt to deal with that. The mechanical watch face set into a hazy sun.

You have kept two sides of your art going simultaneously – the beautifully executed watercolours and the constructions. People are immediately drawn to and find accessible the paintings, but may regard the constructions as difficult; because they do not fit neatly into a frame, they protrude from the wall and use a variety of materials. How do you organise these activities? Do you work on both aspects of your art at the same time?

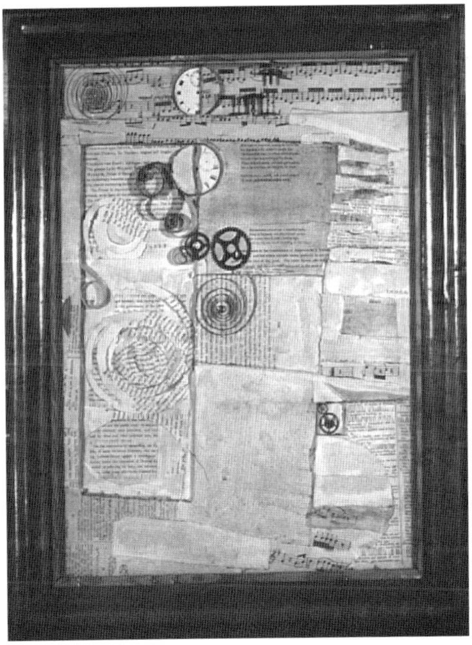

My Pulse Like a Soft Drum
mixed media, 51 x 39.5 cm
1970, coll: the artist

The relief constructions may take three or more months to complete. The drawings and watercolours may well contribute to them, they remind me of the experience of the sea. When I get into my studio, I am trying to remember the essence of things which I have been studying in great detail in the drawings on the shore. the essence emerges for me partly in use of the materials derived from the place – the driftwood, the shells, the slates, the string. They speak of that place in a literal sense, but also visually. The shells are there to say to the viewer, "This is about the sea".

They have an iconic effect then?

That's it.

Though, paradoxically, they are also metaphors, because when you turn the shells over they have that wonderful range of whites, pearls, an opalescent quality. My response to those shells in your current work in the studio was that they were eyes, or open mouths, even to see the shell as a womb. Does that matter, if I interpret such things in my own way?

Well, if I make something which I don't altogether understand myself, then I'm delighted. I don't think that mysticism is vagueness. If you look at a great mystical work of art, a Blake poem, for example, it is very precise, and so it is with the great altar-piece by Grünewald. The opposite of the mystical is that which is vague. The reason why Turner could make those masterpieces at the end was that he had been so precise for such a long time. In that colour there is precision. I am deeply interested in the technique in watercolours. You need imagination, but that must be combined with technique.

Is there something more of the moment in the watercolour; and does that complement the other work with its plans and considerable time commitment?

You must study, intellectualise it, in order to make the sun out of what is at hand – water and some yellow earth. Cadmium yellow is beautiful. But you have to use it properly if it is to retain its identity and also become the sun. Like in a Henry Moore you've got a woman's body, but you've also got the trunk of a tree.

So when Bim and yourself take sacking, shells, torn paper, mechanical parts, you are simply using materials which have not been refined as far as the pigment and oils of traditional painting?

As an artist you are always trying to discover something, aren't you?

CHARLES BURTON

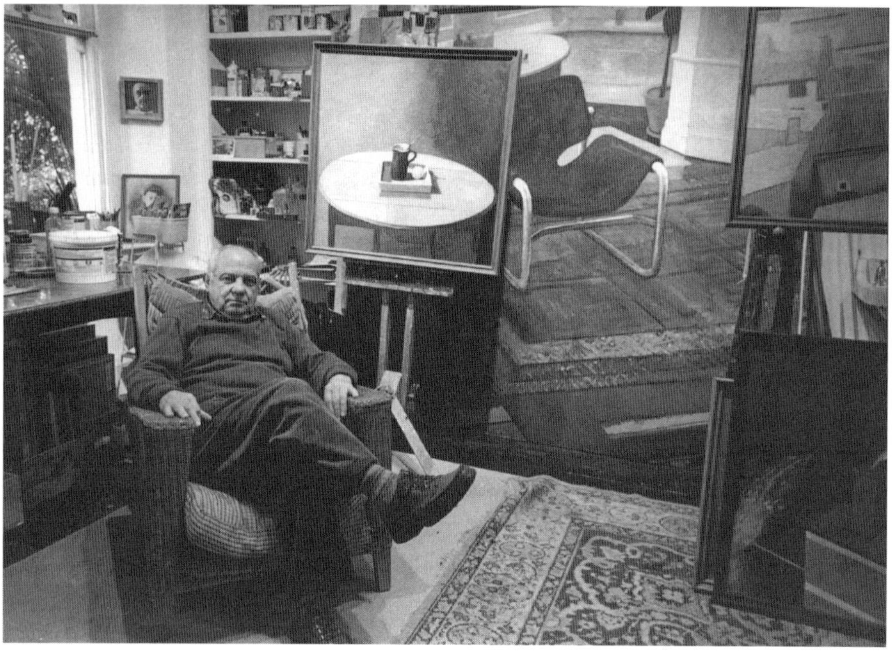

Charles Burton lives in a large Victorian house in Penarth which he bought on his retirement from the Glamorgan College of Education, at which institution we both taught in the 1970s. It is a house which I admire for its light and space; it is a treasure store of paintings by Charlie and his wife Rosemary, Charlie's stacked in apparent disorder in several bedrooms which act as studios for the two painters. I recorded the bulk of this interview in 1996 but have talked with him about art and life regularly, if infrequently, over the years. He is one of the most sociable of friends.

You live in this large Victorian house in Penarth which is as full of art as nearby Turner House. You could hold a full retrospective exhibition here, because there are paintings and drawings from over forty years ago. For you, the art goes on regardless of what goes on outside the house. Would that be fair – that you continue to paint still lifes and works of the memory and imagination without reference to what may be happening beyond your gates?
Yes, that's true. Outside the house has very little influence on my painting, though I have always painted landscapes, recently near Penarth and abroad.

You are still doing what you have always done?
I think it's like a game – chess or rugby – playing within the rules, being clever. You might be able to extend the work slightly; though art is about other art. Painting has been going on for forty thousand years; in a sense there's nothing new. What else has been going on for that length of time?

So painting has more to do with painting than with the rest of the world. It's more self-referential than empirical? But the first paintings must have been to do with a response to the world – the cave paintings of animals and the chase?
But there are a lot of things in those paintings which no-one understands at all. There are unexplained symbols. It is certainly believed that there were specialist painters; not everyone painted. Perhaps it was to do with magic. I think all painting is, in a way, magical in as far as it ought not to be confused with nature. That is always a problem for anyone who paints in a way which might be called representational. There is the dilemma of how much painting is to do with representation, and how much to do with the structure of painting and the development or continuation of painting. Then you come on to the problem of what you actually look at when you look at a painting. Is it about a hat or a sunset or Penarth – what is it? But painting is about arranging pigments on a, usually, flat surface.

Which may or may not attempt to fool the viewer into thinking that it is three dimensional.
I don't think that painting has ever really been three dimensional.

But if the man on the Clapham omnibus expects the mountain to look like a mountain, Churchill to look like Churchill. And if it doesn't, then that's not a good painting.

Yes, and no. You know the problem Constable had was that he had the cheek to paint grass green, when everyone expected it to be brown. Because, stylistically, paintings were made with the grass brown, except in Holland. The problem of idiom comes to the fore. Look at early films; now we expect films to be realistic, but the early ones were obviously not at all realistic. Even so, audiences dived under the seats when trains were filmed running towards the camera. Today's films are no more realistic. The idiom has changed.

The audience willingly suspends its disbelief. So in the early Italian masters one does not expect perspective; and then one reads differently when perspective does become the norm. When you do still life painting, are you not attempting to create an accurate perspective?

No, no, and in fact one couldn't do it; there is no such thing. Even when it is attempted. In the beautiful Vermeer paintings, it cannot be done. Because if you have a system for painting perspective the bottom corners don't work, they become too big. Vermeer and the Dutch painters used to paint a table or something to hide the front corners, because the space would be so distorted that it would be unbelievable. Space is experienced

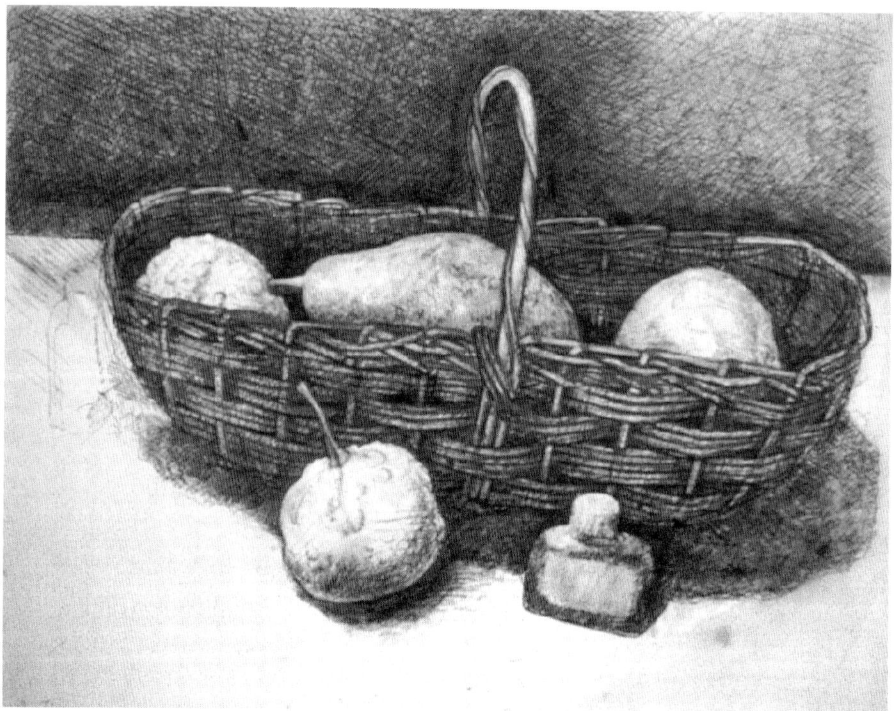

Fruit Basket — ink, 39.5 x 52 cm, 1974, coll: the artist

and it cannot be represented in any way accurately on a flat surface. So if one wanted to do that one would be barking up the wrong tree.

That painting on the wall of a table with those jugs and a pear, that is in no way a naturalistic painting. Is there something iconic about it? Why those things? Do they mean more than they are?

Other people tell me that they mean more than they are, but it's not for me to say. I think that for me the painting to be completely rounded needs the partaker to respond to the work in a creative way. You wouldn't want to write only for another writer, however thrilled you would be with that. It would be absurd to have a doctor only administering to another doctor. So for the whole thing to work there has to be some other response. But I don't think that it's the painter's job to say what the response should be. That side ought to be left quite open.

When I last visited you, you were, it could be said, obsessively drawing fruit. What is the interest in drawing pear after pear?

Every occasion is different, every mark that one makes is different. So it wasn't at all repetitive. It was simply that it was an easy way of beginning some work.

Were they exercises of a sort?

No. I've never believed in exercises. I'm strongly against exercises because I think that if one started exercises it would be to do with a predetermined plan of how one should proceed. It would be like doing weight-lifting when as a swimmer one would be doing completely the wrong thing.

But you spent your working life in education and one might assume that setting exercises would be underpinning that system.

I've never worked that way and it has never been my thinking. One has to take for granted that art students have brought something with them and have something to offer. The idea of imposing set programmes upon them would have to be set against the idea that the students' abilities should be allowed to be used.

You've said to me that one of the earliest things you can remember is the urge to draw things.

Yes, from a very early age, when I could barely walk. I remember being taken to my great grandmother's house, popped on a tin box in the bay window and I did drawings: horses pulling coal trucks across the bridge; the Ynysefio Colliery in Treherbert.

What was that like, growing up in the early Thirties in Treherbert?

Well, I was never aware that there was any kind of financial problem in the area. I was completely comfortable, though my father wasn't in work. He was always there and I had a wonderful relationship with him.

Was he an unemployed miner, out of work after the 1926 strike?

Yes, he was out of work for a long time. I don't know how we got by –

the same way that everybody did, I suppose. But there was enough warmth. I wasn't deprived in any way.

You don't miss what you don't know.

No. I was very lucky, because instead of my father being out at work he was home with me. We wandered round the mountains. It was lovely, wonderful. My father had 'dust', of course, but he is still alive in his ninety-first year and still living in Treherbert.

Was there any art in your family background? Didn't you say that he taught you to draw that bridge?

Yes, and on my mother's side they were quite a remarkable family really. My mother was the youngest of three sisters, the youngest by far. My grandfather was just a labourer, but he managed to send the first two girls to university. In 1912 it was absolutely amazing. One of the principals at Barry Training College, where you and I both taught in the Seventies, was a great friend of my aunt. They had gone through university at Aberystwyth together. I think my aunts must have been the first two girls to go to university from the Rhondda. Both of them died very young and my grandfather believed that this was because they had had a hard time at university, not taking care of themselves and so on, so my mother wasn't allowed to go. She was very bright. She must have been very frustrated because her intelligence was beyond the amount of training and education that she'd had. I've known lots of people who are the opposite and have been educated far beyond their intelligence.

For two working class sisters to go to university before the First World War was a very rare thing, wasn't it?

Certainly. So our house was always full of university books – Latin, Greek and so on. One aunt had read Classics and the other was a musician. One of them taught at Llandovery College.

This is where the Welsh myth of education was born, isn't it? That somehow there was a way out of the labouring classes to the life of education and the professions.

But I still can't see how it was possible. Although I must say that when I went to the Royal College my grandfather was still alive and helped me. I had been a student in Cardiff, and having completed the course I was then encouraged to do the teacher training course, which I did. When I went to the Royal College, after serving my time in the RAF, I was deemed to have been already professionally trained, so I was not eligible for a grant, so my grandfather gave me his life savings, which was twenty pounds. His life savings.

But you had passed the eleven-plus and gone to grammar school?

Yes, to Porth, it was the cream of the schools in the Rhondda.

So at that point you knew that you were going to follow in the footsteps of your aunts?

Yes, I suppose so. But it was exclusively an academic school, there was no art teaching there at all. I think they had someone who came in once a week and carried a bucket of water from room to room. I had been encouraged to draw at the junior school; but at Porth I was the only person at that stage who had ever taken an O Level in Art. I simply said that I wanted to do it, and they must have been nice people there because they let me drop Latin to do that. They really thought that I should have been a mathematician or a scientist, because I was very good at those subjects. Of course, I was given no information about how to proceed in art because no-one had any idea. But, in fact, I did need to matriculate, so I did that with no problem and went to what was called the intermediate year at Cardiff. I got a couple of scholarships and completed my time there. Then I went to Egypt with the Air Force in my National Service time. That was lovely because I taught Art; I set up an Art class and I taught A Level Art. I had never done A Level Art, but the only results I ever had with those classes were Distinctions. It was lovely because I had time off and was paid to paint, draw and to help others.

After National Service, in 1953, I went to the Royal College. I had no grant in my first year, so I had to live by selling paintings – which I did. Because I had no intention of doing any other jobs, otherwise what was the point of being there?

How did you sell them, through a gallery?

Well, there were more outlets then than there are now: there were education authorities and colleges and industrial organisations were happy to buy pictures. People believed that the environment should be human-

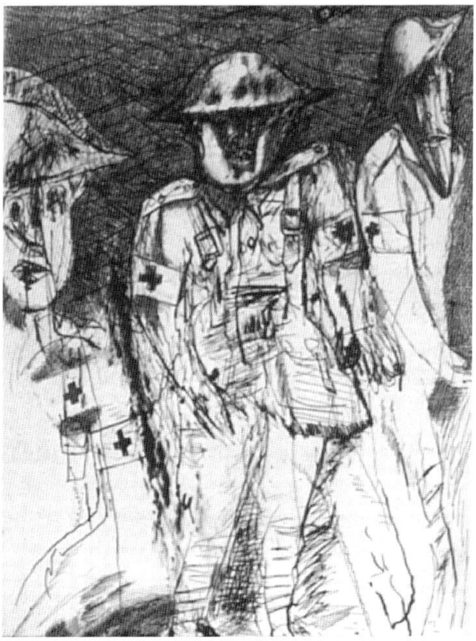

Ambulance Men on the Somme
Pen and ink, 62 x 50 cm
1968, coll: Prof & Mrs Curtis

ised in those days. I think that's been spoilt now.

Who taught you at the Royal College?

In a way, I wasn't taught at the Royal College. There were quite well-known people there, but I don't feel that I was ever taught anything. However, I absorbed quite a lot from the staff and students and from being in London, because I had all my tea breaks in the Victoria and Albert Museum.

So you just used the studio space?

Yes, it was a rather peculiar situation. Quite a few people back here felt that I should have just stayed in the Rhondda and painted. But having gone to the Royal College there wasn't any possible way that I could have gone back – what could I have done?

In any case, at the end of my first year at the Royal College I won a Royal Scholarship, and I won the Gold Medal at the Eisteddfod at the end of 1953. As a result of the Scholarship, the Glamorgan County Council gave me a maintenance grant and the Royal College waived my fees. So I must have been the only student ever to go through there without paying any fees.

What about the first year?

They knew I had no money, so they hadn't billed me; and then they were waived for the rest of the three years.

So how had you got in? By taking your portfolio along?

Yes, and then I said that I didn't want to be denied the opportunity of going by some bakers and builders at the County Hall. They agreed with me and said, "Well, come along". I had done five years at Cardiff and then left the Royal College with the ARCA which had a further degree status.

When people write about you in catalogues and so on, they often characterise you as a member of 'The Rhondda Group'. Is that a fanciful term – what was 'The Rhondda Group'?

That was the group of people from the Rhondda in the Fifties who were art students in Cardiff. We were all fanatical about painting. We caught the same train down from the valleys to Cardiff daily, because we didn't board in Cardiff. These journeys were very important for us.

Ivor Davies, in the introduction to your 1983 Oriel exhibition claims that it was the only art movement, or group, or school that Wales has ever seen. Is that overstating it?

Well, last week I received a card from Leslie Jones which refers to that. I think it is actually true. We painted pictures of the Valleys. But the point is that they were formally well-constructed, so that they were not simply paintings of local scenes, they really were to do with painting, very seriously to do with painting.

The situation was the Valleys, but the impulse was not topographical. So

what happened – you turned up at the station and Ernest Zobole and others were there, and who else?
When I started I think I was on my own. Then Tom Hughes came back from the army. Then Ernie came, then some younger people from school.

So these were Valley boys – and they were boys, not girls – who happened to come down to Cardiff at about the same time and pretty well down the same railway track?
Yes, we spent two hours a day in the train compartment, talking about painting and looking at the drawings and the pictures that we had done. And discussing art at every level we could. We were fanatically keen and I suppose it had some kind of impact.

Was there a shared consciousness that the Valleys had not been painted to any extent, and that you could and should do that?
There was no political implication in any way. I suppose in the air was the fact that the war had ended, and everyone believed at that time that life could be wonderful back home, in your own little patch. So that we felt that we could paint pictures as beautifully as Piero della Francesca, or Cézanne or anybody else, working from our own environment. Young people have high ideals!

Did you hold on to that loyalty to an area because of Cardiff, or despite Cardiff? I mean how did you know about Cézanne?
Painting was always at the centre – there was nothing else. I am still the same, apart from enjoying a good meal and a laugh and the usual things, but from my point of view there's only one thing worth doing in the world, and that's painting. And it's nothing to do with anybody else. I love it if somebody likes the pictures, that's just a bonus. I'm going to paint anyway.

But in the 1950s in south Wales where could you see pictures, in the National Museum?
We went there every lunch-time, although we knew all the pictures inside-out, we still went there. Actually during the war, before I even went to the art school, there were worker settlements, like Maes y Haf just outside Porth and Dowlais. Many fine writers were attached to them. It was a kind of WEA set-up, I'm not sure how they were financed, but I remember seeing lots of good paintings.

They were a sort of community centre which gave people food and education.
Yes, I remember Esther Grainger worked in one in Pontypridd, and Cedric Morris had a lot to do with them. It was Cedric who got Heinz Koppel to come to south Wales after he'd been bombed out in London. But, of course, I was younger than that lot, so I don't really know how it was organised.

So, as with any war, things were thrown up in the air and came down a dif-

ferent shape, so that possibilities were opened up.

Yes, we were so keen to find out anything and everything in the world of art. When the boys came back from the war there was a feeling that you could do something as monumental as the pyramids in your own area.

But there were few travelling exhibitions coming into Wales at that time weren't there, and it has been argued that people like Josef Herman and Heinz Koppel came in and injected a sense of European art into the consciousness of what might have been the limitations of Welsh painters.

I knew Heinz very well. I was introduced to him by Esther Grainger very early on, at the time of the Caerphilly Eisteddfod, 1951. Then when I was the head of painting at Liverpool Art College I had him come to work with me in my department. He was a very fine painter, a brilliant teacher, an absolute gentleman. I know that people could find him awkward because he had the ability to be difficult, but I never met this. I always had the most wonderful relationship with Heinz. As far as the painting is concerned, he had no influence on the actual structure or the making of the paintings for me. He may have done for Ernie Zobole. But he certainly supported the notion of painting, so intellectually he was somebody who was painting pictures and believed in painting, and in that sense he was supportive. We had a good relationship because it was to do with respect. I've got a few small things he made, and I go to look at his paintings. I have an absolute warmth for all his family, so visiting them is always a great pleasure.

There was no professional rivalry. In terms of selling art, there wasn't a gallery even in Cardiff, was there? There was Howard Roberts a bit later in the Fifties.

I never showed with Howard Roberts. But there were South Wales Group shows and exhibitions for schools, and I sold in those when I was a student. But all that is sociological stuff: what interests me is painting. It may even have been a good thing, having to sell paintings to live. I can't say, I'll never know whether that was good or bad. By the time of my final exhibition in the Royal College I had already sold enough for three exhibitions. All the paintings I had left were those I hadn't sold. I've always been in this very peculiar position of painting lots of pictures, and having about me lots of pictures that I haven't sold.

Well, you've certainly got plenty of pictures in this house.

Yes, well, I don't sell pictures.

Though you had to as a student. Was there any compromise in what you did then?

I can remember when I was just going to the Royal College I went to the hotel bar in Treherbert and people were very enthusiastic that I should be going up to London to paint. A collier said to me, "Don't let the buggers bully you up there. You remember that what you want to do is right." That was a very wise bit of encouragement, because so many people got completely bullied into adopting an idiom belonging to a different background and ideology. Painting is about having some idea that's non-verbal, beyond talking. It's become very much the habit now that the artist writes a little bit for the exhibition catalogue. I'm not sure about that. One can be hoodwinked by talk. It's the painting that counts.

But there's also the need for painters to live and sell their work, balancing the painting and the workplace.

You admire Alfred Wallis for his originality and single-minded oddness.
People thought he was mad, but there was a purity of expression, and, you could say, an absolute elegance of presentation. I say "elegant" because he found an elegant solution for what he was saying. There's not a dot or spot that's out of place – they are perfect. I use the words "elegant solution" in the way that a scientist would to balance an equation. There is not a brush-stroke out of place: the form, expression and idea, everything has become one.

Some of your portraits, for example that painting of your aunt and your mother as a girl in the room next door is, well, primitive, isn't it? There's not the elegance of an Augustus John portrait – 'Madame Suggia', let's say. So you mean an elegance of technique?
I mean elegance when expression and form become one. No discrepancy between the actual structure and the expression.

You put things away and store them here and then years later go back to them; are you ever totally satisfied? Is that painting of your aunt and mother finished, or will you ever take it down and work on it again?
I worked on it over ten years. Yes, I'm sure that it is finished. I wouldn't do anything else to it. As soon as a painting can be ignored, really ignored – and it should be ignored for six months at least – until then, it's not finished. It's better to use the word 'resolved'.

Resolved in the sense that you needed to work something out in paint.
Yes, and when you've resolved that – that's it. I'm sure that's exactly like your writing.

Yes, and that's the problem with the education system and assessment deadlines. We have to agree with the student that what they hand in is a stage towards real completion.
I was always very taken with William Blake's "Thank god I was never sent to school to be flogged into following the ways of a fool." I believe that. You have to be exceedingly careful if you are teaching. You can't argue that students are doing everything on their own – they obviously aren't. I think that to be a teacher you have to be like a top quality plumber who opens the taps and gets a kind of controlled flow from the pupil. Trying to get something really new – that's a great prize. And it may be a quite simple thing.

That takes us back to the point of your work. When you draw and paint fruit over and over again, is there a sense in which they are all the same thing – you have, say, two hundred paintings of the plum in the bowl, but is it the ideal plum in the bowl, or is it the curves, the relationship between shape and colour, a sort of Platonic ideal?

No, it's against the Platonic ideal, because that would mean that there was an ideal which was brilliant, and that if you were lucky you could make a copy of that ideal, hence the world is a copy of the idea of God. No, it's the opposite of that: I want to make the drawings so that you couldn't have imagined them. You work on them until you reach the state when you couldn't have imagined the drawing. Then you've got it.

Making the plum newer and newer and newer.

That's right. Out there are these things that you are looking at; and there's this piece of paper and pen or whatever and there is this involvement of working away at the drawing until you arrive, not at a preconceived idea, but until you have arrived at an idea that you couldn't have conceived of.

It's like the novelist saying, I don't know what the end is, I'm on a journey.

Yes, and it's because it's a journey that I could go on painting for ever.

And that's liberating in a way. It's like Peter Prendergast working away at the Bethesda quarry drawings for years. Cézanne's Mont Sainte-Victoire, Morandi's bottles. Not needing to go anywhere else. You stay round here and

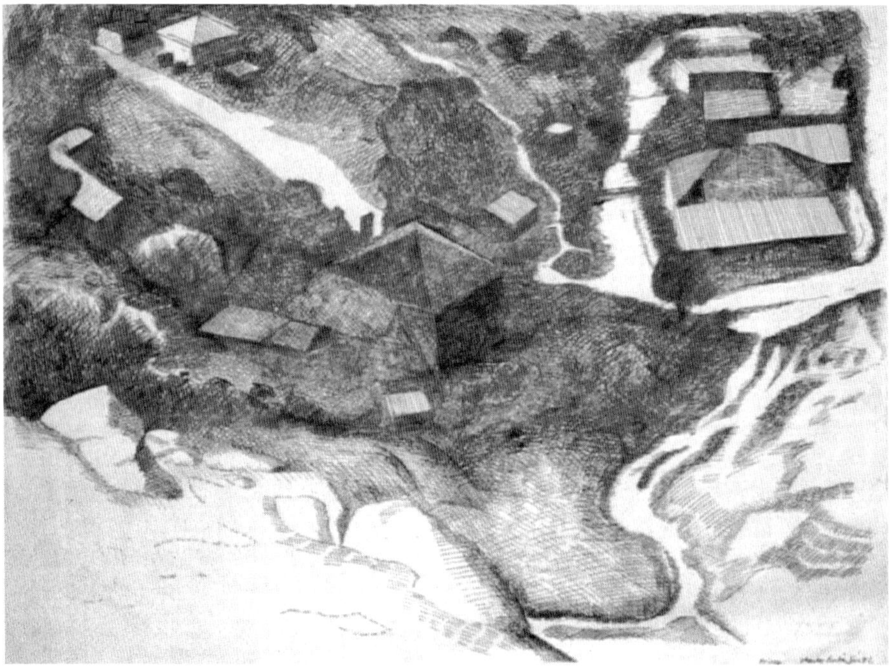

Prilep, Macedonia ink, 43 x 66 cm, 1982, coll: the artist

keep on doing this bit of the world and by getting it right it becomes a sort of travelling.

I could stay in this room for ever. Drawing. That plant. There's much more here than I could ever use. It's a Zimmerlinden, an inside lime tree. Do you want one? Yes, I'll grow one for you. There's no fruit, but they produce little white flowers. This one's a bit weak, it should have lovely big leaves. And if you put it in the dark it's much greener. If you put it by a window it's almost translucent. They were very popular with the central European Jewish community.

Yes, I could do that for ever. I mean Mondrian was doing that with his little squares. This was serious work that he was doing, and there was a very serious philosophy behind it.

It is difficult for the public to see where that sort of work is going, though.

I think art is élitist. I honestly don't think that the general public have any idea at all. I think that as entertainment it's absolutely lousy; you have much more fun watching the television. And if you wanted excitement then watch a rugby match, or boxing, or better still, take part.

Isn't that what Damien Hirst is attempting – excitement? Is he misguided?

That's not for me to say. I haven't seen them, apart from photographs. I haven't seen the real things, but I am sure that I would enjoy them – I love looking at things.

I think painting is for the discriminating few. I'm perfectly happy if people come here and say, I'd love to have that painting. And then, that it looks wonderful in their house.

It reminds me of the occasion when Richard Hughes the novelist was inducted into the American Academy of Writers and he said in his speech how important the novel was; how central such things should be for us. He said that Adolf Hitler was the archetypal non-novel reader. No engagement with the imagination.

I agree. But I don't think that one can succeed as a kind of preacher through art; it doesn't work. Look at all the wonderful art arguing for pacificism: it doesn't change things. Look at recent events in Yugoslavia.

But that is the inability of individuals to make historical changes. I believe that young people, and adults who avoid overwhelming cynicism, can be affected by such art.

And what is clear is that any city, any emerging nation, any community, it seems, in the second half of the twentieth century, does seem to have this impulse to define itself, to confirm its status by building an art gallery and dressing itself with art – paintings, public sculptures and so on.

I agree. Look at the rush to get to the Cézanne at the Tate. You had to get a ticket. Very few people would have an idea about his work. He's not exactly a contemporary. He died ninety years ago, but his work is as new and modern as it was when he painted, and I am delighted that the exhibition is so popular. One can only get to know about painting by rubbing shoulders with it. Best of all is living with it.

And at the level of the individual, when you've got your house and cars and so on, what you buy then is some art. And in a sense that isn't necessarily a bad thing, is it?

It is excellent, because it's to do with the maternal side, it's to do with nest building, to do with the quality of life, and even more importantly it is the best way to learn to read painting.

It used to be common for people to laugh or get annoyed in front of cubist pictures and especially paintings by Matisse, because viewers did not 'see' nature the way they thought painters saw it. One has to learn to read painting. The main reason that the huge American Abstract Expressionist pictures were taken up by the government in America and by big international organisations is that in some way they all represent nothing, so there is no reason to get angry. On the other hand they were designed to influence the environment rather than represent it in some way. They were more matriarchal in spirit. Exactly opposite to the big French paintings of the nineteenth century which were meant to be great heroic statements. However wonderful the 'Raft of Medusa' may be, I'd rather see a Jackson Pollock hanging in the foyer of my bank. I'm straying from the question, however. Yes, there is nothing better than rubbing shoulders with paintings to get to know what they are about. Every painting is an event and every work one responds to is contemporary.

Like your painting the still lifes of fruit. They are in process of decomposing as you are painting them. The art stops time. All the arts are about cheating time. But when, as you say, you have reached that moment of elegance, when it's just right, we still have that problem of the fact that when someone wants your painting they have to prise it from you. But once you've resolved it, it ought to go.

Yes, it should take off, then someone can join in with it. And then it takes on another function. To complete the circle, the viewer is as essential a part as the maker.

Which is how a gallery functions, to bring the two elements together. It's almost ungentlemanly to come here and say, how much is that painting? It's too personal. That's why we need the gallery system to facilitate things.

But it's much nicer to say to someone, Oh, come to breakfast and we'll look at some things. And then if you take something and get fed up with it, you can bring it back and swop it. It's all the same to me. That's very reasonable. I got one of Ernie Zobole's, but because of the scale of the house I couldn't see it, so I swopped it for another one. Everybody should use a little horse sense when it comes to painting.

Felicity Charlton

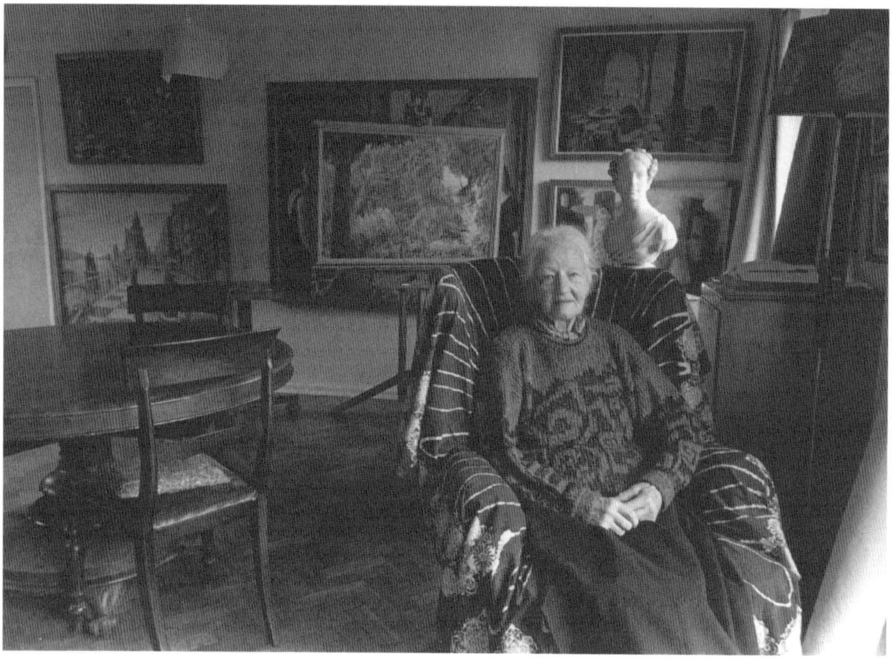

I first interviewed Felicity Charlton in 1994 in her house, The Gables, which stands high above Porthkerry Park in Barry. It is half of a narrow pair of houses from the 1940s that you reach down an unwelcoming track. The long main living room has a remarkable trompe l'oeil *fireplace with a painted sea view decorated with shells by Evan Charlton; it partly complements the dozen or so paintings by Evan and Felicity which cover the walls. In the kitchen hang six striking, original etchings of Rome's antiquities by Piranesi. From the large sliding patio doors the scene spans from the distinctive railway viaduct to the left of the park to the exposed cliffs at Pebble Beach to the west of Barry. The house is set in a marvellous wilderness of trees, shrubs and flowers, though this pastoral is regularly punctuated by the incoming air traffic for Cardiff/Wales airport at Rhoose just a mile away. I have known Felicity for over ten years and visited her several times between 1994 and 1997 to talk about her work.*

We are speaking in the week of your eighty-first birthday. And you've just had a retrospective exhibition in Newport Art Gallery in November and you've sold almost half of your paintings. That must have been very pleasing. When did you first come to Wales?
I was born in Clifton, near Bristol, and came to Wales before the war in 1938, when Evan was made Head of the Art School in Cardiff. I'd met Evan a few years before, about 1935, I think. I was at art school and he was my teacher. An unmarried teacher at an art school wasn't going to last long. We were married in '36.

What sort of family did you come from? And how did you find yourself going to art college?
Well, my father was an architect and so was my brother; and my mother, when she was a young woman, had studied at an art school in Brussels for a few years. But she hadn't continued it because she had four children. Her mother was widowed at a young age and it was cheaper to live in Brussels or Paris than it was in England at the time. My mother was born in 1895. My mother got married when she was twenty-three and so she couldn't continue. We all of us drew as children; I can't remember not drawing. We would get around the table and draw. We were very much encouraged to go on with art.

What did you imagine you would go on to do afterwards?
I didn't really know quite. I had some idea that I would paint portraits, but I was never really any good at that sort of art. Of course it was a time of great unemployment in the thirties; and if your father could support you, then he did support you. You didn't rush out and try to get a job.

Two years after I married Evan he put in for the Headship at Cardiff and got it. Which was remarkable because he was only about thirty-three at the time. He was the only one who applied who was not already the head of an art school.

Was Cardiff a relatively new institution?
No, it had been going for some time. It was on top of that building, the technical college in the centre of Cardiff, near the Temple of Peace. It was on the top floor and the architectural college was there as well, in the floors beneath. Evan was there, of course, during the war. I didn't do any teaching: I didn't need to. Though I don't think I've ever stopped painting and drawing.

It must have been difficult before the war?
Yes. Evan came to Cardiff at the time of Munich when people were more scared, I think. Evan said he thought it was ridiculous signing up art students when it was clear we were going to war. The art school went on, but various people were called up in their age groups. It was very well done, you know, there was no white feather business. Evan, being too old, and head of the school, was not called up, though he was quite prepared to go. That's why Ceri Richards came, because a young member of staff was called up and the art schools in London had been closed. In fact, Ceri was doing farm work, pulling beet in Essex somewhere. Being a Welshman, he applied. And immediately Evan saw his work...

Didn't he know his work before that?
No. But Ceri was a friend of F.E. McWilliam, the sculptor – and Evan was great friends with Mac, they'd been at the Slade together. Mac said to get him if he could. Well, Evan got Ceri through the committee by carefully sorting the drawings out – the more conventional things he put on the top. Ceri was appointed and stayed until 1944. He was a very good teacher.

Of course, this was a terrible time – the docks bombed and Swansea blitzed.
Yes, I remember Graham Sutherland came down to do drawings of the docks. He and his wife came to lunch with us in Llandaff. Evan also did a painting of a factory that had started down in the docks where women were making parachutes. He wasn't an official war artist but they commissioned that one. The women were working with silk at long tables. The strange thing was that Evan went down to draw it – he didn't actually paint it there, of course – but he did these careful drawings on one day and arranged to return the next day. Well, when he went back the next morning the place had been completely destroyed by a bomb. Perhaps that painting is in the Imperial War Museum. Another commission he had was to do the barge boats on the canals, which during the war were manned by women. That was near Windsor and he did several watercolours of these women. One of them is in the National Museum collection of watercolours.

During the war, the art school was quite small, but flourishing. There were some women and the men would stay for as long as they could. Heinz Koppel was there, but I always thought his work was flimsy. I remember that Bert Isaacs and his wife Joan were there, and Bryn Richards. And they all turned up at my recent exhibition!

Now, Evan left Cardiff College to become an H.M.I. didn't he?

Yes, Evan left Cardiff College of Art when he was invited to become an H.M.I. They had never had a separate Inspector for Art, they used to borrow a chap called Peasey from England, and he just used to do the art colleges. But they asked Evan to do all of Wales to start with – every school and every college. He couldn't possibly do it. But he'd run day courses, very much for teachers coming back from the war. They had no art training at all but were expected to teach art in ordinary schools. He had a day, so he made them all draw and paint on huge bits of paper. He'd do a whole week in Bangor, and not having a family I'd go with him and although they didn't pay me I would help with some of the teaching. It was great fun and I enjoyed it. They were very ignorant, though some were older, mature people, coming back from the war. I remember one man saying, "How do you mix green?" We used this awful powder colour. Evan would give them white and black and the three primary colours – yellow, blue and red – and big pieces of paper. And they all had to do something, no-one was allowed not to paint.

So some of them became art teachers in Wales? The basic material doesn't sound very promising.

No, but when Evan first started going into schools many of them didn't have any colour, only pencils.

It's no wonder that there was a problem with Wales developing a strong tradition.

Evan was a very practical person. He'd show them how to take pieces of cardboard and put a layer of oil paint on, commercial paint, you know, so that children had something to mix on. They all used powder paint which he made little containers for. The emphasis was on making do with as little expense as possible.

There was nothing of the fine art here, then?

Yes, but the children did some beautiful work, you know. Evan was keen to get these teachers mixing colour and using it freely. I remember he'd show them very practical things like how to fold paper to create lines. These people were always surprised and pleased to find Evan taking a practical approach. I think it might have been his Chemistry – because his mother insisted that he take Chemistry before going to the Slade. He was at London University first doing a Chemistry degree. They only had two boys and the first had gone into this awful art business.

But George Charlton was an eminent teacher at the Slade.

Yes, but they didn't want another one going that way! Of course, Evan was older than me and I knew his parents when they were retired. His father had the most peculiar business. He bought badger hairs from Russia and they were made into the finest shaving brushes in England. He had a little factory in E.C.1 where Evan was born. He didn't make the brushes, he simply prepared the hair – one of the most skilled jobs you could imagine, that fine hair made into the right lengths, wrapped up in blue paper and then sent off to have the handles fitted.

So did the artistic talent come from that family business of dexterity?

No, but his mother was very interested in painting: I think that she'd worked for a frame-makers at one time. Evan had seen how moody George had got with his art and so he agreed to do the Chemistry degree. He nearly blew himself up at the end, he said! He couldn't get a job as a chemist so just before he went off to training college to be a teacher he went to the Slade to do a bit of drawing. George was five years older and already teaching there and he invited Evan along. One day Tonks, the great Professor there, asked him what he was doing at the Slade. And some days later he told George, "He'll stay," and he did. Then he got a job with the London Council testing gas and that part-time job helped him to pay his way at the Slade. He did portraits for a bit in London, but he didn't like it – people would complain about their noses or something. He did a few – Governor General of the Windward Islands in all his finery. But when the job at Bristol Art School was advertised he went for it. Donald Milner, the head of the school was keen on him, because the Bristol school was very run down and Milner wanted new staff there and he liked Evan's paintings and got him. I was there before Milner arrived and it was very odd, the previous head had let it become very run down and I'd be the only person drawing in the life room. Under Milner the students were put in for the more testing Board's exams for drawing and painting. That's why I took my Board's drawing and painting with John Elwyn, though John is a lot younger than I am. He was from Carmarthen, but came to Bristol to do the Board exams.

So what was John Elwyn like in those days? It must have been quite a move for him from Carmarthen to Bristol.

He was a nice chap, quiet, but very hard working. I think that Evan broadened him in his views.

He's a very romantic painter – all those paintings of west Wales, greens and yellows, like so many Fern Hills.

I love his colours. Another painter that Evan helped a lot was Bert Isaacs, and then there was Joan Baker and Howard Roberts, though that was later at Cardiff.

Yes, I took my Board exam in 1936, the year I was married. I didn't bother to take the teacher training; you could do it at any time later.

Milner always accused me of losing him his best member of staff, because he always thought I had pushed him into the Cardiff job, but it was a much better job – head of painting.

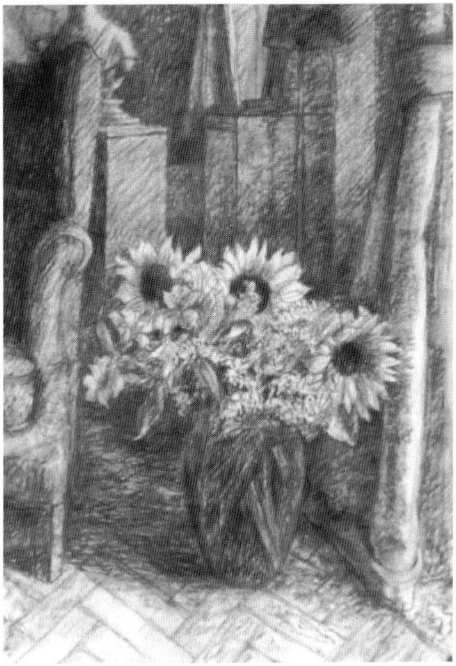

The Vase of Flowers
Pencil, 52 x 38 cm, 1996,
coll: the artist

It must have been like missionary work?

Well, there were good staff there; I remember Bill Pickles who did all the craft. He'd been at the Royal College. He could do anything – weaving, pottery, metalwork. During the war someone gave him a sheepskin and he ended up turning it into a fine wool jacket. No, Evan was keen on Wales because his mother was Welsh. She was born in London, but her parents were Welsh speaking.

So there was a sense of a college community there, and you had the National Museum collection close by.

Yes, we knew people there including Rollo Charles and he bought Evan's paintings and there was a retrospective.

So the Museum was interested in Welsh art? Because they are accused by some of not paying enough attention to the art of Wales?

I think they were. And the Arts Council did a lot – David Bell and Isabel Hitchman. Now with all this cutting down of jobs they don't know where they are.

At the art school there were some interesting students. I remember Heinz Koppel coming along, brought by his father. Heinz was a very quiet, retiring chap. He had the darkest black hair, like a crow when he was young. And Esther Grainger was a very great influence on art in

Cardiff and beyond. She was working in the Settlements and unemployed clubs in the valleys. She met Cedric Morris and went out to his school in East Anglia – that was the saving of her. She had the same disadvantage as myself in that she'd had a very poor start in Cardiff Art School before Evan took it over. She revolutionised the National Eisteddfod. She had exhibitions of young people's work and brought it alive. And there was Frances Bowen who as a patron did a lot for Welsh art. She had a house in Cathedral Road filled with paintings.

So Evan was at the art school through the war and then he was an H.M.I. from 1946 to the Sixties.

Yes, but at the end, for the last four years, England stole him. He was staff inspector for England and some of Wales. He liked that, he found it interesting. He used to go up and stay in the Liberal Club in London from Monday to Friday and just walk across Green Park to Curzon Street, where the offices were at that time. And I'd pick him up from Cardiff station on Friday evenings. He visited the London galleries but said that he didn't want to go back to live in London because it had changed so much.

So you had a lot of time on your own when he was away in other parts of Wales and later in London and you got on with your own painting?

Oh yes. I've had a life of leisure. But I worked jolly hard in the war – at a market garden in Llandaff, just down where the Bishop of Llandaff School is now. I used to kneel for hours weeding onions. I was called up to work because I didn't have a family. I was paid one and six an hour.

We've got that large drawing of yours of Cardiff bus passengers from 1944

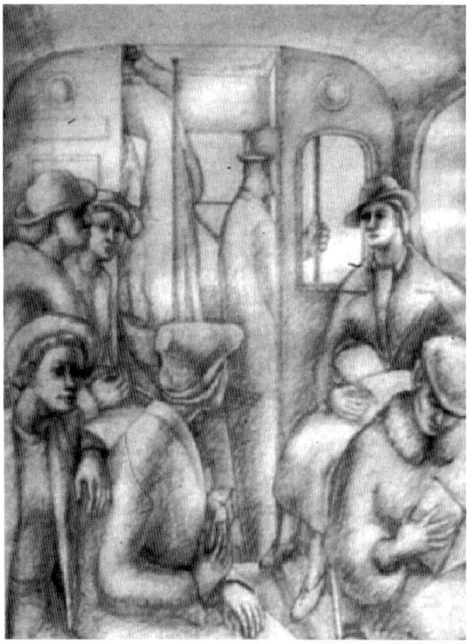

The Cardiff Bus
Pencil, 53 x 40.5 cm, 1944,
coll: Prof & Mrs Curtis

so I suppose that you continued to paint and draw all through the war years? Some early work was included in the recent exhibition. Are you not reluctant to part with things that go that far back?
Oh no. I never feel that at all. If people like a painting I am delighted that they should have it. I see no point in keeping a lot of things just in folios under the bed, or stored in some workroom upstairs. I've always exhibited regularly, sometimes with Evan.

But there must have been periods, in the Fifties, for example, when there was nowhere to show.
The Arts Council had come, of course, and I remember we were invited to paint or draw Welsh chapels. That was very successful and went all over Wales. John Petts was in that, too. And then I exhibited with the South Wales Art Society which was going fairly strong. When we first moved to Cardiff there was nothing apart from that Society; they organised an exhibition once a year in the basement of the City Hall. That was the only thing for years. Then after the war the Arts Council with David Bell as Head of the Painting began exhibitions.

I remember shows in Turner House in the Fifties, I sold a painting there at that time. Then a student of Evan's started up a gallery in St Mary Street. That was the first one, Howard Roberts. We both showed mainly with Howard Roberts. He had a wife who helped him with the gallery, but she wasn't earning, and they had two children to bring up. After a few years he had moved to a very modern gallery opposite the general post office at the bottom of Westgate Street; it was small, but like a smart London gallery. I thought it was delightful. But it didn't go. People didn't care for it. The previous one was on top of this funny hotel where you had to go in this lift, which you felt would at any moment fall apart, but people liked the sense of going up to an artist's studio. Then the Albany Gallery followed. Of course, later the Arts Council started up in Charlotte Street, in Oriel, with Isabel Hitchman organising things.

That was where I bought my first picture after coming back to Wales in 1974. It was a John Selway watercolour 'Twins at Bournemouth' – he was having a sort of studio sale at the end of his exhibition there. These large pictures were twelve pounds, but I couldn't afford both those I wanted.
I remember that exhibition. Of course, Evan was always showing quite widely, but the exhibition in Abergavenny in the seventies was really for me. Then we had one together in Oriel in 1981. After seeing that, Roger Cooksey from Newport offered us a bigger exhibition. He came to the house and cleared it practically. We had the whole gallery to ourselves.

Your paintings are a mixture of the real and the imagined, aren't they?
Yes, I'll use actual things, scenes from the garden here and the figures will be imaginary. I might use an arm, a head, from a magazine. I don't

use models, but I do a bit of life drawing now in Llanover Hall.

Both in your work and Evan's there are almost always doorways, windows, bits of ruins used as part of the setting; the furniture, as it were, of the paintings.

With Evan's paintings, and I try to do the same, we don't want it to be a record of a real place. He got that more strongly than I did.

Take that room in Evan's 'The Crate' hanging there. It's not a painting of a real room – it's a dream room. And that is very important. The way he puts that gap in the floor. It's equivalent to you writing a poem about something, rather than you writing just a piece of prose, just a record. One's trying to do an imaginative parallel of the real world. And that what's your poems are doing, aren't they?

Robert Lowell said that a poem is not a record of an event, it is an event.

But your work up to and including the war is conventional, isn't it? Like the drawing of people on a bus which we have in our house. Why did that change?

I think because I was living with Evan. He was a very big influence on me. His work has this extra thing, it's not quite symbolic. That one there – 'The Crate' – for example.

Yes, there are the four women in the corners, but then the floor is like a chess-

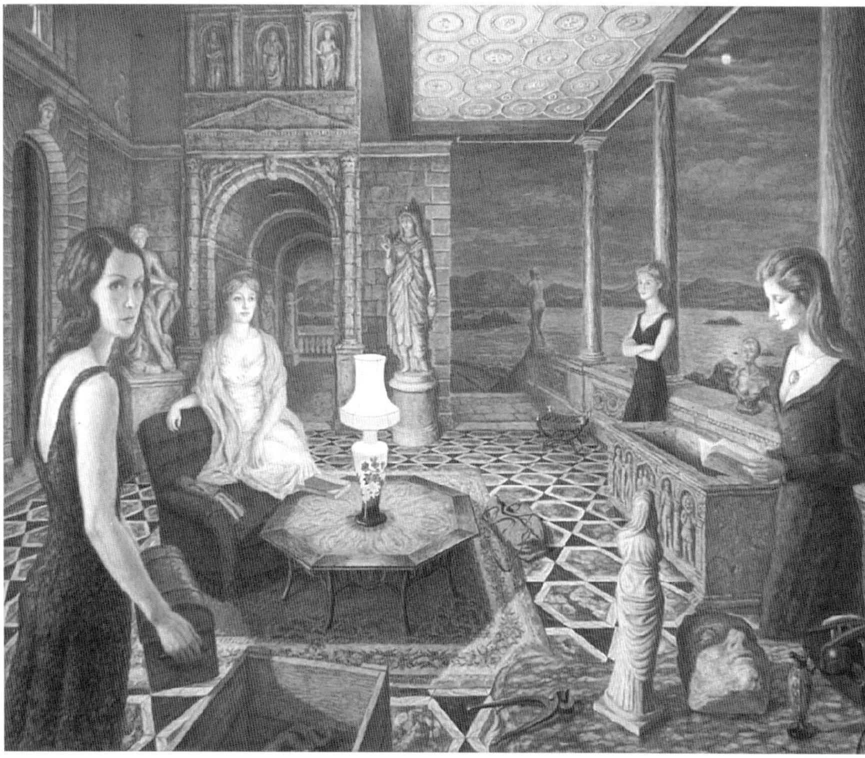

The Crate by Evan Charlton oil, 122 x 152 cm, 1974, coll. Felicity Charlton

board, as if a game is to be played.

Yes, he loved those floors and that perspective. He was always very good at perspective. But you couldn't possibly imagine that was a real place. It's very, very strange. Look, there's a sort of workman's bag there. What is it doing?

And she's looking defiantly out at the viewer. I find the same sort thing in the earlier work of Harry Holland. They have the same sort of dramatic intrigue.

Well, when people would ask Evan about a picture he'd make up some ridiculous story. A few months ago there was a fire in the house up the hill here and a policeman came to ask me about it. He saw this picture and said, "Were they your four daughters?" Now wasn't that interesting? Because people want there to be an explanation, a reason.

This other one, 'Comus and the Lady' has the anagram of Evan Charlton as the name of the Metro station. The statue is, of course, of Comus and was in the Great Exhibition of Victorian times. I remember when we did a talk for the sixth form in the girls' school here in Barry a girl asked Evan where the buildings came from. And he said, "Liverpool, Manchester, London." And that last one is from Newport, though it's sliced in half. He took an enormous number of photographs just for buildings. He did his own developing and enlarging.

When Evan left the Art School and became an HMI he felt much more free to paint what he wanted. When he was teaching students it was as if he was painting for them. When he saw what the children were doing there was a freedom there. Despite the bureaucracy and the travelling, he never gave up painting, you know. We spent a lot of time on our painting. Both in this room at either end. This was our living room and our studio.

The view over Porthkerry and the sea from this remarkable house is used by you, but not by Evan? He is more of a city person, isn't he?

But we used to go on holiday abroad quite a lot. A year or two after we were married we went down to the Dordogne before English people went there and he took a lot from that. Some friends in London told us about it – it was cheap and unspoiled. It was in 1937, I think. I remember, we took all our own oils and canvases with us on the train. We got lost on the way there and had to take a long taxi ride. It was an amazing journey up and down these hills. It was a full moon and the driver was just like a brigand with a huge moustache. We arrived at the hotel about eleven o'clock at night and Evan asked if we could just have a cup of something and a sandwich. But, oh no – into the dining room and a complete dinner was laid out for us.

How long did you stay?

About three weeks. We did landscapes. In order to get a cheaper rail fare we went through Paris and there was a huge international exhibition on at the time. Of course, the Spanish Civil War was being fought and Picasso, who was in Paris, had just finished 'Guernica' and we saw it there in Paris. Just recently I saw it for the second time in Spain.

The architecture in Evan's work is very grand, isn't it? But in that painting of yours, 'The Scarves' you have appropriated two of Evan's paintings in the background.

It's a strange picture, really. I've got all the things in it. They do exist. At first I thought I would have someone sitting in that chair, but there's not the space, so I put in that picture of Evan's with the moon in it. And do you know when I was painting that the phone rang and it was Isabel Hitchman from Oriel to say that someone wanted the one with the moon in it. So I've never sold it.

When you paint, do you ever think that there is something particularly feminine, womanly, in what you do?

No, I don't think so. I've never thought that.

Let's talk about the painting which you are currently working on. It's a painting which you are developing from a drawing that was on your 1996 Christmas card, isn't it?

It's different from the drawing on the card. And also from the last painting which is over here. This one you saw last time you visited – it hasn't got a title. The figure is supposed to a be a Greek soldier and his helmet. David Alston liked that when he came, but suggested that I slightly change the tree on the left; the trunk was too dark, so I added these touches of blue and that ivy creeping up it.

Yes, the ivy adds a sense of mortality. Perhaps the title should be simply 'The Helmet'?

Yes, let's call it that. This picture started after I'd been to some life classes at Llanover Hall with a friend and the figure was lying down facing us on the dais. The trees come from around this house, of course.

But when you are painting you are primarily concerned with the visual effects you are creating, not the narrative and symbolic elements that I as a viewer will take from it?

Yes. This one on the easel I started four months ago and I am working to paint out some of the detail that was in the original drawing. The table, for instance, was crowded with what could be a meal or something, but now I've just got a book.

You've got a group of what seem to be female figures surrounding a patriarch sitting with the book at the table. He's a sort of King Lear figure, I think. The landscape here is more Grecian or Mediterranean. But if one tries to weave a story from the painting, the reading of a will, or a family Bible, do you accept that?

I want ambiguity. The trees at each side may be curtains. I've put in that full moon, taken from Evan's painting 'The Crate'.

Yes, I can see how painting in this room, as you both did, the other, previous work is an influential background to whatever new work you are doing. You had a trunk on the floor in the foreground of your painting, but it's now been replaced by an almost sinister shadow. And the moon seems to draw upwards that female, ghostly figure on the right.

That's another of your works, next to 'The Crate'.

Yes, there's classical ruins in that one too. It's 'The Excursion' [see colour plate], the lovers are visiting a classical site and are walking away from the guide because they're bored stiff.

They want a life more immediate than the history of that place.

Well, I can't paint for so long – about an hour usually. But we always kept the materials here in this room, so I can begin in about five minutes when I feel like it at any time. I still use this spotlight which Evan fixed up. Because he painted from the imagination he could do it at any time, even at night under electric light. I may work at any time, but you have to be careful of the yellows under electric light; they become too bright.

And you tend to work at one thing at a time, except for the drawings, of course. That drawing of you and the Georgian marble bust is very strong, I think. Will that become a painting in due course?

I used a mirror to do that.

There's a strong tension between your face and the Georgian lady, with that plant between those curtains, which again make the thing almost theatrical. That sense of theatre is certainly in the new painting. And that one is so different in texture and subject from what we shall call 'The Helmet' which you completed at the end of last year.

I want to use more paint, 'The Helmet' is much thinner. The whole point is to paint it much broader. I'm striving for a mystery.

You're going on a cruise to the Arctic Circle in the summer; will you take a sketch book with you?

I've never worked abroad much, but being on the ship constantly I will probably draw something. Although Evan and I went to France a lot we didn't stay for long. Now I go abroad with the Contemporary Art Society. Although I went to Turkey last year with a niece.

Evan was very much a town person, living in London and Bristol before we came here. It was a joke between us that I would offer to paint a tree in his pictures if he wanted one. He very rarely put in a tree. Though he liked living here in Porthkerry.

Have you ever painted that view over the park precisely?

Yes, I have one upstairs. And there's one in the National Library in Aberystwyth. The funny thing is they sell quickly when I do one.

And there's that very good one in the Glynn Vivian.

Yes 'Sinararia', after the plant. It is a good one. But the funny thing is that the buildings in that one are not from Wales at all, they're from all over the place.

When will you have finished that new painting?

I don't know. My friend Edward is coming to see me tomorrow and I'll talk to him. Evan and I used to discuss each other's work a lot, and it was an awful blank in my life when he died. The queer thing was that quite soon after I met Edward. He saw our joint exhibition in the West of England Academy and was bowled over by Evan's painting; he wrote to ask to see more of Evan's work. We've been friends ever since. I visit Edward and his wife in Salisbury. Edward trained as a print maker and illustrator at Southampton. He is very honest about my work and I need that response. What do you think about that painting?

Well, I like the intrigue you've created. I love the colours and the texture. The figures are shadowy, rather like Samuel Palmer's, though this scene is a long way removed from Palmer's England. But I am a little worried by the glass bowl on the right of the table. It's almost hovering like an apparition and I think it should be more solid, so that it doesn't detract from the spectral figure of the woman by the table.

Yes, I have worried about that. I put it in last week and it isn't right. Perhaps it could be a spray of flowers just picked, transitory things. No, it's good to have someone else say that. I shall work on that.

Clearly, your biggest influence was Evan, but who else really influenced you?

I admired Bonnard, a very wonderful painter. And in my student days the Renaissance painters, though they haven't influenced my own painting. Also Palmer and Claude and Poussin. Claude influenced Evan with his use of water. I should love to possess his 'Enchanted Castle'. David Jones's work is wonderful, full of poetry and romance.

You are still painting into your eighties. Is there anything you regret not having done in your work? What is there still to do?

I've never been ambitious. Some people regret not having a London show. Perhaps I would have liked to do something really big, a mural or something. But then ten or twenty years later you'd look at it and think, Christ what is that on the wall? I shall just go on painting these pictures. I don't think I've stopped painting since I was four, so I really ought to be better!

SALLY MOORE

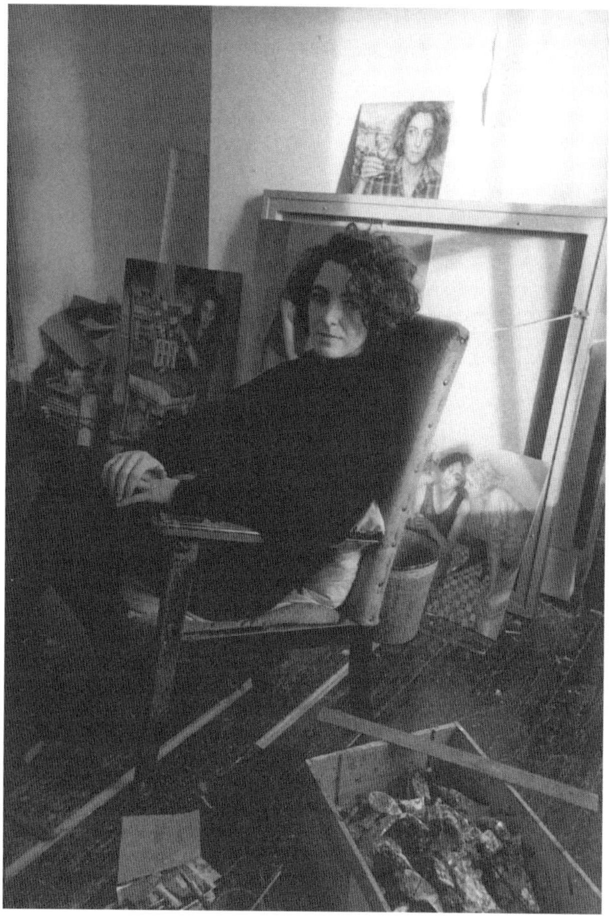

I remember Leslie and Eira Moore bringing their son Simon and daughter Sally to play at the Barry Island Tennis Club in the middle Seventies. I recognised Eira as a part-time teacher of dance at the Glamorgan College of Education where I taught, but I never really knew Leslie. A few years later he died and both children went off to college, Simon to read Biology and to become a successful rock guitarist and composer, and Sally to Oxford, Birmingham and a professional artist's studio in London. I talked to and formally interviewed Sally at Eira's house in Romilly Park, Barry, in February 1995. It is a house full of Leslie's strongest paintings; a striking large early oil of Sally's, 'In the Blue Room' which reminded me of a Bonnard, also hangs in the front room where we sat.

Charles Hall in his catalogue notes to your 1995 exhibition at the Martin Tinney Gallery sees strong personal statements in your work. Do you agree?
I think he stresses that too much, particularly in the last paragraph. He talks about me as if I have some personal problem: he talks about "the spontaneous life she does not have". Too many people read autobiographical things into what you do. It's an easy trap to get into.

People want that because it gives them something they can control in the art.
The nicest response is when people look at the work and say: "I feel exactly like her; I know what she feels like".

But do you feel exactly like her? Because the people in your paintings often look exactly like you.
Yes, they are about how I feel, but also about the human condition and how lots of people feel. They are about obstacles that you face as you go through life. Feelings of being lonely, because you can feel very lonely working as a painter; feelings of being trapped, in the studio you are very removed from the outside world. But people can feel that in all sorts of situations, in bed-sit land or whatever.

There's that sense in the painting which has you, the woman, looking at the goldfish in the tumbler. And it's too small for the fish to survive: you bend down to look at that with an empathy. But then in the background there's a rather stagey violin with a broken string, as if inspiration has gone. Or there's a discordant note.
There's a hint that things have gone wrong. But that's the amusing part in the painting; there's an element of melodrama in them, something slightly staged, false, contrived.

They certainly are contrived because baboons don't turn up at most people's breakfast tables; lions actually don't come at you in a stately garden.
But does the humour come from the fact that these figures are acting out a role, that it's not really happening?

So you like people to come to your shows and take them lightly, rather than to feel intellectually challenged by trying to make sense of what they are seeing?

No, I like the combinations, because the subject matter is seriously based on people's anxieties and the problems people face. It's treated lightly, with humour, and that makes it easier to deal with, to look at and to enjoy.

One of the biggest and most impressive paintings in the 1995 show is 'The House of Cards' [see colour plate]. Hall says that this painting is typical – a female protagonist who is enclosing herself in something that appears to be trivial – building a house of cards – but with elements of the ritualistic about it. While outside, he says, there's a storm gathering, there are forces at work. Is he overplaying that?

That one is not as playful as the others. It's about having a conversation with someone and the two of you not getting on at all. Everything in the painting is to do with that relationship – an awkwardness and tension and they can't relax. In the foreground there's a game of chess – and it's checkmate. That's where the humour is.

So that game's over and the clock has stopped, and one of the characters is looking out for something, or is aware that something is going on outside.

I wanted to create a sense of a precarious feeling and a tense atmosphere.

It's also a stupid solitary thing to do, like crosswords or patience. The point of building the house of cards is to eventually topple them over. So she's saying "I'm not dealing with you at the moment, I'm doing this thing with cards; you go and stand by the window". And there's potential for confrontation with the two cats there.

Yes, that's why I like to have animals in the paintings. I love the way Hogarth used objects in his paintings, because he would have objects surrounding the character on shelves and every object has a purpose. One object might be pointing at one of the characters, or a painting within a painting might reflect the state of mind of the character.

Still, people read all sorts of things into my work; I can't mind that, and have no control over it really.

But you do have control over the world within the frame of the painting; you can open some possibilities of narrative and close off others.

Yes, of course. You learn from people's responses to them and take that into account. Though there can be quite bizarre responses to the paintings, with people imposing their own lives on them.

Once the work is on show, never mind what happens when people buy them and hang them in their own houses, goodness knows what their minds will make of them and how close that remains to what you intended.

In many of your paintings one is not allowed to forget that this is a painting – in terms of the painterly quality. The large early canvas hanging above us here in your mother's house has bold brush strokes and a texture that is quite different from your recent work, which is smooth and spare.

Now I'm trying to create an illusion that draws the viewer into something that they can feel part of. The larger paintings in the exhibition work better, the figures being almost life-size; or you could be entering the interior yourself. So with 'The House of Cards' the table comes right out in front of you so you could be almost touching it. I often take a low viewpoint. I'll be sitting on the floor, which makes you feel more on a level with the figures, the floor and the interior. In the one with the owls, you could be entering through that door, an extension of your own space; and there's inevitably more of a psychological link.

But that realist perspective is broken up by this stump of a tree with two owls on it, which cannot be in the actual room.

I like making the viewer feel uncomfortable, the two owls glaring out at you, confrontational.

But these are not owls as in the Welsh art and literature of Ceri Richards and Dylan Thomas. They exist essentially to break up the perspective and the reality. How could the door have opened if the owls are positioned there?

I wanted it to be believable because it's painted there. I want the painting to work so that the viewer will not want to question that too much. I want those confusions not to be in the painting, not to be an issue. The owls are supposed to keep you out, to be confrontational.

There's a drama in there – the woman either putting something in or taking something out of the bowl, yourself emerging from under the table as if there's been an air-raid.

But that's the female view. It's based on the early Italian Annunciation paintings, where the angel comes in to visit Mary; and she's quite often reading a book, or she's quiet and composed. It's always to do with good will, bringing good news. I've done that in paintings before, people pushing a door closed. It's to do with change, things are about to change: that pushing of the door is to do with pushing things into the past.

This kitchen is similar to your mother's in this house, isn't it?

Yes it is. I use interiors which I'd like to live in. Though they are out of my reach. The one called 'The Intruder', with the projector, is set in the royal palace in Amsterdam. I love the richness of the fabrics.

That takes us on to where the elements come from. Some of them are places you've visited or lived in, but then you rearrange these elements by using photographs of other art and furniture.

Well, my method of working is that I'll start by doodling in a sketch book, so the idea is the main thing. Then there seem to be several themes that I develop and try to do better. There is the theme of feeling trapped; the tiger theme, which is the feeling of being brave and scared at the same time; another one is the interacting of people, conversations which aren't communicating; people whispering and the viewer is the third party who is excluded.

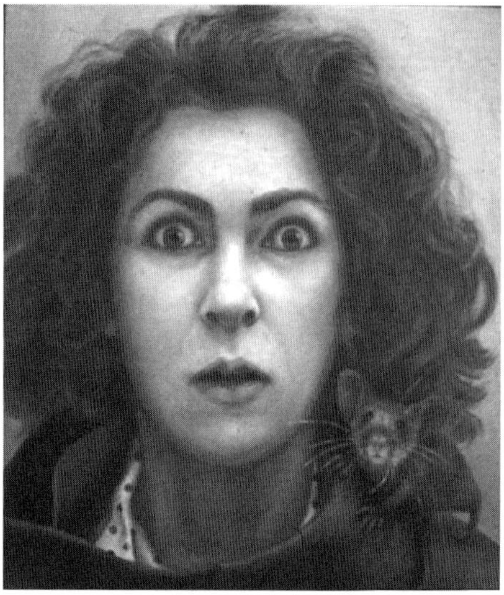

Touch and Go
Oil on panel, 32 x 24 cm, 1995
private collection

Some of them are confrontational. I'm thinking of the small painting of yourself where you have a mouse on your shoulder and you are staring out at us, as if we have caught you unawares and you want us to feel embarrassed about that. And with the others the viewer feels more of a witness, a voyeur. 'House of Cards' works in that way. As does 'The Crossing'.

In 'The Visitor' [see colour plate] the two figures are gossiping and their two heads are almost life-size, and that's you being excluded, though you are sitting at the table with your wine glass.

Yes, you place us there. It's not like Edward Hopper in that famous 'Nighthawks', where one is looking in at a lit space containing someone else's life, something private going on that you can privately view. In your work we are in private houses, rooms lived in by people, so that we are implicated in those lives.

Also, there might be somebody behind a door and the person may not be aware of this figure that the viewer can see. Dramatic irony. Though I don't want them to be too theatrical. As I say, I start with my idea, and the poses have to be spot on. That's why I use myself, I practice in the mirror. You have to be like an actress, I suppose. I know what expressions I want. And then I get someone to take photographs of me; and then it's a matter of finding the setting. That can be using photographs together, playing around with the size of the figures in the interior. Then from that I will do a line drawing which uses a collage of the photographs from a photocopying machine to enlarge or reduce things. It's a quick way of sorting that out. And I end up with a very careful line drawing, much like Botticelli or other early Italian artists used to work in their frescoes. I find it very laborious setting the drawing up. I want to get on with the drawing as soon as possible. The photographs help me to get the linear design, the composition, sorted out, so that I don't have to rearrange things later on. I transpose the line drawing on to the board and then begin the painting. I don't want them to look photographic at all: the way light falls on the faces is linked far more with the way earlier Italian Renaissance artists like Piero della Francesca had the light falling.

All your faces are lit, aren't they? There are no faces in shadow, and they are all artificially lit.

I want that frozen, still quality which comes from not having shadows: that permanent 'caught' quality.

And that sort of lighting is revelatory: you are saying that it's all there to be seen. The personal things about these characters, the significant and humorous things are all in focus.

And you always work on board now?

Yes, I get a smoother, sharper line.

But over the last few months you've been producing smaller pictures, faster paintings, and you claim that's improved your technique?

I think it's confidence. Technically I've got a lot better; and just knowing a lot more about materials. I would varnish things and alter colours as I went along and now I get closer to the colours I want from the beginning. I think it has been a natural development. Harry Holland was helpful in pointing out some of those things to me.

I am not fascinated as, say, Lucian Freud is in being there and getting involved with the flesh and the presence. Mine aren't about that. In the past I have worked with a model, but now I feel uncomfortable with that keeping the pose. I am interested in the effect and use the best means.

Your paintings have tremendous detail – if there's a lion or a monkey then the hairs have that real quality that I admire so much in Andrew Wyeth. You are quite meticulous in what you do.

I want to capture the quality of things – I want fur to look like fur. I want to paint a pearl and get the light shining right, the glint in the eye so that suddenly you realise that something is moist. I want everything to have its own quality, like in some of the recent paintings I've got the wood right – the table in 'House of Cards'.

And that hinge down the middle of the table, which is also about things splitting and folding.

Colour is a very important part of the work; I was very influenced by Matisse in the early eighties, and those influences are still there in the organisation of colour.

There is a strong narrative and theatrical element in what you paint, and you set the stage and the agenda.

That's why I don't paint men, because people will immediately assume that it's about a relationship between that woman and a man. But they are not about that at all. They are concerned with how I feel in certain situations; I'm sure that men feel the same. I don't know what it's like to be a man, so I paint myself.

Is a sexual frisson likely to be part of what you do at some point?
Maybe, but it hasn't been one of the themes. People seem to latch on to sexual significance in so much work – there's my riding of the tiger – but that's too obvious.

Are you playing games with the critics and the viewers?
No, I think the tiger-riding was me being naïve. When I'd finished it I thought, "Oh no, what have I done?"

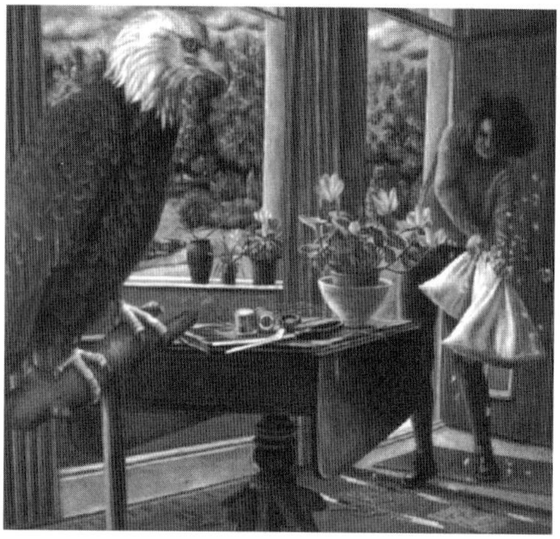

The Nestbuilder
oil on panel, 29 x 28 cm, 1994
private collection

But so often your paintings are of interiors decorated or appointed in a certain way and then you introduce an owl or a baboon or that eagle in 'The Nestbuilder'. By doing that, aren't you challenging the critic to read some significance into the work?
Yes, the animals could be seen to be representing something frightening that needs to be overcome. I think that was to do with moving away from home, meeting new people; having new, but quite scary things in your life. The animals always have a certain characteristic: monkeys, for example, because they are childlike. In 'The Lesson' it's as if I am chopping the heads off roses in a tantrum and the monkey is watching in a very childlike way. It reminds me of a beautiful Chardin painting in the National Gallery where a teacher is teaching a child. They are looking at a book and the child, beautifully painted, is somehow not concentrating.

I hear so many people criticising young painters, that they haven't involved themselves in the great tradition of Western European art. But you have, haven't you?
Yes, I travelled a lot before and after my degree and before I started to channel myself. I saw Botticelli, Titian, all those people, and I still

thought I wanted to slap on paint in a very gestural way. But then I started to refine it down until it felt right. Details like eyes and expressions, the faces are very important. I want them to have a timeless feel; people have said that they come from a different age. But I think they belong now, but that they have several references. They mustn't be too fashion conscious; I want things to last and then belong to the past. They are about things that are timeless, the way that people are and behave.

You mix elements, don't you? You take a wonderful house that you've seen and bring it down in size to make it one of your character's houses. Few people have gardens like those in your paintings. Yours have vistas and mature, manicured lawns and topiary. For example, in 'The Breakfast', inside it's bedsit land and outside it's stately home.

It's a mad combination: I've always loved stately homes and very ordered gardens. I like the fact that the turmoil going on in the lives of figures is contrasted with the ordered environment in which they are placed. I like films like *Dangerous Liaisons* and *The Draughtsman's Contract.*

You have an almost eighteenth century, Age of Enlightenment ordering of the world, but then there is this personal turmoil and confusion and oddness and humour going on against that. And the other things you've got are references to classical art – Renaissance art and pre-Renaissance art – to do with the age of faith, where you have religious icons almost, you've got saints, gestures, that are set in a banal context, a bedsit kitchen context. There's an angelic figure in 'The Sleeper'.

Yes, it's based on a de Chirico drawing. It is reflecting on what is in the mind of the main character. She is asleep, but when she is asleep the bestiary comes into her mind. I like the dog on top because you're not quite sure whether it's yawning or screaming, it's not clear. There's a big cat and you're not sure whether it's catching or feeding. I adore painting goldfish, mainly through Matisse.

Though it's a fairly obvious metaphor for entrapment and being cut off yourself.

I use caged birds too. A lot of it is to do with when I had a studio in this house. You can feel very removed; the studio can also be a complete comfort – it's your room, you feel right there. I suppose they are well-worn symbols, but I hope that I use them in a new way.

You don't live in your studio now, do you? You go to it.

I still need to be in contact with other artists. My present studio is part of a complex with people whom I've known for about five years, who work there every day. If I work exclusively on my own, I get to feel rather nervous of going out. It's good to leave the studio.

When you've done your planning and preparation, how long does a painting take?

A small one takes a week, larger ones a month. I always finish one at a time; I don't work on them simultaneously. The problems I have can't be left; they are problems to do with the light on a cup and I have to get that finished before I go on.

But you used to take such a long time to complete works.
Yes, that's because I was working from a model. At the end of my MA in Birmingham I had four paintings and each had taken me about three months. And I did line-drawings which were incredibly slow.

You say that you have been commissioned to paint a picture; that's a new departure, isn't it?
Yes, that's because I think my drawing had got better. I was in Rome for four months. A man saw me working and wants me to paint him and his car. I've since had a tutorial with Stephen McKenna who is a figurative artist who lives in Florence. I'd always been snooty about portraits, but technically I knew that I could do them now. It does mean earning some money. It's a 1930s Rolls Royce, with the Savoy in the background. He won a big competition in Pebble Beach for best car. It's absurd really.

But here you are saying that you don't paint men and with this you are celebrating the most macho, possessive aspect of a successful man with his prized car.
I suppose I'm showing my expertise in depicting it – the shine on the paintwork and lights. But Martin Tinney has commissioned me to do a portrait of his friend Nick as a character in one of my strange dramas, and that's the perfect commission. But I wouldn't want to do too many; they would get in the way of my own work.

But you are intrigued by this challenge?
Yes, I've got three this year. A man is commissioning one of his wife. It will be a big painting; I shall go to their house and she will be wearing a beautiful dress, with wonderful furniture in the background – I will enjoy doing that.

I suppose that your visits to the Savoy and this grand house will all go in the file for future use in your own paintings?
Portraits are a way of keeping going, because paintings don't sell regularly. Many people teach; and the ideal would be two days a week, but they've cut back on posts recently.

I can remember you as a girl being a good tennis player. You played for Wales and then just gave it up.
Yes, my brother Simon was good and I just tagged along. But then O Levels came and I wanted to do well. I wanted to go to university because my friends were, but I should have gone to a proper art college. I went to the Ruskin on a three year art degree. But there was nowhere for the artists to get together. I was in Somerville and there seemed to

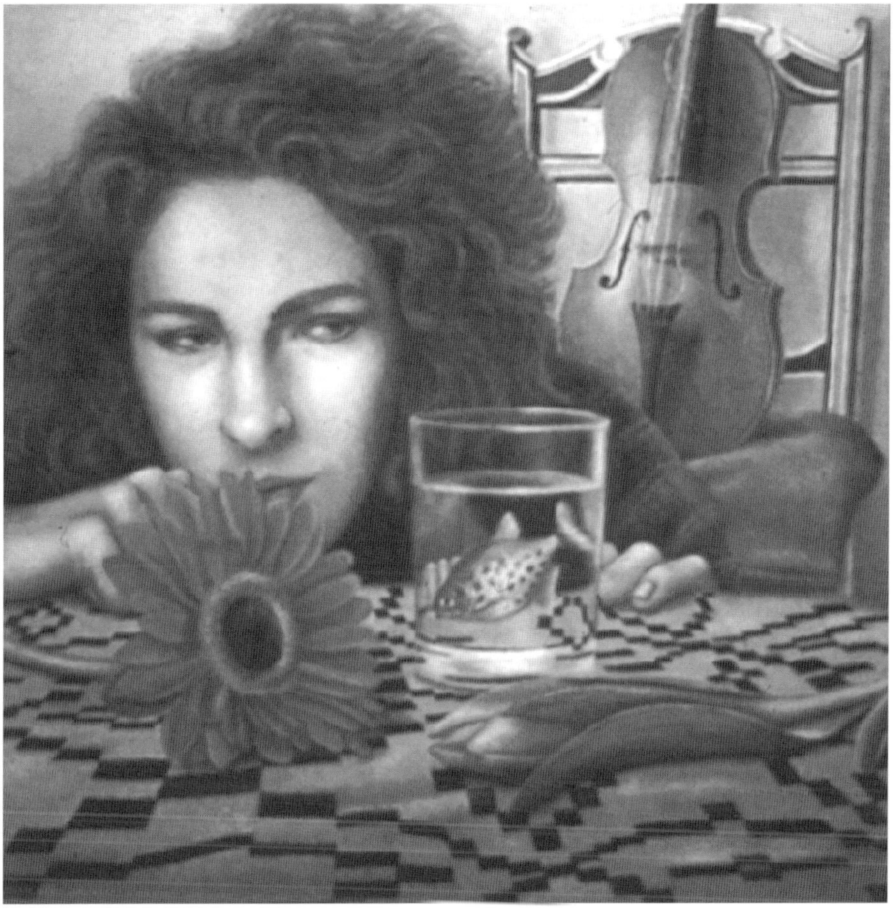

Trapped oil on panel, 32 24 cm, 1995, private collection

be nothing to share with the academic students there. Oxford was full of very bright, articulate people and I felt intimidated. My language was visual and the learning was what happening on canvas, not talking about it. I think that I needed more guidance and my finals show must have seemed very confused and inconsistent. I really moved on when I returned to my mother's house in Barry. For two years I was applying for MA courses.

I got a studio in Cardiff and had a show in the Cardiff University Viriamu Jones Gallery before I eventually got a place on the MA in Birmingham. That was a good year; I got on with my tutor and began to sort out the construction of the paintings. I was influenced by the colours in Bonnard, but needed more in the sense of structure. I stayed on in Birmingham because I found a cheap studio. A friend worked for a magazine *The World of Interiors* and one of my paintings was used in a photograph in the magazine. I got a big response. I sold the painting and received phone calls from galleries. Nothing specific came of that, but it made me aware that people were buying work and that I should try to get to London.

Do you have to live in London?

I think that things are becoming more dispersed, and that's good. There are many more good galleries outside London now. When I was in Oxford and Birmingham I didn't feel part of anything and thought that it was important to experience London. Then I got this Delphina Studios Trust Award.

And the Delphina Trust was set up by a wealthy woman in a building which provided free studio space for ten artists.

Yes, at the end of the year each of the ten artists gave her a painting. that was a good arrangement. This was 1988-89 and there was yuppie money around and people were buying work. Her friends would come to our shows and buy. And she never took commission.

The studio I'm in now is with people I met at the Delphina Studios. At the end of the two years we set up our own space in another part of that warehouse building called the Maryland Studio.

There's something of the Renaissance isn't there, the generous patron?

Yes, and there's nothing wrong with that. But I feel that in London now the Royal College students expect to make a living straight away. They are so obsessed with money. They think they have to get a gallery immediately. They need a few years to get out and see what it's like to survive, to appreciate having a free studio. That is the only problem with the Delphina Trust scheme; they take too many people straight after their MAs.

Does that pressure lead to young artists producing work which they think will sell?

Yes, if a gallery sees your work at the Royal College and wants you to do that, how are you, in your early twenties, to move on? Too much success too soon can be dangerous.

After my two years at Delphina I did manage to have a solo show at Long & Ryle Gallery and they'd seen my work at Delphina.

And now you are showing with Martin Tinney in Cardiff?

Yes, I'd shown with the Welsh Group and I did have some work at St David's Hall in Cardiff. He'd seen my work and asked for two more pieces for the Summer show and then the Christmas show and sold them. The offer of a solo show came and the pressure of producing for that deadline made me work hard.

How important was it for you to go abroad?

I had enjoyed the two years of the Delphina and then the two years of the same people in the Maryland Studios; that was quite rare in London to be able to meet the same people working alongside you every day.

But it seemed that after two years people were beginning to apply for other things and move on. So the Rome scholarship was good timing. After I went to Rome for four months the paintings got stronger, more confident, the colours fresher. I hadn't used varnish in the past but now I use it to heighten the colour and protect the painting.

So elements of that different light, different culture, that different tradition would now feed into your work, because many of your paintings are clearly British.

It's strange because I did a painting in Rome and it had a British light. I was only there for four months, under that beautiful blue winter sky. Some of the Italian light in my paintings has more to do with Italian paintings than being in Italy.

When you got there did you feel you already knew the place from your knowledge of the art?

Yes, that's the light you see in the paintings. It's great when you go down to Sienna and the Uffizi and see those places.

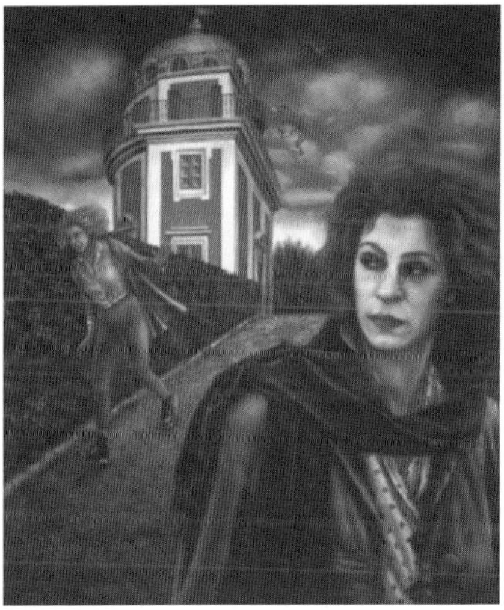

Runaway
oil on panel, 44 x 37 cm, 1994
coll: private collection

Classical statues occur in your work; and the other person who used those a lot in Wales was Evan Charlton. He would take bits of building to assemble what he wanted, rather as you do with your preparatory collages. In 'Runaway' for example.

There's an influence of Munch there, red Virginia creeper and something's happened there, but you don't know what. But in order to stop the painting becoming too sweet with the flowers you see; I wanted something more mysterious; there's something of a film like *Psycho*, staged and melodramatic, with birds flapping. That's the most sinister work in the exhibition really.

What about 'The Intruder', in which you have that old, cranky slide projector?
I like old things, like the old HP sauce bottle I've included. A new projector wouldn't be at all threatening. The intruder is a theme I've used before. Somebody being secretive. I wanted that painting to be able looking inside yourself – with all those objects, the use of mirrors. You have to decide whether she is looking around for an intruder or whether she is the intruder.

There is an echo of the woman in the painting above her which shows a nude on a chaise-longue. The woman is on a chaise-longue, but it's not an exotic pose.
Yes, the woman I paint is the exact opposite of the woman in the painting above her: a classical nude.

Yes, she's a sort of odalisque. Yet your women are never odalisques, merely decorative objects, although there may be a frieze or a painting in the painting which may have represent the past, but they are not like that now.
Yes, a woman would stare out and say, "Why are you looking at me?" in one of my paintings. Though I have used nudes in the past. But now that I am painting flesh so much better, that naked presence would be too much, too powerful.

All your women are properly dressed, sensibly dressed, one might say. Though they may be riding wild animals, or have monkeys on their shoulders.
Yes, sensible. I certainly don't want to have flowery dresses, though that would be nice to paint: I would put that in a curtain or something. I don't want them to look fashion-conscious.

You must be riding on the success of this last show and the increased confidence which you say that you feel now. So the next show will be easier.
Well, I want to do some large paintings now, after the small work of the last two years. I want to be brave. I like the way in which the smaller ones are intimate, and that you can live with them. But I want to work larger now.

Kyffin Williams

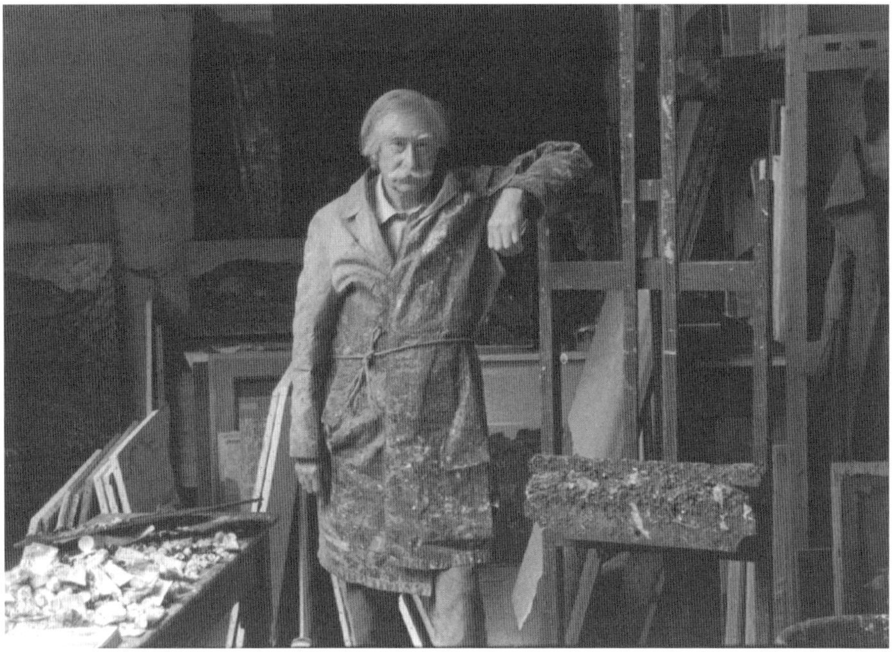

I visited Kyffin Williams in October 1996 in his cottage on the Angleseys' estate near Llanfairpwllgwyngyll. It is on the banks of the Menai Straits, near the bridge and greets you with the tang of the garden's fennel after which it is named, Pwllfanogl. Kyffin works in a studio to the rear of the house. It is large and workmanlike with its big canvases and rich patina of oil spills, but gives no view onto the mountains and sea which have occupied him for fifty years. When we entered the local pub for lunch he was instantly and warmly greeted as a famous personality.

You have always been forthright in your criticisms of trends in contemporary art haven't you?

I don't blame those so-called artists in the current British Art Show, it's not their fault. They only do that because they can't paint and they can't draw or sculpt; they haven't been taught to in their art schools. It's the art schools one should attack. I've got a letter from a student at Cardiff School of Art which is frightening – saying that students were taught that landscape is a fascist art, being a mindless love of nature. Portraiture is finished as there is no such thing as an individual. When you receive a letter like that from the student, you must feel that it's a cry for help – like being in the Samaritans or something.

I get a lot like that from art students. Of course, I can't do anything about it. I was never allowed to teach in an art school, that's why I taught all my time in a boys' school. I was lucky, I was left on my own and I didn't get mixed up with this terrible art school business. I taught there for twenty-nine years. When the Coldstream report came out in the Fifties, it inferred that there should be no drawing or representational painting or sculpture. The man behind this was, oddly enough, a man I admire tremendously, Victor Pasmore, and he honestly thinks that drawing is a thing that holds art back. He influenced Coldstream in this. I was put on a committee in the House of Commons opposing the Coldstream Report and of course we didn't have the clout and it went through. And that was the beginning of the end. To my way of thinking, what Coldstream was saying was that we were moving into the Twenty-first Century and we had to have this new art for the robot age. The only way that they could do that was by destroying tradition. Tradition was holding everything back, they thought. But they will never destroy humanity in art. They didn't realise that tradition is the outward expression of humanity.

Over the last thirty or so years too many lecturers have been appointed who do not care about the future of their students. Too many were given jobs because certain people thought they should be given a salary to advance their own work at the expense of their students's progress and education. They were ruthless, these people in the art schools, and few of them actually taught anything. Several of my pupils from

Highgate went on to art schools and the only instruction they got was, "Go away and express yourselves". I sent one boy to the Royal College and in all his four years there not one of the staff ever went to see his work. And at the end of four years one of them put his head around the door and said, "You've all got your ARCAs", and that was that.

You were trained as an artist during the war. You went to the Slade didn't you? And you were recommended to do art because it would help your epileptic condition and not strain your brain.

Yes, a land girl came to our place in the war, a lovely girl called Gwyneth Griffith and she had been the best student of her generation at the Slade. She advised me to go to the Slade, because they were desperate for men as everyone had gone to the War. She wrote to the secretary of the Slade who said, "For God's sake send him". I didn't know what to do, but I had always been keen on birds and got some pictures by Peter Scott of ducks coming in over the mud flats and I copied them. I took them along and met the Professor in Oxford, where the Slade had been evacuated. He was a bit shocked when he saw them but said that I could try it for one term. It was very interesting because they were all so good there, all these girls who could draw like angels, and I couldn't draw at all.

But you were taught there, not stuck in a room and left to get on with it?

Really properly, thoroughly taught. Every day they came around and showed you how to draw. They sat on your donkey and they taught you how to do it – old Professor Schwabe, Albert Rutherston, George Charlton who came from Penarth, Allan Gwynne-Jones, Barnett Freedman, they made you work. In the second year I had a sort of 'Road to Damascus' conversion after seeing a Piero della Francesca, and then something changed and I sort of muddled my way through. They evidently liked me because I was made President of the Slade Society, I was an older man there and I commanded a platoon of undergraduates in the Oxford City Home Guard. Finally I got a portrait prize: I did learn a hell of a lot, but I never wanted to be a professional artist, I just wanted to get a job in some sleepy public school, get married and have some children and sleep my way through life.

But that didn't happen, did it? You got the job in Highgate which you eventually negotiated as a part-time post, but from your book it seemed that you lived in a succession of seedy digs.

Well, I didn't have any money. And it had something to do with my epilepsy. I was getting anything up to nine attacks a day, which used to throw me a bit, having to teach as well. I remember one day I wanted to paint so I didn't go to school – I was teaching six days a week on a salary of £325 per annum – and I went out on to the Heath and painted. The next morning I went in and the Headmaster said, "Oh, Kyffin, you didn't come in yesterday, did you?" I said no and that I had gone out painting. He said, "You know Kyffin, it is rather difficult if you do that because we have to get someone in to take your classes." I did feel that I really had to paint in a way that I had never felt in the Slade. So I went to him and said that I was leaving. He said, "Have you got a private income? Why not get a friend and share the job?" It was his suggestion, so I did that and came down to £200 a year, which wasn't particularly easy to live on. I had a series of friends to do the work with me and it worked out very well, especially for my senior students, two of whom are now members of the Royal Academy – Anthony Green and Patrick Proctor. Anthony came to me in short pants; his parents were divorced so I understand why he is obsessed with painting his family. He used to paint huge canvases then. A very nice chap, very sensitive. I suggested that he go to the Slade. At that time he was painting very much like I did, and they broke him of that – quite rightly – and he started painting in his own way. I said to him that after the Slade he really ought to have a year in Paris. After that he came back and worked with me as my assistant at the school. After a while I felt that his work was getting a little stylised and suggested that he go to America., which Coldstream helped him do. He never really looked back after America and got a job in the Slade. He lives in Cambridgeshire now.

And the other boy who is an RA was Patrick Proctor. I never really taught him much. I helped him to get to the Slade and four years later he had a one man show in the Redfern, upstairs and downstairs and in the passage, and every picture was sold before it opened!

You lived all those years in a place which couldn't have been more different from this north Wales landscape, but there you were in north London for decades and you were painting this landscape in Wales. That must have been a Wales of the memory, a Wales of the imagination.

In holiday time I was always back in Wales and I was doing drawings and painting on the spot, so that on my return I had a whole sheet of drawings to work from and I would paint my pictures from those.

Did you paint much in London? Did you paint the city itself?

Oh, yes. I set myself two pictures a week. I taught Thursday, Friday, Saturday and the rest of the time I painted. And I did paint London: I did quite a few pictures of Hampstead Heath, around the Thames, Lower Thames Street, St. Paul's, Billingsgate, Kew.

There was a painting I did of lovers on Hampstead Heath which I re-discovered in a strange way. Do you know Dewi Z. Phillips?

The Professor of Philosophy at Swansea? Yes, he taught me in the Sixties.

Well, he wrote to me several years ago and said that he had bought a painting in Hay on Wye which wasn't signed and which he'd like me to sign. His friend had bought another. I said that he had unknowingly bought stolen property, but I didn't mind except that I quite liked the picture he had bought, but I couldn't stand the picture his friend had bought. The first one was of lovers arm in arm crossing Hampstead Heath. It's quite unlike what people think of me now, but I like it.

What were the circumstances of it being stolen?

Well, I was thrown out of my lodgings by some bloody woman and the only place I could find to work was the first floor of a semi-detached in Woodside Park. Now on the ground floor a couple of unmarried mothers had been put in by the council. One of them was a good-looking dark-haired girl called Sandy, which was rather incongruous. I didn't lock the door to my place and one day after I'd moved from there, when I'd got a studio off the Fulham Road, I got a call from someone called Fred Amies who said, "I've just bought fifteen of your paintings from a sale room in Broxborne." He went on to say that fifteen had been sold the day before and, "Could I bring mine over for you to title them?" I refused to believe they were by me, but when he turned up they were all by me. I presumed that the regrettable Sandy had been able to go up to my store-room and take them one at a time and take them to flog at a junk shop in Tally Ho Corner for a quid a piece, and they eventually got into the sale room. I told Fred Amies that I felt that I still had rights to these pictures but would do a deal whereby he gave to me all those which were so bad that I felt that they should not see the light of day and I would destroy them and he could keep the rest. He agreed and that was the deal we had.

So you will do that – your practice is to paint things within the Greek unity of a single place and a day or so and if a few days later you are not satisfied with them you will scrape them off? And you don't sign anything until you are certain of it?

Yes, if it lasts more than two days the canvas will be ruined for painting on. I hate signing. Painting a picture is rather like doing a crossword puzzle, it's all got to be worked out and after finishing it, if you put a mark on it, it mucks it up. But people want a *KW* on it. And sometimes, *KW* helps the balance of a picture, particularly if it's a portrait. But with landscapes I hate signing, but I've got to do it. Though anyone can do a *KW* if they want to.

There's a market in bogus Kyffin Williamses is there?

Yes, I get photographs from dealers of paintings supposed to be by me and often they are not. I've even been to the saleroom in Gaerwen and seen the catalogue with some of my work there which was not by me. They've had to withdraw them – mainly drawings.

I suppose in a way that's flattering, isn't it? Rather like being an author and someone steals your book from the library.

Your roots are here and as the genealogical table in Across the Straits *shows you clearly feel part of a very ancient tradition of notable Welshmen in this area.*

Well, not that notable, though my great, great grandfather was a Fellow of Jesus College, Oxford, a cleric who was interested in English Literature, had a brother Thomas who cornered the whole of the copper in Britain and became the copper king of Britain, the first millionaire of the industrial revolution. All that side of the family married into the aristocracy and all led riotous lives and the average age of death was about fifty. Whereas my side of the family went rumbling on as clerics in Anglesey and their average age of death was eighty-five, I think. The others only went on the sea when it was calm and they were members of the Royal Yacht Squadron; and my side only went on the sea when there was a wreck in a storm, and we seemed to survive. They have all passed out now, except for a cousin of mine who says that her grandfather was in fact Edward VII. I think she's probably right too, because when he was Prince of Wales he used to come and stay in the family home along the Straits there. And she doesn't look like my side of the family.

So you feel part of a long and reasonably distinguished line here. Was that part of your thinking as a painter? That you were part of this landscape's heritage and might contribute something to that?

No, it was never anything as noble as that. What happened was that quite unconsciously, in my genes I suppose, as my ancestor parsons ministered to the people and all loved the landscape, I've always thought it was so obvious that I should paint this place, unlike others leaving art school and wondering what to do. As a boy I was brought up to hunt with a pack of foot hounds in the mountains which was really doing a job for the farmers in keeping down the foxes. I would, when quite young, go into the furthest recesses of the mountains following the foxes in all weathers because they were decimating the flocks of sheep. What people don't realise is that foxes are rural rats, but they look beautiful and that influences people. Certainly with hunting in England it is the people who go hunting who are the problem.

The unspeakable in pursuit of the inedible. So you knew the landscape long before you knew that you would be a painter.

When we lived in south Caernarfonshire there was a small hill in front of the house called Moel y Gadair and I was always out in the fields with my small dog and used to sit on the hill there sometimes as the sun was going down, that wonderful panorama, a cyclorama back and front. I knew all the names of the mountains. People don't understand how vital a knowledge of the scene is. I have looked at so many waterfalls that I know how the water flops from one rock surface to a lower rock surface, fanning out with fingers of water. And also the sun coming through cloud, coming from behind ridges and bursting through a cloud and hitting onto the green breasts of mountains – explosions – those are very exciting. As I was really born without any talent, just as van Gogh was born without talent, and we were both epileptics, we just had to make a go of it by obsession. If you are talented it doesn't mean that you will be obsessed, but if you are obsessed then it forces you to have talent because you want to do something so much.

You are best known for your landscapes of Wales, but as the book Portraits *shows, you have painted many notable portraits over the years When we were in your studio just now it struck me that there was preponderance of landscapes there, but do you make a conscious decision to paint a portrait because you may not have done so for a while, is there any allocation of your time between the two forms?*

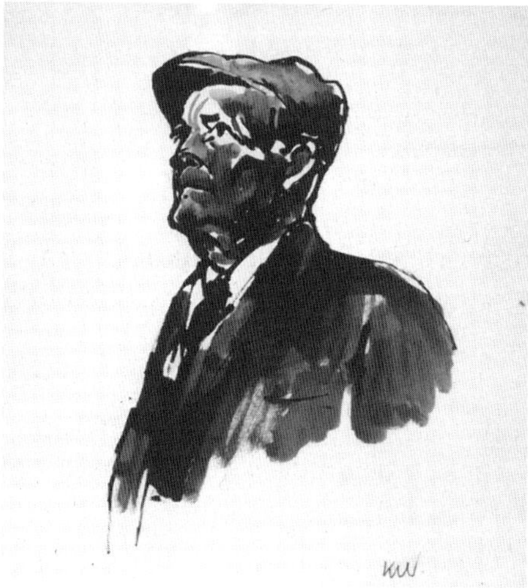

Henry Morris
pencil and watercolour, 41.5 x 34.5 cm
1979, coll: National Library of Wales

Well, I have a typically Welsh love of people and I like communication with people. If a cross-bred Serbo-Croat came to live in Llanfairpwll all the village would be anxious to see what sort of a man he was and they'd go and talk to him. That wouldn't happen in England. With this fascination it seems strange that in Wales there have been so few portrait painters. I mean I've never been a portrait painter, but rather a painter who painted portraits. I've always done it on a take it or leave it basis. I have accepted commissions, because in a puritanical way I thought it was good for me, having to do something; that was difficult. But I am a congenital worrier, like my mother, and I would very often take on a commission and then pray that the person would get flu or something and not turn up. But when I reached seventy I thought I really must stop this worrying. So after seventy I've only painted people I really wanted to paint. I got so neurotic about these portraits even though it was on a take it or leave it basis.

And some were disliked by people, weren't they?

Oh, yes. I painted Alun Oldfield Davies for the BBC. And he came and sat in this chair with his huge legs crossed and I painted him and I sent a photograph of it to the BBC who replied that they considered it to be *repellent.* So I said, "Alright, get Tom Rathmell to do it." Tom was much better at doing cobwebs than I was and poor old Alun Oldfield Davies had a face like interwoven cobwebs. Alun was a very nice man and insisted I did it. So in order to put him off I said that he would have to stand for me to do it. Anyway, he came and stood like an Atlas missile all day long. I painted this six-foot canvas and I painted it on the easel and the floor. And this time they accepted it. It's not an attractive picture, but in a way I think it is very like him.

That's the difficulty isn't it? Sometimes people dislike a portrait because they are being shown something of themselves that they don't want to see, and as long as they stare into a mirror they will never see for themselves.

It's very odd – husbands invariably like my portraits of their wives, but wives invariably dislike my portraits of their husbands. I don't know why that is.

Do you prefer painting women?

I like painting women, though it's much more difficult. I didn't paint a girl for years after leaving art school because painting as I do with a knife it's difficult to get the subtlety and smoothness of the skin. The best portrait of a girl I have ever painted was of the writer Alice Thomas Ellis. She came from Penmaenmawr and she's a friend I've known for a very long time. That portrait I sent to the Royal Academy and it was bought on the private view day by some old gent. He left it to his housekeeper and so I couldn't have it for any exhibitions. If you are a painter you are bound to lose some of your paintings. I had a photograph of it for the first edition of *Across the Straits*. When I painted her she hadn't started writing. She had been a student at Liverpool School of Art.

And she went on to marry into the Haycraft family who owned the publishing house Duckworths.

Yes, that was important: I gave that book manuscript to Curtis Brown and after a year they returned it because every London publisher they sent it to said that it was unpublishable. Then I got a letter from Duckworth (I think Anna had been working behind the scenes) and they published it. Anna, who hadn't started writing as Alice Thomas Ellis then, looked at it and said, "Kyffin, some of this is awful, it needs re-writing", and she was right, so I did some re-writing.

There was a time in London when you painted some nudes. But then there were no more for some years because you had a problem with one, didn't you?

I never had a problem with the nudes, I had a problem with the client. What appalled me was that I had a very good model called Sandra and I sent a very big nude of her – 3ft by 4ft – to the Academy and the number of letters and calls I received wanting her telephone number!

That painting was bought by a little American called Herford Sharon. He rang me up and asked if he could come over and see me with his wife. One day there was a knock on the door and he entered with this huge woman – a Daughter of the Revolution. She said, "Mr Kyffin Williams, I want to make it plain that my husband did not buy that painting because it was nude, but because he's genuinely interested in works of art." Little Herford was busily straightening his bow tie and looking embarrassed. There was another man from Purley who was a collector of nudes who called me and said in a broad middle European voice, "Haf you any more of zat little girl?" I said I had and he came around and bought it. It put me off painting more nudes.

You had a bachelor existence in London, didn't you? You never did marry, did you?

Well, the epilepsy always got in the way. There was nothing I wanted more than to get married. My ideal was always to get married and to have a nice sedentary life.

You said that before and it strikes me that you have a very idealised view of married life. My experience is that a family takes up huge amounts of energy and commitment and money, and both my children are in their twenties!

Oh, I am an idealist.

You have said in one of your books that in order to be an artist you have to clear most other things out of the way. Is it a sacrifice?

It's not a conscious sacrifice; obviously things go on behind the scenes, in your mind, but I suppose that basically I've been very lucky. I was lucky that I was ordered to take up art, I was lucky that I taught at a boys' school, even though I wanted to teach at an art school, and I was lucky, maybe, not to have got married.

Did you come close?

Oh, I came very close. I got involved with two girls and each time I discovered that they had fathers who were epileptics. Now that is incredible coincidence. One was a German girl. But somehow I've struggled on with things. And the luckiest thing of all was that somehow my paintings seemed to get through to the people of Wales.

It's true that you do have this central position as an interpreter, as a champion of the north Wales landscape particularly. North Wales is Kyffin Williams: but Kyffin Williams is not necessarily north Wales, you have done other things, portraits and so on. But I suppose that those ponies, those walls, those mountains are, for many people, yours. Are you happy with occupying that position?

I am very happy, because I was never ambitious to be a great artist. Obviously I could never be a great artist, painting as I did for the benefit of my health. Thereby I didn't take myself very seriously and nobody else took me very seriously, and that was ideal. People buy my work, but I've never been taken up by the art world. Luckily.

Except that becoming an RA is one of the great accolades, isn't it?

That was an incredible piece of luck. But no galleries would buy my paintings. Though the National Museum of Wales have some bad ones, but have recently bought a better one.

They have that big one in the restaurant though.

That was bought for the restaurant, not for the Gallery. The Welsh artists there – Terry Setch, Peter Prendergast, Emrys Williams – were bought specifically as decorations for the restaurant, not for the Gallery.

Is that a disappointment for you, because it seems to me that any exhibition of art from Wales in the twentieth century would have to include your work, wouldn't it?

I don't think that I have ever been in any exhibition of Welsh art sent abroad by the Welsh Arts Council.

Well, to a layman, that sounds quite remarkable.

I don't fit in in any way, I am a total loner in art; the Tate have never bought a painting, in fact no public art collection in England for years and years and years has bought my paintings.

But you are represented in major collections, aren't you? The University of Wales colleges have some work and HTV and so on.

I have one in the Walker Art Gallery, bought for them by the Liverpool/Rotterdam Mutual Assistance Association or something. But I don't think it's ever shown. There are very few places that buy my work. But that is not important, because if you are bought by a gallery the chances are that you are put in the basement; if you are bought by people they are put up on the wall. and if people see one in someone's house they are likely to want one as well.

As far as the Royal Academy is concerned, I have tried to get elected other artists with connections in Wales like Colin See-Paynton, but it seems that they don't want wood engravers.

Well I think that engravers such as Gertrude Hermes and Claire Leighton are superb artists of the mid-century.

Yes, and Agnes Miller Parker; the women were very good. Old Gertrude Hermes was one of my very best friends. One year she said she'd cook me a meal for my birthday. She'd seen a lino-cut of mine of black cattle in a field and said she'd give me one of her wood-cuts for one of these lino-cuts. So I took along the black cattle, but she died before giving me her piece. I've got some of her prints in the *Selbourne* book that Gregynog Press did a few years back. She was a lovely, gentle person. She came to Gregynog in the first years of the press with Blair Hughes-Stanton. She said that Gregynog ruined their marriage.

You have been attracted by the combination of words and images, haven't you?

Yes, I like the idea of paintings interspersed with writings. I once put the idea to the Welsh Arts Council that they should organise an exhibition of R.S. Thomas's poems blown up and combined with his wife's paintings. I have a feeling that it wasn't the Council's fault that it didn't go ahead.

There was an exhibition in 1995 of paintings supposedly related to R.S.'s poems. Weren't you in that?
Well, he told me about that. A pretty daft idea, he thought.

I saw it in Oriel Plas Glyn y Weddw. It didn't hold together very convincingly, I thought. It's got to be the sharpness you get with wood engravings to work effectively in proximity to words, I think. As a writer, I feel that Colin See-Paynton would be good to work with. Both Ceri Richards and David Jones involved literature and music in their art, especially music in Richards's case; do you play music while you paint?
I always used to have music on when painting, but what I used to enjoy was to paint and then go to the piano and play. I never learned to play, but I loved it, though it must have been absolutely awful; what I was actually playing and what I thought I was playing were totally different things. I thoroughly enjoyed my playing, but to anyone who knew music it would have been intolerable. When I was teaching in Highgate I always refused to eat and went into the school chapel and play the organ. No-one was listening and I thought that I was playing beautifully! Great joy.

You've mentioned some of your former pupils who have become notable, but I sense that you didn't greatly enjoy teaching, did you?
No, I never enjoyed teaching; though I had lots of interesting pupils. For example, Martin Gilbert, the Churchill and Holocaust historian. Then there was Anthony Howard the journalist. He was a great talker, always arguing with other boys over ideas. His father was vicar of Highgate, then he moved on to St John's in Kensington and Anthony went to St. Paul's school. There were the composers John Rutter and John Taverner, who now has a tremendous reputation. I thought little of his stuff immediately after he left, but he later became influenced by Russian choral music and his work became very impressive.

Were you never tempted to return to Wales to teach?
Oh, I could never get a teaching job in Wales. It's interesting, because the same thing has happened to David Carpanini, because he couldn't get a job in an art school and has ended up eventually in Oundle. He found, as I found, that once you have taught in a boys' school you have had it, you can't move on.

Once I heard that there was a job going in the painting school in St. Martin's School of Art in London so I thought that I would go down and see the Principal. I got a porter to tell the Principal what I had come for. He went in to the office and I heard a bit of talking before he returned to hand me a bit of paper and he said, "Write down your qualifications." So I wrote them down and when he came back he said, "Sorry, mate, qualifications inadequate." Six months later I was elected to the Royal Academy and they appointed me to the governing body of St. Martin's School of Art! A delightful little triumph.

Did election to the Academy make a great difference? Your reputation and your prices went up, I suppose?

No difference at all, but it did enable me to leave Highgate School. When I told the boys that I was leaving they protested; it seems that I was the only master who didn't believe in punishing them.

But Proctor and Green are distinguished artists so you must have had a very real effect as a teacher.

There was a great advantage to teaching in such a school. If I had been at an art school the students would not have been in a position to buy my work, but the parents at Highgate did, and when boys left to work in daddy's firm they could buy for themselves. One boy went out to Hong Kong and made a lot of money and bought one a year practically. The boys turn up here from time to time, and seem to be very loyal to their old art master.

For much of your time in London there was nowhere to show work back in Wales, was there? Though Howard Roberts ran that gallery in Cardiff in the Sixties.

Howard Roberts's gallery was wonderful. They had a good eye for art and showed very good work. I was very lucky to show with him. There has never been a gallery quite like his, because he used to go up to

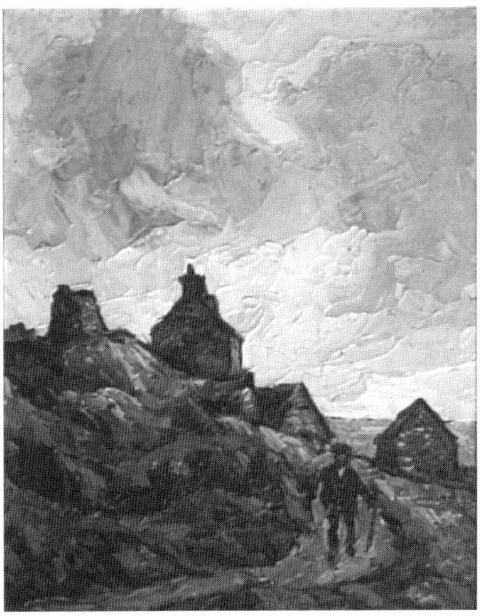

Farm above the Sea
oil on canvas, 24 x 20 inches,
1950s, coll: Prof & Mrs Curtis

London and get work to show too. I am lucky now that the Albany Gallery has taken its place to my benefit.

Well, in addition to the Albany with whom you mainly show in Wales, there is too the Martin Tinney Gallery in Cardiff and he brings work down from London. There was a very successful show there by the young painter Sally Moore, who is based in London and whom I have interviewed. Did you know her father Leslie Moore?

Oh really, is she Leslie's daughter? Yes I knew him, a nice man. I always loved the way he called Pontarddulais "Pont a du lais" as if it were a French town.

Peter Prendergast points out in his interview that Leslie Moore was a great help to him and assisted him in gaining entry to the foundation course in Cardiff. Men like Leslie Moore and Prendergast's teacher Gomer Lewis can make a huge difference, can't they? So there are people who can perform marvellous acts within an academic or arts administration role and help people significantly. Though you are not complimentary about the Welsh Arts Council are you? You feel that they've not done enough for Welsh art in Wales?

Yes. (Incidentally, I met Gomer Lewis because he moved up to Anglesey eventually. A fine man.) And I suppose I must not be too hard on the Arts Council: there must be some good things that they've done.

You have also said that the 56 Group had concentrated too much on looking out from Wales and bringing European work of quality in and not tending to the roots here.

Well, I was never invited to join the group. Because I was very much a Welsh artist. They showed a lot in Czechoslovakia, Italy and other countries. I think that it has changed very much now and it is more Welsh in its orientation.

You can see that there was an argument which logically said that as artists in Wales were not doing very well internationally and making waves, that they needed to plug into international influences in order to make those waves. "Let's look outside ourselves to see what we might be doing wrong."

But I think that they did that too wholeheartedly.

Your most significant experience abroad must have been the Patagonia visit. How did that come about?

The whole idea of the Welsh in Patagonia had always fascinated me. It was such a romantic story and being a romantic myself I was always deeply moved at the thought of my fellow-countrymen so far away from their homeland. I was extremely lucky to be able to go there and to Tierra del Fuego with the aid of a Winston Churchill Fellowship. It was the greatest experience of my life. The Welsh out there were so friendly, but everything else was so different. The sky was different, the light was different and so were the birds, the animals and the vegetation. All this was so exciting and during my four months there I made seven hundred drawings and took seven hundred photographs. I made many friends out there with whom I am still in touch.

That must have changed your work in some profound way, didn't it?
No, my work did not change. I suppose that as I was fifty when I went out there, my style was too set. Nevertheless, I had to change my palette because of the different light, but then I change my palette when I go to Venice. Black is the colour I discard, as it would hardly be suitable for such places. It is interesting that, after painting about fifty Patagonian oils in strong colours, I reverted to the manner of my work before I left for South America. I am delighted that so much of my record of Patagonia is now in the National Library of Wales.

The Lord and Lady Angleseys have always been your patrons haven't they?
They have been very good to me and this is their cottage in which I live. The family had been the sponsors of Rex Whistler too and they have introduced me and my work to so many people over the years. They have been tremendously supportive.

That is the traditional role of patronage which was probably lacking in Wales for so long. Welsh art needed sustaining in that way didn't it?
There were also a group of people who founded the Contemporary Art Society for Wales. They were patrons – Geoffrey Crawshay, Leonard Twiston-Davies, Wynn Cemlyn Jones and Brynmor Anthony. And Lord Howard de Walden who lived in Chirk Castle. He commissioned Eric Gill to do the war memorial in Chirk. And they got the Society going, which has done a lot for Welsh artists.

Is there a sense in which your dissatisfaction and that of others with the National Museum in Cardiff is that because the Elizabeth and Gwendolyn Davies bequest brought these internationally renowned painters in to Cardiff – Renoir, Cézanne, van Gogh that everything else was rather swamped by that. And that it set a different agenda for what the museum should be?
I think that the Museum has a dilemma. They want to be seen alongside the Louvre and the Prado and the Albertina: well, it will never be, we haven't got the money. The danger is that we will be a pale reflection of the others, a second rate European gallery, and what we lack is character. And I think a museum should have character. As our charter says, it is there to show the world the best of Welsh art. We should concentrate more on Welsh art, because even if our art is not as good as the best English art, it would be different, and people would see something new if they came to our National Museum.

And if one came new to the country one would want to see what was characteristic of Wales, what was indigenous to this people. That's part of what one experiences when coming to the country. It's good to see Renoir's 'Blue Lady' and Monet's Water Lilies, but surely visitors need more to take back with them?

The Museum does its best. It is unfortunate that the people who get slated all the time are the landowners of Monmouth and Glamorgan. Like Paul Flynn, the M.P. for Newport, criticising people who live in their castles. But if it hadn't been for them nothing would have happened at all. They have been running the National Museum when no-one else seemed to be interested. The whole of the literature of Wales written in Welsh in the eighteenth century and the beginning of the nineteenth was paid for by the landowners of Wales. They subscribed to the literature in Welsh. Yet people slate the squirearchy.

You do need patronage and although we now have a state patronage, arts councils and committees, there is no perfect solution to this necessity for an interface between the artist and the public. The one thing which the Arts Council in Wales unquestionably has done for the visual arts is their Collectorplan.

Yes, that was created by a man who was half blind too – Mike Pearson.

It's a wonderful idea. I know so many people – the chattering classes or whatever – who haven't got a lot of money, but they have a little bit they can spend, and through Collectorplan works of art by living artists hang on the walls of those people. The artist gets paid, the person enjoys living with the painting and the gallery is happy. As I travel abroad and visit galleries they all say that they wish they had such a scheme. That's a state patronage, in terms of the subsidising of the interest-free loan – which does work for both the public and the artist. As you say, you want, of course, to be represented in the public collections, but you get enormous pleasure from knowing that your work is in people's houses, that they are living with it, their friends are seeing it, they feel proud of it.

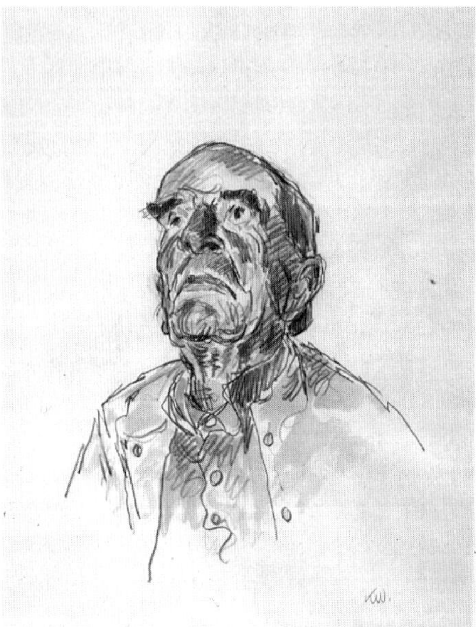

Evan Roberts
pencil and watercolour, 58 x 46.5 cm
1992, coll: National Library of Wales

They all say they grow on them. It is astonishing. Especially as I paint them so quickly!

It must be the case that when someone has walked off with one of your canvases, they will come to know it much better than you do.

And they do chemically improve. I mean two years after I've painted it it's a better painting than when I painted it. The paint seems to knit in some way.

Well, they do go quickly, and you don't keep them long because you do sell a lot of work. And you lose track of them.

Because I took up art for the benefit of my health, I didn't take myself seriously and I never kept any records. I have trouble remembering everything.

Though some artists keep a record of everything they sell – John Knapp-Fisher, for example, knows where almost everything is.

He's a good artist, I think I got him made a member of the Royal Cambrian Academy. And another man in Pembrokeshire called Denis Curry. I've got a bronze of a sheep by him upstairs.

So you've always acquired the work of other artists?

No, no, I never had the money. I even had to sell those pictures I'd inherited. I once bought a lovely Richard Wilson for fourteen quid. I knew I had to sell it, and I took it up to all the London galleries, who said it wasn't by Wilson, but I knew it was. Then I went to see an old friend of the family called Ralph Edwards, he was the father of Nicholas Edwards, and head of the woodwork at the Victoria and Albert. He in turn showed it to Willy Constable, the man who'd written the definitive work on Wilson. When he came over from Boston, he saw it and said, "Ah, the missing Wilson! I wanted that picture for my book." So he wrote an article about it in the *Burlington Magazine* under the title 'The Kyffin Williams Wilson'. And I flogged it. But it wasn't a Welsh one: it was the Temple of Vesta in Italy. I found it in a junk shop in Chester. I used to go there when I was terribly hard up and I bought a lot of things there.

I bought a painting in a junk shop there which the man tried to sell me as an El Greco. I asked him how much, and he said three pounds! I was in the army and in hospital outside Chester. And then I went to the Slade and attended lectures on the history of art given by the greatest expert on European art in the world, Professor Tancred Borenius. And the work of Domenichino would come up on the slides. On the back of my work there was that name. So I showed it to old Tancred one day and asked him if it could possibly be by Domenichino. All he said was, "Of course, of course. I must hurry, I must get my train". And then I showed it to Sir Karl Parker, head of the Ashmolean, whom I knew from my Oxford Home Guard duties, I was a lieutenant and he was a sergeant. And he was an expert on old master drawings. I had bought a drawing in Chester in another junk shop, obviously an Italian drawing, by Carlo Maratta, and that was a good buy. He agreed about the Domenichino.

I inherited a number of works from some old cousins – a Marco Ricci and others – I knew that I had to sell it. I took the Ricci to one of the leading London auction houses and I was shown into a room and a young man came in and proclaimed it a beautiful Robert. I knew there was an engraving of it and that it was a Ricci. He called in a senior partner. "What a beautiful Robert!" he said. "We have been in business for two hundred years, we do know what we are talking about." I said that I knew what I was talking about. Then he came up to me and whispered in my ear, "Do not be such an idiot. We will get more for it if we catalogue it as by Robert." I was so shocked. I said, "Good day," and I took the picture away, which was rather stupid.

So don't trust the auction houses.

Oh, God no. So I took it round the corner to the Hazlitt Gallery which was run by a friend of mine, Jack Baer, and he knew bloody well what it was. He sold it for me to an important Italian collection as a Marco Ricci.

So you grew up in a family which had lots of art, which was great privilege.

Oh, yes. My great-grandmother was a good artist and I had cousins who had studied under artists in Paris. So when I was told that I had to take up painting there was no parental opposition. I was privileged in that way, and I've always loved paintings with a real passion.

There is a Ben Bowen Thomas Memorial Lecture given every year to the North Wales Association for the Arts. It's always published, and mine attacking this attempt to destroy tradition was out of print immediately. It was one of the most popular there's ever been.

Yes, you certainly laid out a manifesto in that. I remember you expressed the opinion that Abstract Art had run its course and that there was probably nothing left for it to do that was original. It's funny how the wheel turns, isn't it? Here you are castigating an officialdom which is against tradition, and you are the rebel speaking up for traditional paintings.

I've been lucky, really, because I've always had security; not financial security. But if you come from an island, oddly enough you have security. That's why the English are snooty about the continentals. If you live on an island you know exactly where you are, where the coast is. And as my family have been here so long – five hundred years, maybe a thousand years – I can go round the island and see where all my ancestors were. As I am secure I can say what I think. The odd thing is now that with so much better health and so much better education people are not more secure, they are frightened of saying what they think. It may be that they have an inferiority complex about taste. And taste is the Achilles heel of everybody. These people in the art world so lay it on that they know and the public know nothing. They really despise the public. And they hide behind a veil of incomprehensibility and obscurity; and I know damn well that they are naked behind that veil. But the public doesn't know that.

But the media are guilty too. The only time that the media get interested in the visual arts is when something like the Turner Prize is announced and how ludicrous they feel the decision has been – Damien Hirst for example.

And rightly so. I blame the education system for creating such artists. If you are creative – and Damien Hirst is creative – you've got to create. But I doubt if he can draw. If he saw something that he thought was beautiful he couldn't put it down, because he couldn't draw. And then Anthony Gormley and his little pot figures, five thousand and more of them, he didn't make them himself. That has nothing to do with the visual arts, it's inanimate theatre.

But it is effective. I've seen Gormley's 'Field' twice and it is strangely affecting.

Anything which is duplicated is impressive. Like Field Marshall Montgomery repeating phrases over and over to motivate the troops. Anthony Gormley certainly has got something, but it's something to do with the theatre.

An event, a performance or event art.

And from what I've seen the angel which is going to be shoved up near Gateshead is a disaster. It seems to be to be singularly insensitive.

It certainly looks like the locals don't want it. That fits in with your argument – that the high priests of art think they know best. People may want a Kyffin Williams but what they should have is a huge angel.

Oh, the public is ignored by those people.

As you say, the fact that your work is sought after by a wide public in Wales is the strongest argument for your commitment to the tradition in painting.

I am extremely lucky that the public in Wales likes my work, but that is incidental. In truth, I am a very selfish painter indulging myself on the landscape and the people. The fact that my work is popular is a tremendous bonus.

Before the war there were few people in Wales who bought original paintings. The farmers, the miners and the minister were never in a position to do so, but their children, who were able to go to our universities, eventually to become doctors, engineers or lecturers, became a new buying public.

I was lucky because, although I painted entirely for my own satisfaction, the subject matter that appealed to me obviously meant much to them. My mountains and my farm houses were their mountains and their farm houses. They knew my stone cottages and the people who lived in them

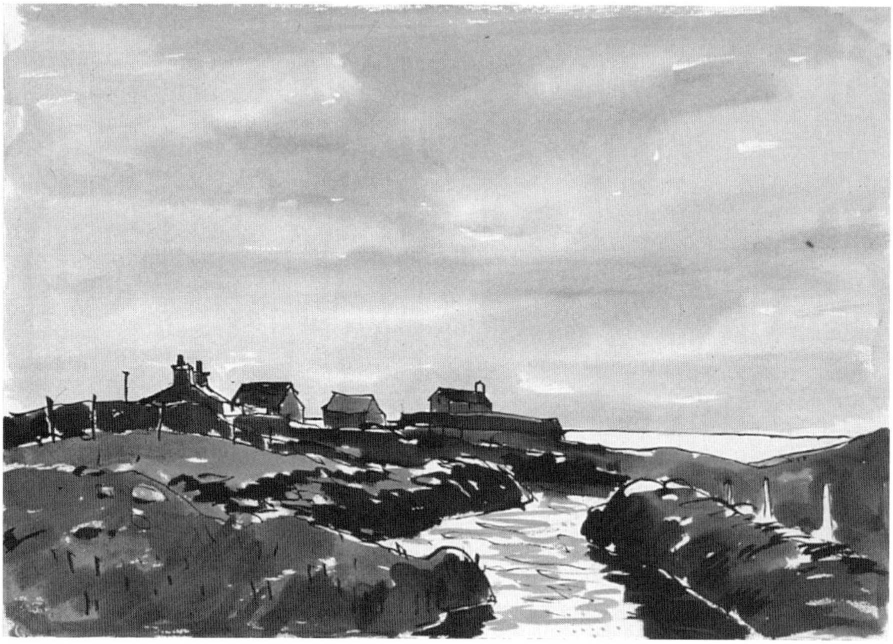

Stream, Porth Cwysan ink and wash, 12 x 19 inches, 1994, coll: the artist

and they bought my pictures because they represented what they knew and loved.

The act of buying a painting naturally stimulates an interest in art so it may have been that, having done so, their interest may have led them to buy more contemporary art, sometimes of a more international and adventurous kind. This may have been important in the context of the attitude of the art establishment towards the public, which is "We know and you don't, so belt up". Unfortunately, the public does just that and the so called elite have it their own way. Private patronage has given way to council patronage. It has been a disaster: but I would say that, wouldn't I?

WILL ROBERTS

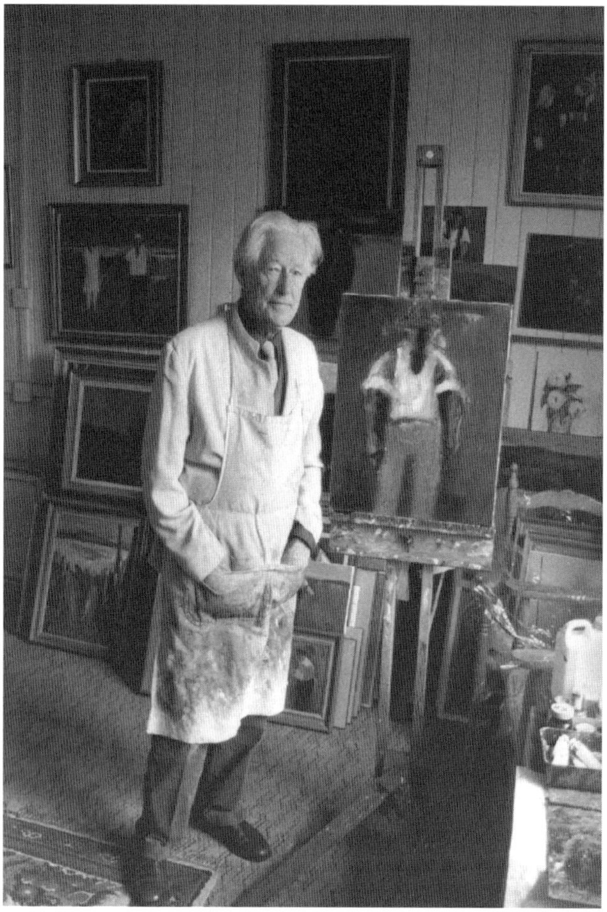

I visited Will Roberts first in November 1994, meeting him one morning in his studio in a converted shop in the middle of Neath. You enter the apparently abandoned premises, noting a painting propped in the window, and climb the stairs to his studio, a compact room with books, an easel, kettle and sink, and many of his works in various stages of completion. I also spoke to him on several occasions between then and 1997 in his house in Neath. It is a small, neat terrace with a fine selection of his and his friends' paintings and drawings on its walls.

You must be very pleased with the large exhibition of your work currently touring Wales?
Yes thanks to Susan Daniel, the Director of Oriel Mostyn Llandudno: she has produced an excellent exhibition

You've never been linked with a gallery as such?
I am 'linked', as you put it, with several Welsh galleries with whom I show regularly as well as other galleries outside Wales – English and Scottish galleries and likewise in London

But you were part of the 56 Group?
My role in the 56 Group was not important to me at all. In fact I left them very soon.

The Arts Council was in being sometime after the war ended and I did show in certain exhibitions mounted by them in the 1950s and, as I remember, was purchased by the Arts Council. I travelled quite frequently to London both with my paintings and to visit the National Galleries. In 1953 Roland, Browse & Delbanco in Cork Street showed some of my work and followed that with a one-man show in 1954. I then also became a member of the Artists International Association and too showed with the London group. All of these were important to me. My work was well received and reviewed in London. I continued to show and sell reasonably until, in due course, abstract work became fashionable and realist painting and the like was not wanted. I never had any difficulty in selling my work in Wales. The 56 Group was set up by art school teachers who wanted to sell their work. In the first two years it was my work which sold from the exhibitions and, in fact, from the first of those exhibitions the National Museum bought my 'Farm at Cimla' [see colour plate].

We are surrounded in this studio by your paintings – landscapes and working figures – a wonderful collage of images. Are they recent?
Some of what you see are current and recent works. There are also some older works that are still with me for various reasons. I can re-consider them and possibly re-work them.

Do you paint at all from nature direct, or only in the studio?
I paint in the studio only. This I have done almost all my painting life

– at least since the 1950s, working from, mainly, pencil sketches made out of doors. Earlier I had used watercolour outdoors, but found this quite unnecessary later. Still life subjects, flowers etc, I paint direct from the subject; my landscapes and figures are painted entirely from sketches. I would never use photography, as some do today.

You've worked in Wales most of your life, haven't you? Though you studied at some art colleges in England?

Mostly I've worked in Wales – I still do. During the war, when I was in the RAF, I did two tours of duty near Bath at a training camp and any free time from the camp (which was a technical training camp) I attended art school at Bath. That was both pleasant and useful. I was also stationed later quite near Bath. During the bombing of the city the art school was lost.

Would you say you had a 'good' war? At one point you were at Biggin Hill, and you included some sketches of Biggin Hill in your retrospective exhibition. Were you drawing throughout your time in the RAF?

My war-time service in the RAF was as a technician, mainly with Fighter Command, servicing and maintaining fighter aircraft, mainly Spitfires at Biggin Hill. Good war? There were good moments. Off duty I could (from Biggin Hill in Kent, for instance) nip up to London for concerts – the National Gallery lunch-time concerts were always an attraction when I had a day off duty. In camp life all was not work, entertainment was essential: there was usually a concert party on camp made up of musicians, actors, dancers, now in uniform. I was the violinist usually in these concert parties, and sometimes played in camp bands. Out of camp I caught any art school available where I could attend – mainly life classes. I kept on sketching wherever I went. I even managed some landscape watercolours.

It's strange how the war changed things. Ceri Richards was teaching in London and then they closed the art colleges and he found himself picking swedes in Essex. It was Evan Charlton who got him a job at Cardiff. But he did some war artist work – those tin-plate workers in Dunvant.

I did no official war drawing or painting. What I was doing was purely private, but I was, in a small way, recording Britain as it was: country churches, farms, barns, landscape.

Some of the drawings I did then are in the exhibition. And the Biggin Hill fire-place in the billet. I had that billet to myself at one time so it was like a studio. When I went out with my water-colours, what I drew and painted were recording Britain which was a common practice at that time, in case of loss through bombing. I like the watercolour of a barn done at Comberton, just outside Cambridge. A beautiful barn – that could have disappeared. I was then stationed at Lordsbridge, and was able to attend art school at Cambridge.

WILL ROBERTS

You had been at Swansea Art School before the war, and it had a good reputation.

Yes, it was the only art school in west Wales. I'm not sure of the reputation. Ceri Richards and Evan Walters had been there before us, when Fred Janes and myself were contemporaries. Howard Martin, who started what is now a reputed stained glass school and workshop, was also there.

What effect did the discovery of Picasso have on you?

I am looking at one of my paintings, painted thirty-five years ago. And I can see that Picasso possibly lies beneath it. I went several times to the great Picasso exhibition in London in 1945. They bowled me over. It was hair-raising. But you don't simply imitate Picasso: you just learn. The mind was so lively and the subject-matter was vast. He said something like, "The man who sees a tree and paints a tree has done nothing: but the man who sees a tree and draws an elephant. . .". None of my paintings copy nature. Practically everything I do is in some way changed by distortion of shape; then the change of colour might follow; because they have to comply with my feelings about the things. I am trying to get at the greater truth of the thing.

What you are talking about is Expressionism, isn't it?

Yes. I was well aware of the German Expressionists before the war. Rouault was also interesting. I love to paint on paint, as he did, rather than a new canvas. When you look at Rouault's world you can see under

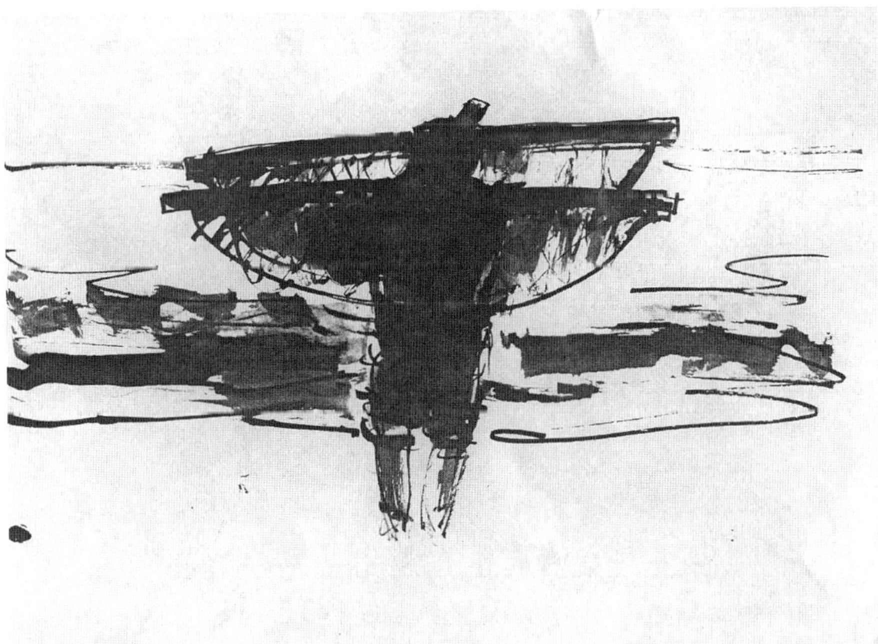

The Shrimper ink and wash, 20 x 25.5 cm, 1970, coll: the artist

the layers of paint. The act of painting on old paint has its use and can be a satisfying practice.

Abstraction, as I see it, is 'normal' painting. That is realism, if you care to use that word, a means of making clear, emphasising, seizing what is important and apparent in the appearance of the subject. One finds this in most great paintings; for example, in Rembrandt's portrait of Titus, his son, the fine rendering of a hand which does not display anatomy but the full meaning – at that moment – of that hand and its intent.

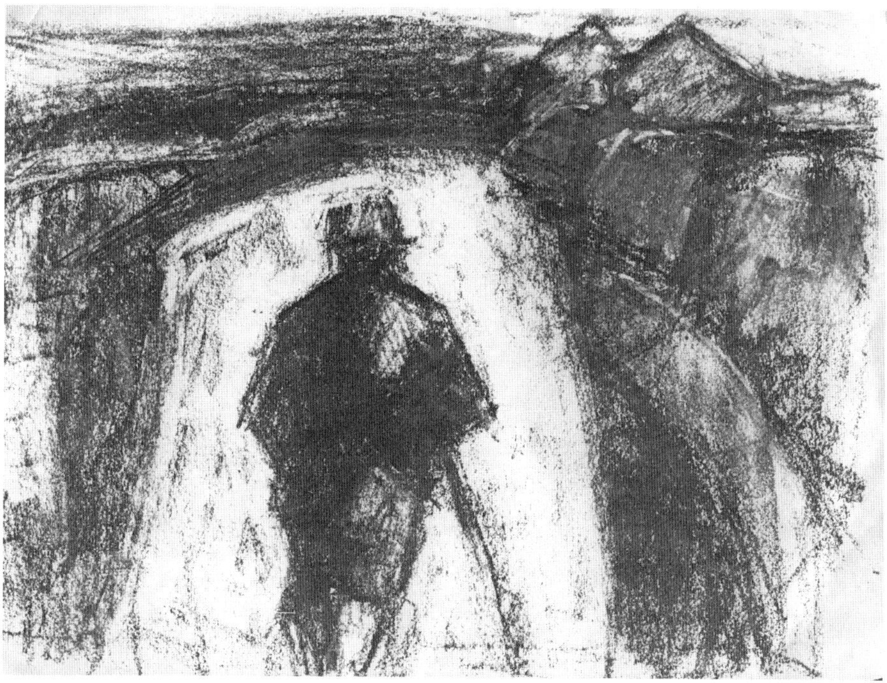

Farmer pencil, 20 x 25.5 cm, 1986, coll: the artist

Your subjects are 'ordinary people', and you've never undertaken a portrait commission, have you?

I have never really wanted to. Only on a rare occasion have I made a portrait as a request. The ordinary people are part of – often the main part – in my paintings of the commonplace, everyday subject. People as I see and draw and paint them, are of main importance and do reflect for me the commonplace of life. I am not interested in just painting pretty landscapes, even when I paint flowers in vases I am aware of the "ordinary" in our lives. And the ordinary is more than just ordinary.

Ceri Richards played the piano and included pianists in many of his works. Have you ever used the subject of violinists?

I've never used music as a theme in the way that he did. Though I was as much in love with my violin as Richards was, apparently, with his piano.

Music is very important to me. I work to Bach and Brahms and the others. The painting, too, must have music in it. Harmony is incomplete without discord. So with painting as in music.

I thought that your contribution to Meic Stephens's Artists in Wales *was very well written. Have you ever thought of writing an autobiography?*

Not really. I'd have to give myself fully to that, perhaps at the expense of the painting. If I made time for it I am sure that I would enjoy writing an autobiography. I might make the time someday!

Your childhood in Ruabon was written about very evocatively in that essay for Stephens. Is there a sense in which you are still inspired by it when you work down here in Neath?

Early memories are likely to remain with you all your life. The first ten years must be important – an important episode in the whole. I have very clear visual memories of my childhood in Ruabon and the Vale of Llangollen and Clwyd, some of which might play some small part in the range of my painting. This seems usual in others; a good example in the extreme, being Chagall.

In all these years living in Neath, you don't look to the industry, you look to the hills and farms, don't you?

That was a choice that I made. Though I did quite a lot of sketching in the tin-plate, sheet steel and galvanising works, in the Sixties. I've still got a number of sketches. Likewise in Gowerton I sketched the open-hearth furnaces, and that was quite an exciting thing. The likelihood of them disappearing was apparent.

Neath had heavy industry on the one hand but the town was also a market town which held weekly sales of cattle, pigs and poultry. Alongside this environment in the town itself one saw the tinworker coming and going wearing his white apron and a towel around his neck I made some drawings of these men as well as sketches in the cattle market. I was, however, drawn to the hills, for I loved walking and found more to my liking in variety of subject in the hills and farms than in the town and its industry. Finally, of course, by the 1960s industry had practically disappeared, as had the mines.

That's like Jack Crabtree in the Seventies going to the mines and recording them before they were closed.

I would not go to the mines – they belonged to Herman, and Herman closed the book on this subject. Earlier, the only artist showing any interest in the subject was Evan Walters, who painted the collier, as he was then known, on several occasions. I think he was a fine painter. I cannot recall any other painter being interested.

Was it in 1945 that you met Josef Herman?

Briefly, yes. I was still in uniform. He would come into Neath. We became fully acquainted later.

You say in Meic Stephens's book that you were his "pupil" and Alistair Crawford in the exhibition catalogue takes issue with that. Do you regret using the word "pupil"?

No, of course not. He looked on me as his pupil and a chosen one. He obviously recognised something in my work that mattered. Much that I learned from him one would not learn in an English art school. Remember, he came from eastern Europe. In Belgium he had been influenced by Permeke and so on. It was chance that he ended up in Ystradgynlais.

That story of him seeing the miners coming out of the sunset at Ystradgynlais and thinking that was the place from him, that was fanciful was it?

Well, he did romanticise sometimes. I know exactly what he was talking about. I was with him often on the footbridge, looking at the road bridge over the river – towards the sunset and the Varteg mountain. We both painted it. I don't know where my painting is: it's one I never got returned from an exhibition in London. I was a member of the AIA and some of my work was in the lending library there. Finally it closed down and I lost certain paintings.

My involvement with the AIA was friendly, interesting and quite productive. I showed regularly with them, including one-man exhibitions and received good press comments at times. I was sorry when the AIA came an end. When Josef was living in Wales we worked together, as equals. I did learn an awful lot about the art of the Continent by talking with him. He had attitudes and ideas that didn't exist in this country. Through Josef I met Martin Bloch in London and other artists and writers too.

Your contemporary, the writer Glyn Jones wrote that he found Josef Herman's figures to be "lumpish and impassive" not at all like the Welsh miners on whom they are based. Looking at those figures of yours here on the wall, I think I know them as Welsh. I know them from my years growing up in a council house at the back of Carmarthen mart. I can see a sense of Wales coming through the landscapes.

Of course, my people were country people from north Wales, Merionydd and Clwyd. I used to go on holiday to the farm at Denbigh. My mother's people were the Lloyds of Clwyd. I remember the traditional long-house with people and animals under one roof. They were artisans, too, farming and smithing. Stephens of Tyn-y-Waun, Neath, was really a reflection of John Lloyd in Bryn Mulan, Denbigh.

(Looking at a painting on his studio wall.) That's Tyn y Waun. I would be there several times in a week when they were milking, making my sketches. These paintings are all really Stephens, though he's been dead for about fifteen years.

(Points to another painting) And that's Dai Rabbits, as he was called. Dai used to call with his hand-cart, selling fresh vegetables.

And that other one's a Pembrokeshire farm – East Williamson. Every year for the last forty years we've taken holidays there. My man with the scythe is Tom Davies with whom we'd stay at Saundersfoot. A fine old man.

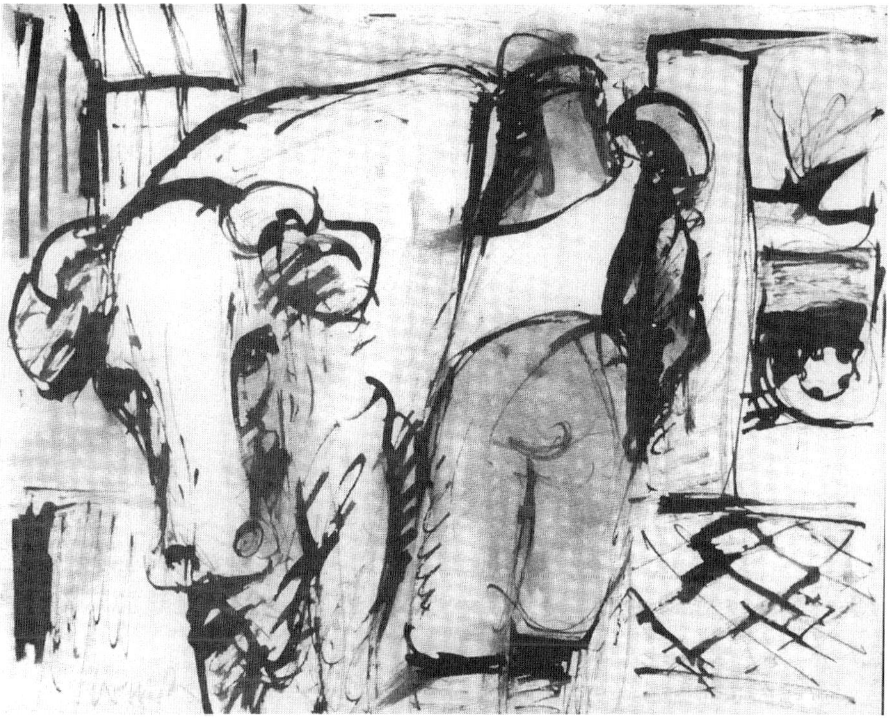

Washing the Cow — pen and wash, 30 x 40 cm, 1960s, coll: the artist

I've always liked your farm scenes, and they have been generally very popular. Let's look at 'Washing the cow', which you've used as a Christmas card.

Yes, this is the drawing from which I did a painting. It was bought from the RA exhibition by an Icelander living in New York. It's good that the work is seen and appreciated and understood by someone who seriously collects art. I remember that in 1970 a Canadian senator was visiting Swansea for a conference and staying in the Dragon Hotel. There were some of my paintings on the walls there and he wanted to buy them. He got my telephone number and came over to visit me. That was Senator Grosshart and he stayed all day and bought five large oils. He wanted to arrange an exhibition of my work in Canada, but I think he died before that was fixed. I never followed it up – perhaps I've been too laid back in that way.

Sutherland is now closely associated with Pembrokeshire – and I've written a poem about his work down there – but his paintings, good as they are, don't move me.

His paintings would not move you, perhaps. His drawings, done on the spot, I love. I've walked along that estuary at Picton Ferry. But when he transcribes those things into paint they tend to become mechanical things. I am not always moved by his paintings; at the same time I recognise the great artist he was.

So who else influenced you?

Rembrandt, Millet, van Gogh, Bonnard and others. And, indeed, Picasso. The German Expressionists I've mentioned already. Also some of the people I met through Herman – Martin Bloch and Heinz Koppel. Koppel was a Berlin-born boy who was evacuated from London. He was one of the true painters in Wales, I think. He was one of the twelve original members of the 56 Group.

I thought that the religious drawings in your exhibition were very strong. Are you a Christian artist?

Yes. I was a member of a Christian Art Society some time ago. I don't show with them now. I have dealt with the Stations of the Cross. It's a tremendous subject and I've recently been thinking of returning to it.

Important and unchanging. I saw one of your Penclawdd drawings recently, a woman and a horse, and there was something about it – the figure of humanity in a bigger world.

Herman said years ago, "Roberts's work has a spirituality in it, whether the subject has it, or not." Now, what did he mean by "Spirituality"? Not in a religious sense – he is not a religious man. But talking about the human spirit, which can almost be divine. So we are coming back to the simple fact that what I am painting is a serious work. It is serious in this sense, that I am expressing my own feelings in response to the subject.

Perhaps the "spiritual" is twofold, religious and secular; sometimes they might merge. The religious part, of course, is in one's belief, in my case Christian faith. I have over many years, produced such religious paintings and drawings, including the stations of the Cross. The stations drawn in charcoal (really as preliminary drawings for painting) hang permanently in St David's Church, Neath.

The secular works as they might be called, might be suitably considered as having 'hwyl', to use the favourite Welsh expression that seems to cover so much that pours from one when moved by some thought or experience. Indeed, the 'grand experience' upon seeing something commonplace that stirs the imagination is enough to produce this spiritual response – 'hwyl'. Any work without 'hwyl' must be somewhat tame. The drawing of 'The Shrimper' [see p.95] which I did on Saundersfoot beach in the 1940s fully expresses the subject and has never needed to become a painting. It's like a writer working from notes. It would have been done on a Saturday, the quiet time of the week in the summer.

It's certainly very elemental – simple, but intriguing in a way that a cruciform is made from the man's outstretched arms and his nets. Christ the fisherman.

It is a sort of crucifixion, though vague in its lack of details. It was a working man with his hands up to a load that started one of my first crucifixions.

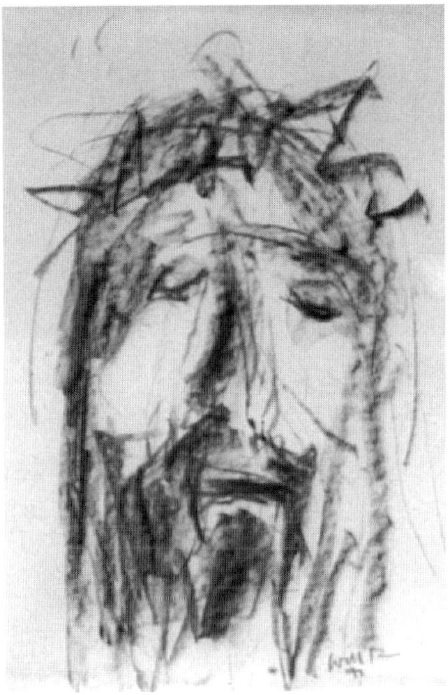

Crown of thorns
charcoal on card, 48 x 35.5 cm,
1997, coll: the artist

Now, this recent head of Christ with a crown of thorns is done on a card with a stick of charcoal.

It's again very simple. The elemental burnt wood, I think, is the fitting medium for the subject. From across the room it seems at first to be an abstract. And then, suddenly, it comes into focus and meaning. Very powerful.

Drawing is done through the heart rather than the head; it's the original grand thing. Often a charcoal drawing is superior to a painting.

A lot of your men and women look isolated: they are looking away, they are not looking at the viewer. The ones of your family are different. I love the one from 1946 of your mother reading – just a couple of slabs of paint and everything is there: tiredness.

Yes, that was painted soon after my de-mob after the war. I am fond of it.

You must be very proud that your 'Deposition' is in the local Anglican church?
That's only one. The one you see in the exhibition belongs to a private collector.

Is there a sense that you could hang one of your farmers, one of your people, in the church. It might take a bit of explaining, perhaps. But you are celebrating. . .
For what reason might such a work hang in church? It would have to be sanctioned by the diocese to be permanently there.

Dylan Thomas said, "I write for the celebration of man, which is also the celebration of God".
Well, this is it. Yes.

Is the work here in your studio recent?
A studio is never free of paintings. Some finished, some partly finished, a good many cast aside temporarily, or finally. I like having works about for longish periods that I can continue to work on or re-work from time time. When is a work finished?

PETER PRENDERGAST

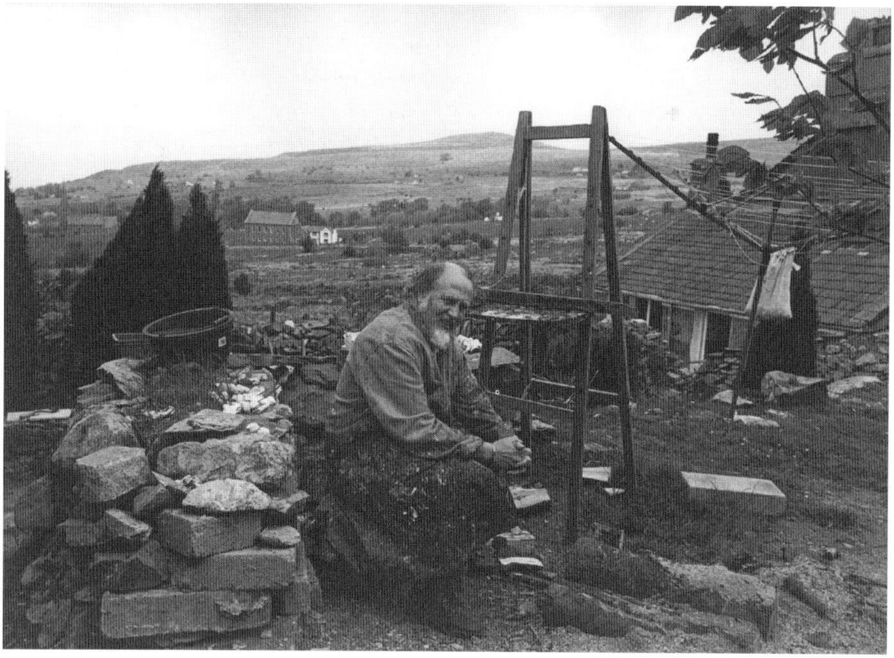

I had been struck by Peter Prendergast's large touring exhibition through Agnew's and the National Museums & Galleries of Wales in 1993, and in June the following year, I visited him in Bangor. We drove up to his studio in the hills and talked. I have since visited him in his new house and studio in Deiniolen which looks out on one of the views from which he draws his inspiration. He drove me to the exact spot at the Bethesda Quarry from which he worked his important series of drawings and paintings in late Seventies and early Eighties.

You were born in Abertridwr and your father was a coal miner, wasn't he? And just now in your house in Bangor you showed me some early drawings and a painting of the hills at Abertridwr which were not unrecognisable from your later and more famous landscapes of north Wales. Is there a sense in which your childhood continued to inform your mature work?

Yes, I was born in 1946 in the Aber valley, twelve miles north of Cardiff. My childhood was typical of the Fifties, carefree, spending one's time playing on coaltips; cowboys and Indians, camping – all activities based upon the village, the rivers, the streams and so on. I first started to paint pictures when I was in school at twelve or thirteen years of age, with a man called Gomer Lewis. He was a painter who had been in Java as a prisoner of war under the Japanese. He taught painting in an art room we called the Old Shanty, which was a tin shed at the bottom of the school yard. This was a secondary modern – we had all failed the eleven-plus examination and were destined for the coal mine, or the factory, or nothing at all. And this man came along and had us all painting and making sculpture, not for any exam, but serious paintings. He had us looking about us at our own environment; he had us carving stone and making plaster sculpture. He himself would be at the back of the room painting big pictures of his experiences in the war and in the prisoner-of-war camp, where he had seen his best friend beheaded in front of him, simply for falling out of line in parade. He was painting to make sense of his life, but at the same time he was communicating to us the beauty of painting and drawing and its value as a form of expression.

Did that disturb you? I ask that because I too was born immediately after the war and those images haunted my childhood.

I was curious and moved but it didn't disturb me at all. The man had an enormous amount of compassion. He taught us that being in that camp wasn't like we thought it was – barbed wire and turrets – because it was on the island of Java, it was just a few huts and guards and he would actually risk his life by going out to get food from the village for the sick. He was evolving in his own life because he'd started out as a PE teacher, trained at Caerleon. After the war he was in such a bad physical state he'd started drawing and painting as a way of expressing himself, as a therapy. Because he was a communicator, he became one of the best art teachers I ever met. The whole point of that beginning for me was that we started by looking at our own environment, our own landscape, which happened to be the Aber valley.

We played in it, camped in it, played football and rugby and grew to know that place intimately. Painting the coal mine had nothing to do with Josef Herman's influence or any other artists. I hadn't even heard of him at that time. I feel that this influence of Josef Herman in Wales is misplaced. It would seem to me that he arrived in Wales and its spirit and character, the landscape and the miners, rang a bell that reminded him of Poland; the effect was as much beneficial to him as to Welsh art. You have to remember that our influence in art was England, particularly as most of the art school teachers were English. Possibly what Josef Herman might have done was to encourage what was indigenous, what was rooted in the valleys' environment. I think that it is important for us in Wales to recognise that we did have a visual character which was waiting to be developed. Perhaps the paintings of Josef Herman did help to give us confidence in our own work.

I painted the mining valley because it was my environment, I grew up in it. It was my thing. I knew that my father got up at five in the morning with no fire or hot water or bathroom. He made the porridge before going to work and left it for us. And I used to hear the hooter going at half-past ten. If he hadn't come home perhaps it was because he'd been in an accident underground. That's not nostalgia or romanticism, it was a way of life which all coalmining families grew up with.

There is a problem in looking back at those times because of How Green Was My Valley *and other works. That man Llewellyn did Wales a service and a disservice it seems.*

Yes of course, he over-romanticised the way of life, yet on the other hand he made the miners heroes, but so did Josef Herman. I must say that from here my childhood does seem idyllic. My brother has now built a house on the very place on the mountainside where we used to go camping as kids. Life was simple, there wasn't much money, but life was rich and had meaning.

There was a community too.

Yes, I still don't know who were really my aunties and uncles and who were the friends. Doors were always open. That south Wales thing was actually real: that's how it was – not a myth. That's what Gomer Lewis did – he made us start from our own lives and find out who we were and where we were coming from. And to have pride in it.

Did he show you the great names in painting though?

Oh yes, he was a great experimenter. Can you imagine in the Fifties in an old tin shed, we were shown Jackson Pollock, Van Gogh, Rouault. He even put down canvases on the floor and used tins of paint to drip the paint, simply because he wanted us to find out what Pollock's paintings were about. In his own way Gomer Lewis was attempting to be an original, unique artist, and to do this he investigated the painting technique of the artists that interested him. Pollock was one of many.

At what point did you think – I enjoy this more than anything else in school – I want to do this?

Well, a lot of things happened when I was thirteen. I was what was known as a late developer. I started to do athletics and rugby, I captained both teams, and then I started making paintings. I was really surprised when Gomer began to suggest that I should go to art college. Then I grew to like the idea and began to live the life – wearing chef's trousers! At fourteen I would talk with Gomer Lewis about serious painting, searching for something you didn't know. We'd have philosophical discussions. I thought that I would work as a commercial artist and make my own paintings in my own time. But it didn't take me long to realise that I didn't have that kind of commercial talent. Because of Gomer's example, I felt that I'd like to teach. If you can teach and you can paint, then you have two vocations in one lifetime, that's a privilege.

It seems that we have a lot in common, both late starters from working-class backgrounds and both recognising the importance of sport and being encouraged by that. I turned myself around at fifteen after playing rugby for Pembrokeshire and seeing my name in the paper.

Yes, sport was important, and still is important to me. At the time it helped to give me confidence, and a belief in myself. Whereas the failure of the eleven plus exam had for a time destroyed my confidence, sport helped me find myself as a person and painting became the thing that put meaning into my life. And luckily now my paintings have begun to sell at good prices.

You're an overnight sensation after thirty years?

I don't know about sensation, but it's certainly been a long haul. You see, at the age of fifteen I won a county art scholarship. Leslie Moore, the County Art Adviser, was a friend of Gomer Lewis and they both recommended me for a scholarship. The Glamorgan County Art Scholarship was £300 and enabled me to go to art school. So that was the next step. I went to a two-year foundation course, without any O Levels. The people at Cardiff were marvellous to me. I pretended to be going in for commercial art. They saw what I could do as a painter and supported my application to the Slade, as Leslie Moore had earlier suggested. It all came from Gomer Lewis – he changed me and all the people I've taught, and my family.

So the Slade was the next stage for you. Did you realise what that would mean?

Well I knew Augustus John and Stanley Spencer had gone there. But I didn't really know anything about the Slade. I arrived in London, Paddington station, seventeen years of age, with my easel and suitcase. It cost me half my grant on a taxi ride to Woodside Park!

At the Slade there was my name on a notice which said: 'Tutor – Frank Auerbach'. I was to see him in a month's time. And that was it. Nobody cared whether you were there. Of course, at the Slade at that time were Jeff Camp, Euan Uglow and Robyn Denny; William Coldstream was the Professor. As the year went by I got used to what it was about. Looking back on it, I can see that it was the best training for a painter, because you had to be dependent on yourself, not on anyone else. It was teaching you not to be a good student, but to be able to survive, as a painter, in the real world.

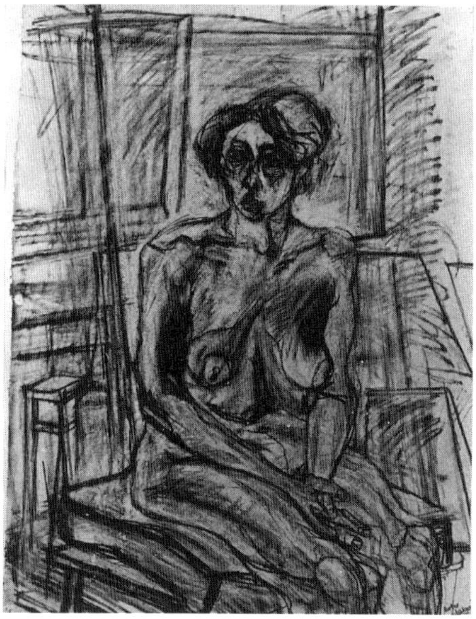

Paula
conte on paper, 101.5 x 81 cm
1982, coll: National Gallery of Bratislava

But surely was there a timetable – Life Class on a Wednesday afternoon, and so on?

No, there was no structure. You chose where you wanted to go. They had four life classes, and many visiting teachers. Professor Coldstream would assign you a tutor who would see you once a month. The tutor was allocated according to one's talent and sympathies. Frank Auerbach was my tutor perhaps because of the way I painted, which was intuitive and energetic working from Nature, from the landscape and figures. Frank Auerbach painted the landscape; his teaching was objective and constructive. It was not about expressionism or any other label. It was more concerned with integrity, structure, geometry and drawing, painting things more convincingly and inventively. It certainly wasn't about copying or mirroring Nature.

That sounds fine. But some people must have failed to cope as well as you did?

Yes, the Slade was notorious for students dropping out of the first year. Some suicides even. Some people think that I met Auerbach and started to paint expressionistic paintings. As I've said, my paintings started in Wales.

The Slade in the Sixties, like other art schools, was inundated by American Abstract painting, to the extent that the philosophy was that anyone who was painting from the object was old hat. I ended up painting from the figure because that was feet on the ground stuff. I was very homesick at times and spent a lot of time outside the Slade. I was educating myself, reading Dylan Thomas for example. I needed to keep in touch with where I was from.

I began to look at and paint London. I'd seen an Auerbach exhibition of London, and also Ceri Richards's Trafalgar Square paintings, but also because that was now my environment too. Frank Auerbach encouraged us to look at things about us. Again, as with Gomer Lewis, we began with drawing. I grew in confidence, but I still wasn't sure that I would pass. Then at the end of my final year when the list went up I was "Highly Commended for Painting". I went to the prize-giving and was surprised to be given the prize for figure painting. These were all pleasant experiences. I was totally naïve at that time.

I met my wife in that last year in the Slade and we got married a year later. I worked as a teacher for three days a week. After a year teaching I went to Reading University for a two-year MA course. Terry Frost and Claude Rogers taught there. It was one of the only places where one could do an MA in Fine Art at that time. I met Len Tabner there, a painter from north Yorkshire, and we have been close friends ever since. The important thing they gave to me was the time to develop as a painter, and it allowed me to work out a strategy to live my life.

Everyone seemed to be going from Reading to seek fame and fortune in London. But I'd already been in London, so I chose to live in an environment which I wanted to paint. Len Tabner left to live in Yorkshire and I decided to return to Wales. I chose north Wales, Bethesda. It was much like the Aber valley, but in a different place. It was a quarry town, a working environment vital and alive, and I liked that.

Why up here in the north? Did you know the area?

Not at all. I had passed through on the way to Ireland! But in 1969 we came to Bethesda. I rang up the only place there seemed to be to teach. And a bloke put the phone down on me saying, "Teach? I do all the teaching round here."

I eventually got a post at Liverpool School of Art for two days a week. After four years the School decided that drawing was out of date, not needed in art schools any more, so they ended my contract. So at twenty-seven I was out of work, with two children. Out of date, out of touch. But we didn't want to leave Bethesda: the kids were at school; we liked the place, and I was starting to make serious paintings of north Wales.

You were Welsh-speaking too, then?
No, no, but like so many south Wales Welsh I felt conscious of not speaking my language and I wanted my children to have what I had lost. I feel that I express my Welshness by being a painter in Wales.

So I stayed in Bethesda and taught at the local school. I continued to paint seriously and exhibit. Wearing jeans and no tie meant that there was no career for me in the school. But they were sympathetic to me being an artist and allowed me to change my contract to permanent part-time so that I could keep painting. This was unique in Gwynedd at the time. My winning the Eisteddfod in Wrexham in 1977 certainly would have helped this decision. Later I was given a job teaching on the foundation course which started at Bangor. At that time I was making drawings in the slate quarry at Bethesda.

The quarry at Bethesda has fascinated you for a number of years, hasn't it?
The quarry at Bethesda was an extremely exciting big hole – the biggest man-made hole in the world. Like Breughel's 'Tower of Babel', except in reverse. I started in 1971, but couldn't do anything with it. Then I began again in 1975 and worked there continually into the early 1980s.

What do you mean? In what way couldn't you do anything with it?
I didn't know how to draw it. There's always a right time to do things. At this period of time I actually moved house three or four times. I liked to move house every few years to pay off my debts. I moved to live in a house near to where Martin Bloch painted. I used to take materials to the quarry in a wheelbarrow to work. One of the main drawings is owned by Lewis and Eileen Allen. I should say that money hasn't been my driving force. I've just wanted to develop as a painter and become the best that I could; and I wanted to do it living in Wales – that was an important commitment and challenge.

I believe that the things that excited you as a child don't ever leave you. Drawing the quarry was again a working man's environment, like the slag heaps of my childhood. Bethesda was like the valleys, but with slate instead of coal.

Did you ever worry that these quarry pieces would not interest anyone? Was there a sense of an audience, or a market, when you were working?
Never. In fact, the opposite. Because people would ask me why I kept on drawing the quarry. But everything I've done there has sold. And when that began to happen I became suspicious. Also, I began to tire of it, and needed to move on. I suppose that, commercially, I should have produced a print of the quarry, of Lewis and Eileen's drawing, but such ideas never interested me, only doing the work.

Yes, I first encountered your work in the Allen's house where that large and impressive quarry drawing hangs.

Lewis Allen has been an important supporter. When I won a prize in the Wrexham Eisteddfod in 1977 Lewis bought a picture for the Contemporary Art Society for Wales. Then Eileen and Lewis came to see me and bought more pictures for themselves. I've been lucky in that I have met a lot of people who have given me continuous support, and that means buying pictures.

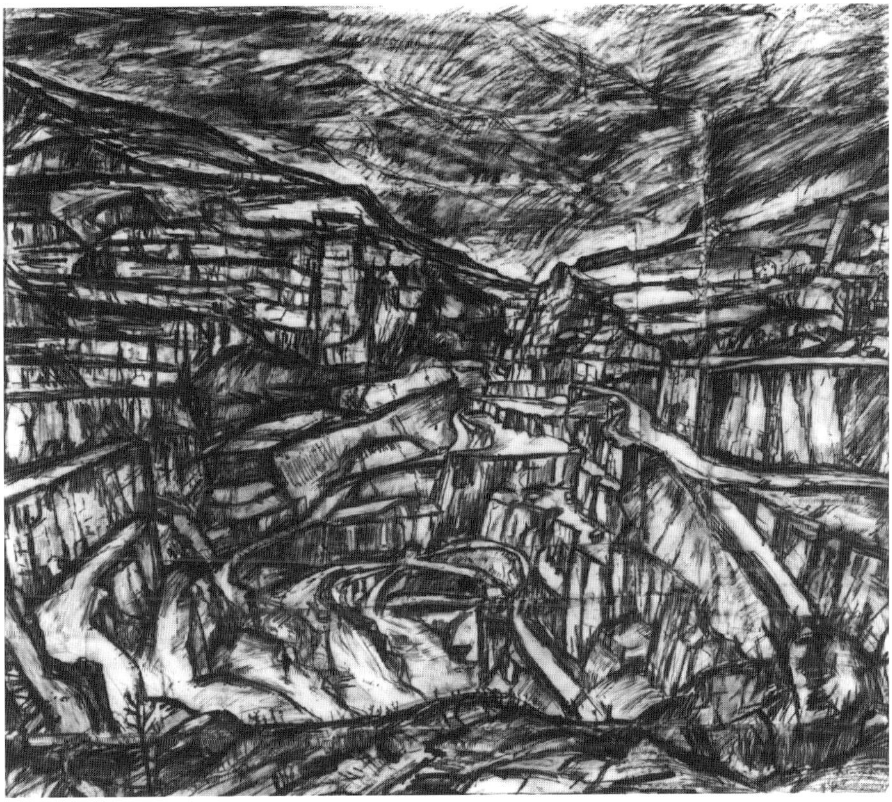

Study for Penrhyn Quarry Painting mixed media, 97.7 x 115 cm, 1980, coll: L.& E. Allen

Yes, they have a fine collection. I went to see a Ceri Richards which they have when I got interested in Richards a couple of years ago.

I'm glad you've mentioned Ceri Richards. I think he's a fine painter, not simply derivative of Picasso and Matisse, as people have said. I used to feel scornful of a reliance on literature as a source for artists. Where would David Jones be without it? There are other Welsh artists who rely on literature – anything can be a source really. I think that Ceri Richards didn't have enough support from Wales. Someone needs to organise a major retrospective. Augustus John, Gwen John, Ceri Richards, these are some of our major artists and Wales should promote them. There are people in the visual arts in Wales who are more concerned about political issues than promoting the best of the visual arts to the rest of the UK and beyond. If we don't believe in our own art how can we expect anyone to believe in it?

Can you say anything about influences from other Welsh painters? Whose work you would you have seen?

I wasn't influenced by other Welsh painters, but I was aware of contemporary artists such as Ernie Zobole, Eric Malthouse and Robin Hunter in Wales and working in Wales.

I remember mostly the *Monitor* film on television of George Chapman, travelling the Rhondda Valley making drawings of everyday life, and the Ceri Richards cathedral paintings that one could see in the Howard Roberts Gallery in Cardiff.

But my finest memory was seeing the van Gogh painting 'Rain in Auvers' at the National Museum of Wales. I suppose therefore my greatest influences were European.

Of course, one gets the feeling that there's a nationalist agenda which plays a part in arts decision-making.

Well, of course, there should be a nationalist agenda, a Welsh nationalist agenda. And there should be an awareness of visual art made in Wales, but it should be like in the USA of the nineteen hundreds up until the present. It should involve all artists that work, live and contribute to art in Wales; but we should all know what Wales is about, for Wales does have a culture, a language and the roots of a visual language that simply needs encouraging in order to grow. I have always believed that the visual language in Wales should be a way of uniting and expressing the spirit of Wales. In other words, bridging the gap that we have by having two spoken languages. I simply feel that my best way of expressing my commitment to Wales by living here and teaching and trying to paint good pictures which hopefully will compete outside Wales.

So you see yourself as a Wales painter, not a Welsh painter? You want to paint the best painting of Wales that you can.

Yes. I suppose that I could paint safe paintings and make a decent living in Wales, couldn't I? But at the end of the day, however limited I am as a painter, I still want to attempt to make radical images. Painting is not about confirming people's pre-conceptions. It's about attempting to discover and express something new.

There's a problem in becoming too predictable, isn't there? What about Kyffin Williams? I suppose one could say that you are the two outstanding painters of north Wales.

I don't know about that. Kyffin will tell you that he has been lucky in that the Welsh people like his work. I suspect that he confirms their nostalgia and feelings of what they think is Wales. He has had a big influence, but of course there are other ways of seeing Wales. For me, painting isn't about confirming what you think is there, but telling what hasn't been seen, what's beneath the surface. The problem for the painter is to find imagery which isn't predictable, imagery which develops in some way.

I think that your landscapes move people in a different way to his.

Of course, we say different things! I certainly don't adhere to a system. But I think that Kyffin Williams has done a lot of good for Welsh painting. And of course in other ways made it difficult for us too! But perhaps that's also the challenge.

Yes, he's got the R.A. and he's legitimised again the business of painting the landscape of north Wales.

Yes, unfortunately most people in Wales see that as the only way of seeing Wales. That is just one way. Whereas a painter such as Terry Setch, who I regard as one of the more interesting painters in Wales, because his work isn't accessible, isn't as popular.

I've seen his large pieces which use flotsam and debris from the seashore at Penarth. And those murals in the restaurant of the National Museum in Cardiff.

Yes, they're big works which don't fit nicely into your dining room. Welshness in art is a side-issue. The older I get the more I question: Am I Welsh? Am I Irish? I tried to learn the language, but I'm no linguist. Whatever I am, whomever I am, I want it to be expressed through my painting – no excuses, simply pure image-making.

Let's look at a painting here. How does a large canvas like this of Nant Ffrancon start?

There are probably two or three pictures done on this major theme. I made drawings on the spot. Some large drawings, one was six foot by four. I worked on a big pencil drawing for three months through all kinds of weather. They are now in people's collections. Then all that information is fed into the picture. When making a picture the intention is not simply to make a recording of what's there, I'm trying to make a comment on the energy, my feelings. I don't know whether the painting is about the valley, or my personality. Maybe these are just vehicles for it. I'm trying to make an exciting structure. But the painting hopefully is independent of the valley and at its best should have a life of its own.

If it were about personality, what would be there – angst or exuberance?

I don't know because people have said before that they were about angst. But I feel that they are just as much about exuberance. Life changes you: when you're younger you have worries about your kids growing up and affording things. But you don't really know what your paintings are about. Hopefully they are a mystery!

Money comes with middle age.

Clouds do lift when one can at last start paying one's way and getting out of debt.

In crude terms, that is a twelve thousand pound painting, which price puts it out of the range of most people.

Yes, but that's irrelevant. I worked on that one every day for two years, perhaps for an hour or for much longer. Obviously, I did other things at the same time. But the money value of it is neither here or there. It's having the time to paint that's important, not money; but of course money means time! It's painting that I'm interested in, and the time to do it.

I know what you mean. When people ask me how long it took to write that poem, I say forty-seven years.

I never think of a painting as having a particular value. I tried with that painting to keep the light as that of a clear winter day, and hopefully more than that.

Is that your favourite season?

I like all the seasons, but I don't like the summer as much. Though it's lovely to have a sunny day like today, looking out at the Menai Straits. A lot of my pictures have been done from here recently. Lots of small things. But at all times of the year.

You have painted subjects away from Wales recently, haven't you? I am thinking of those large works from Cork and America in the 1993 touring show.

Yes, there was a painting of West 53rd Street, New York City. It shows the scene from an apartment on the thirty-first floor, right next-door to the Museum of Modern Art. I was fortunate that my then London dealers, Agnew's, own that apartment and made it available for me, so that I could go the the Matisse exhibition. The first couple of nights in New York I couldn't sleep, being away from home. So I would get up at about three in the morning and look down on this marvellous street thirty-one floors below where you could see the yellow cabs and then the scene towards the Hudson river. I made a large drawing which, when I brought it back to Wales, became the basis for the painting. I was trying to get some sense of the chaos and spaciousness of New York. It was like a canyon; it was a canyon in the sense of the Penrhyn Quarry in Bethesda. I deliberately called on my earlier experiences of Bethesda in order to make that painting.

You had a drawing show, mostly drawings of figures. There are very few people in your bigger works, are there?

I don't seem to want to put figures in paintings. It's quite interesting, when you are painting or drawing landscape, you know, you very rarely see people. Perhaps I just don't want to see them! Yet I have sketch books full of drawings of the family.

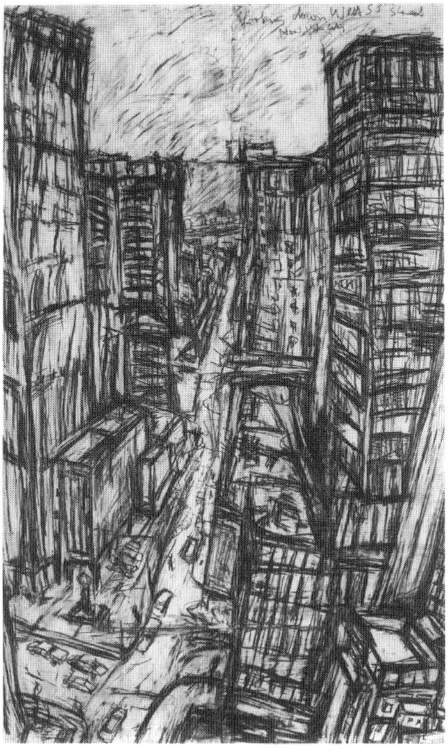

Study for West 53rd Street,
looking towards the Hudson
pencil and chalk,
154.9 x 99.1 cm, 1993
courtesy of Agnews

Not even a car passing? In a sense, do you block them out?
They're never in a position where I need to draw them. But they are in my New York painting!

So it's an occupied landscape, but by a community rather than individuals?
Maybe, but I don't really think about it. When I paint landscape I like to get away from people, away from teaching and family. The landscape creates another world, and that other world is about getting away from people. But I like houses in the landscape; maybe I just like traces of people.

When I paint my concerns are about structure, design, etc, but of course content is important and if you are going to make a painting it has to be a special event. Something important. You have to surprise yourself.

It's a meditative thing, a pulling back into yourself?
Perhaps, but I don't really know. The reason that I moved house again is that I felt a need to be near nature. To be a painter I needed to live in that landscape all the time. And there need to be periods when I do nothing but stare at it. And merge into it. That's why I've got the studio up here now. Where I live now I've got the mountains and the sea in the distance. And the next part of my work – it will be the mature part of my work, at fifty, won't it – the next period. If I've got the time.

I feel that by now I've done all the ground work, all the homework, I know who I am as a person. And – God sparing – I have around me the kind of imagery I need: I have rugged mountains, rocks, hawthorn – the same sort of imagery which comes from being in south Wales or in north Wales. The sea in the distance – and the sea at Barry Island wasn't that far away from Abertridwr – so all the images which are important to me will be on my doorstep. So, hopefully I'll make a few ambitious pictures.

You are a Catholic. How important is that faith to you? Is there a sense in which your paintings are religious?

No, I don't think my pictures are religious, but I think having gone to church has helped to make some sense of my life. I believe we have talents and that we have a responsibility to use them and that our convictions and beliefs should come through in one's painting. There are many kinds of religions and we are all accidents of our birth. My accident of birth was Irish Catholic, born in south Wales. What that has given me is a structure, a way of living, a way of seeing the world. From a kid I was going into Catholic churches which were full of colour – blues and golds.

For me I believe that the nature of landscape is important. I believe that if you could pull the earth back you could find out where the world came from. The picture is made out of some sort of glorification, celebration of nature. I don't know what they do for other people.

Do you care if others like them?

Well, we all like to be liked. But I've never painted a picture with anything else in mind except to try and paint the most ambitious and inventive image that I could.

Is there a moral purpose to your art?

I don't know what that means. I personally feel the need to make paintings, and feel strongly that people should have the right to express themselves. And I have felt so strongly as to commit my life to it. But that's my own selfish need; I know that painting helps me to make sense of my life, as a way of trying to understand myself, to see the world and justify myself in it.

To see paintings, to visit great galleries, to be in the presence of wonderful pictures is important for my existence, I would like to think it means the same for other people – clearly it doesn't, but then bingo was important to my mother!

The only purpose for my art is to make something exciting or to discover something exciting that might convey something vital and mysterious to someone else.

KEVIN SINNOTT

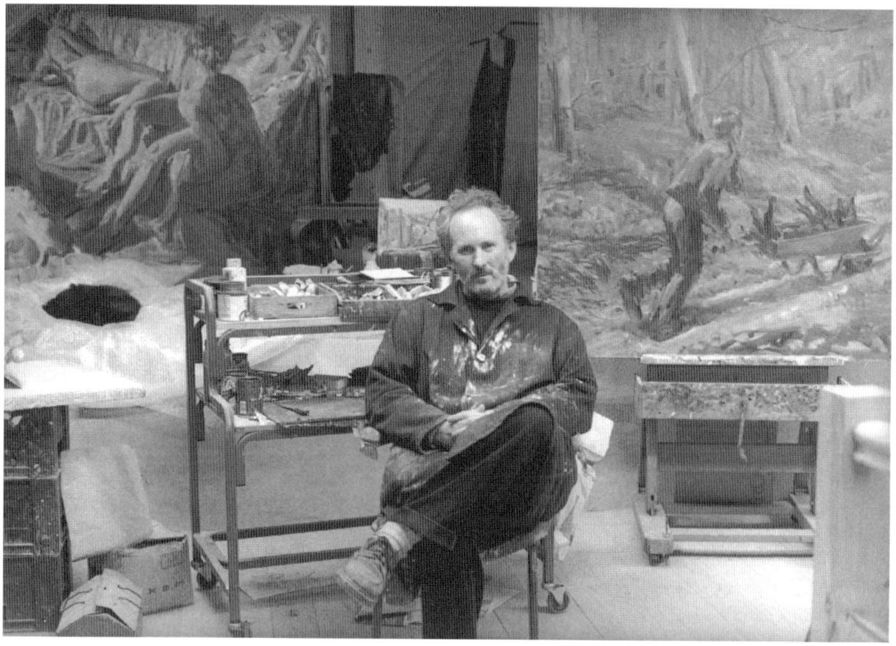

I interviewed Kevin Sinnott in his house, Ty'r y Santes Mair, in the Garw valley just north of Bridgend, through an afternoon in January 1997. It is a remarkable house converted from a church and retaining many of its window arches as well as its roof. The front door has been replaced by a large glassed door and panels which pull light into the building. Kevin's studio occupies the whole of the roof space above the family's living rooms and, despite being packed with his large canvases, allows him plenty of room to work.

You have returned to Wales to live in the area where you grew up and went to school haven't you?

Yes, I was born in Sarn, near Bridgend and went to what was called an elementary school, a poorly funded Catholic school. I went into the infants and came out of that school when I was fifteen. As it happened I wasn't a great performer in school so had no qualifications of any sort. I think that in those days that wasn't unusual, if you hadn't managed to pass the eleven plus. I got a job at Evans & Phillips, a carpet and furniture shop in Bridgend. I joined them as a kind of trainee furniture salesman and then later became a carpet fitter. When I was about sixteen I remember being disheartened and sad; I knew something was wrong. About this time I started going to a youth club in Aberkenfig and met a man called Mike Watkins. He told me that the eleven plus wasn't the end of the world, and he told me about correspondence courses. I'd always been drawing and painting anyway, but he told me about art school. Through the correspondence course I got some O levels and went to do the foundation course at Cardiff Art College when I was nineteen. There had been an art class in school, but it was the place for scoundrels, I suppose.

Yes, the eleven plus was the deciding thing in so many people's lives. I scraped through and got a bike as a reward. But the boy next door I'd played with since we were toddlers, failed and we went our separate ways, literally; I turned right in the morning and he turned left. We hardly met again. Sheep and goats. But this Mike Watkins changed your fate.

Yes, and after Cardiff I went to Gloucester School of Art based in Cheltenham. Again events took a turn for me. I would have liked to have stayed in Cardiff, but they had a strict quota, a very small percentage of their foundation course students, perhaps something to do with the funding, I think. Cardiff was run by Tom Hudson, who was a very dogmatic person with firm ideas about what an art school ought to do. I thought it was very Bauhaus inspired and very modern in its aesthetics. Traditional drawing was frowned on, but they had good disciplines in other ways – an incredible work ethic. Three nights a week working late was compulsory on the student timetable. They were excellent teaching colour to us.

Had the construction and installation stuff started then?
Cardiff was the sort of place at that time where it would emerge, an avant garde college. It was at the cutting edge in that respect; though foundation students who didn't get into the diploma course found it difficult to gain a place elsewhere, having come from Cardiff. Although I haven't reflected on that before now, I can see that it was a harsh regime, and there was an injustice in it. They equipped them well in order to progress onto the Cardiff diploma course, but not for other colleges. For myself, once I'd got through the interviewing procedure at Cheltenham I found myself well-equipped to make a mark, because of the commitment I'd learned in Cardiff. Hudson instilled that.

When you finished at Cheltenham what did you think you would do? Was it to be teaching or a work as a professional painter?
Well that's interesting, you see, students didn't have this new professional view of things, they weren't so precocious as they are now. You just took one stage at a time. Though something happened at the end of my course and pressure was put on to apply for post-graduate places and also to apply for the A.T.D. teaching diploma. I got an interview for the Royal College and failed to go for an interview for Hornsey A.T.D. Subsequently I got into the Royal College and the tutors thought that I'd been arrogant or confident in only going for the Royal, but in fact I'd missed the train for the Hornsey interview.

But someone must have recommended that you go for the Royal, that you were good enough?
I had worked very hard in Cheltenham and was happy there. I suppose I was among that handful that they expected to go on to the Royal College or the Slade. I was advised.

So you did the MA at the Royal College; Peter Prendergast talks about going up to the Slade at that time and rather stumbling through at first. Auerbach was his tutor, but much seemed to be done on his own. What was your experience, who was your tutor?
London took me by surprise. I was already married, in the middle of the Cheltenham course, and our first child had been born. But in those days we could get by with grants as a mature student with a child allowance. By today's standards it was generous. I also sold a few pictures while at the Royal College. I sold one to the North Riding Education Authority. People like that would go along to the college and meet the students and buy work off them at a reasonable price to start a collection or add to one. It seemed to be a service which the Royal provided to first year students. We were able to get by, though the scale and pace of London was incredible. At first I spent some time politicking and caught some air of change at the RCA as Carel Weight was retiring, the climate was changing. I wasted some time in the first year. When de Francia arrived he

got people like John Golding in from the Courtauld and others who proved far more sympathetic to me. It wasn't until my third year that I was settled enough to build up a momentum and I started to really work. I think that work meant that I defined myself as a figurative painter. Until then I had been involved in a kind of information processing of things, Warhol-influenced. I can remember clearly that summer between the second and third year. I can show you a painting from that time which represents a turning point.

What occasioned that change, because these things aren't decided upon are they? It's more likely to be a realisation that is then articulated.

It's interesting, a period in your life. Things that involve building things, like painting, take a longer time to evolve than thinking and writing. Look, this picture is a very simple picture – a can opener on the wall of our flat – I just stopped doing what I was doing and started to look. These weren't complicated pictures that involved shading and illusion; I just wanted to do a simple line of what I saw. I didn't edit out or compose.

It looks as if it had been influenced by Patrick Caulfield, in subject matter and its simple outlines.

It was before I knew Caulfield, but yes, there must have been influences around me – more kitchen sink art than pop art – Fifties art. Very much based in the Royal College.

So who was your tutor and did you have to work through his influence?

John Golding was my tutor, an abstract painter. And John had a very open approach, he had an excellent eye and was unpredictable. So when Peter de Francia assigned John to be my tutor it was an inspired act; it wasn't an obvious choice, but he helped me enormously in that last year. In many ways he was a stranger there and stayed only a short time. Also Ruskin Spear was a good artist and a help, and Carel Weight. But while you can see the impression that Auerbach made on Peter at the Slade, there was no-one who did that for me, there was a range of things happening in the RCA.

When you were in London there was so much going on and so many paintings to see. But when you were growing up in Wales where were you painting and what art did you see? Did your family assist you?

Well, I threw myself into the correspondence course and began to discover things about myself. I thought that I could go into a profession or something. My father came over from Ireland when he was eighteen and worked as a nurse in a mental hospital, Glan Rhyd, just outside Bridgend. Whether there was anything in the genes, I don't know. One of Mike Watkins's interests was art and my first trip up to London was with him. We went to the National Gallery. I saw art in library books – Sidney Nolan and so on – and the pocket library art books that Smiths would do. So you'd go into Bridgend at the weekend and start reading about somebody like Cézanne. When other lads were off kicking about,

I was engrossed with this chap from Aix.

It was a kind of escape, but at the same time a deepening of the world. Because there was no art in Bridgend.

But there was in Smiths. And the coach to Cardiff would take me on my half-day off to the National Museum to stand in front of three actual Cézannes. One of them one of the best landscapes he ever painted.

That is an interesting contribution to the debate about the Museum and the role of Welsh art. There is the argument that it was overshadowed by a concern for these European modern masters. But it was there magically for that boy from Bridgend.

It was an accident. My gradual awareness of art gave me so much, because it gave me an awareness of history, of the sequence of things, of what the nineteenth century was. I became aware of time in a way that I had never been aware of it in school. When I went on to read about the Classical world I could place it not just because of the look of it but I could place it before the Dark Ages, the Renaissance. I realised there was this massive world with more of it to be discovered. I was in the National Museum of Wales walking through and then I crossed the landing to where they used to have the Davies Bequest and when I walked into this room it was an extraordinary, moving experience. I went back on the bus to Bridgend and was full of this experience for days after. I was sixteen, but in developmental terms I was still thirteen or fourteen, because I had been so slow at things.

Was there any way of articulating that then?

No, it was my secret. I can remember going out to do a watercolour of the farm nearby at Sarn and seeing things, fences and trees as Cézanne saw them, wedged into the landscape like he saw them in Aix. That should never devalue your backyard experience – to see something like that.

Because it's not the place, it's the way of looking, and you can take that away with you. You've got to in a way. Maybe that's being patriotic or true to your roots, to bring it back on the bus with you to Bridgend and to see the place transformed. But you still have to get materials to paint, it's not like being a writer. How did you do that?

Well, I could get stuff in Bridgend, but that first time was a big thrill, the first oil paintings. Because I didn't know what you put oil on. They had to order me the canvas on stretchers. I had tried the Daler boards but then I graduated quite quickly to canvas. Even Bridgend has got art shops.

But you didn't think of joining an art club or something?

I would have done if there had been one I was aware of. I was ploughing my own furrow. I did do an art O Level on the correspondence course, but it didn't tell me anything about painting because I did pen and ink drawings for the entire course. And when I went to sit the O

Level in school, in Maesteg the rest of the candidates had paint. But I could paint anyway. I managed to put a portfolio together.

How did your family react? I mean, you had a job which you were giving up to do art?

There was no resistance, though they thought I was dreaming. There was a feeling in those days that ordinary people couldn't do that. I remember that one of my older brothers came home from the army and he said, "You're dreaming"; he'd picked that up from my parents. I think that there was a great deal of emotion and pride when I went off to college, and England. I used to write lots of letters from the RCA and used all sorts of coloured pens. They must have thought it was very arty. Once I was established in London I was fuelled up with ambition, in that third year I decided that I would not teach, that I would be a full-time painter. I was almost bloody-minded about it. I spent five years then working as a postman, painting in the afternoons. In Stepney Green and then Clerkenwell.

There was no thought of coming back to Wales at that time?

No, not until twenty years later. My influences were then around me in London, they weren't in my past. But I didn't even enter the Whitechapel competitions for artists in the East End, in a funny sort of way I put myself out of touch, being determined to be on my own.

What were you painting during that time as a postman?

They were paintings about the post office. But semi-abstract paintings, a flat space, executed quickly, slight with a dry pigment and acrylic paints and egg tempera – I wasn't even painting oils in those days. And they were, by 1980, starting to be noticed. I won a prize in the John Moores in Liverpool; I had a few exhibitions in the Arts Council spaces, in the Ikon in Birmingham and the Riverside Studios in Hammersmith, a gallery in Leeds. After years out in the cold it all started to happen. A dealer in London, Jonathan Blond, exhibited my work for a number of years. And then, funnily enough I started to teach a bit at St Martin's. I'd left the Post Office before doing five years in order to cash my pension in. It was very tight for about six months with a small mortgage and two children, but then things began to happen. Much of the publicity following the John Moores was based on the fact that it was in the post office, it made good copy. About that time I appeared in an American art magazine in a feature by Bill Feaver on the working art scene in Britain.

But then in 1986 you were showing in Los Angeles and New York?

Something different happened then, I had started to visit St Martin's and Canterbury School of Art to teach regularly. I managed on that until 1985 when Bernard Jacobson took me on, and he had the American connections. In America relatively ordinary people in the cities buy art

– office workers and so on. When I delivered mail to some of the biggest houses in London, in Hadley Wood, and these extremely wealthy people had reproductions of Constable on the wall. They could have afforded good contemporary art but their social milieu gave no credit for that. I sold a drawing to a woman in Germany at that time. I corresponded with her and found that she was young and couldn't even afford a car, but she collected art. She had a small collection of contemporary drawings.

I can believe that. We need a new suite at home, but I keep spending the money on art. Some people would think that was crazy. They'd think you were crazy for painting it, but people like me were even crazier for buying it, before a car or something. That must be a good feeling for you?

The incident with the German woman underlined the fact that artists were up against it in Britain.

Not to mention in Wales. Though now we are not so badly off for galleries. There's even a good one – Oriel Myrddyn – in Carmarthen where I grew up and where I never saw a painting.

Well, the middle classes leave Wales – they get educated and leave and don't come back.

Were you seduced by that?

Yes, it had to be London. I don't know whether it's different now, perhaps in Glasgow or Edinburgh.

But you have succeeded in America. Was it Bernard Jacobson that took you there?

Yes, until Bernard got me over there to New York in 1987. I'd never flown. I was forty and had never been in a plane; we'd never been on package holidays as a family. That year I went to Rome and America. I had been to Paris and Italy, by train of course. I actually found it harder to get by in New York, although the language is the same, than in Rome; the cultural gap is large because we are Europeans. It's easier to order things in a restaurant or use public transport in Europe than in New York, at least at first. The taxi drivers hardly ever talk English! Still I got to all the galleries, I loved the Frick especially. I stayed with Bernie at his father-in law's house on 57th Street. I didn't paint while I was there, but the exhibition was a sell out. In the last week a Swiss man came in and bought six large paintings. He put them away as an investment, figurative art was 'on a roll'. There were some good reviews too. The next time I went back it was on my own to Chicago, that was in '89 and it wasn't a success. The biggest success was in the New York in 1991, the *New British Painting* show and people were coming up to me and asking for me by name. The *New British Painting* which was associated with that exhibition was published at the time. Since then I've been regularly in the Art Fair in Chicago and the Welsh paintings have done extremely well there – I don't know who buys them.

Are you interested to know that? Does it matter to you where they go?
Now that my paintings have this Welsh aspect to them I wonder now where they go. A painting I sold recently in my London gallery Flowers East was called 'The Last Bard' and they changed the title to 'The Last Poet', but it was a big painting and I was fascinated to find out who had bought it – the London Welsh crowd, I thought. But it wasn't – they probably didn't realise it was Welsh painting.

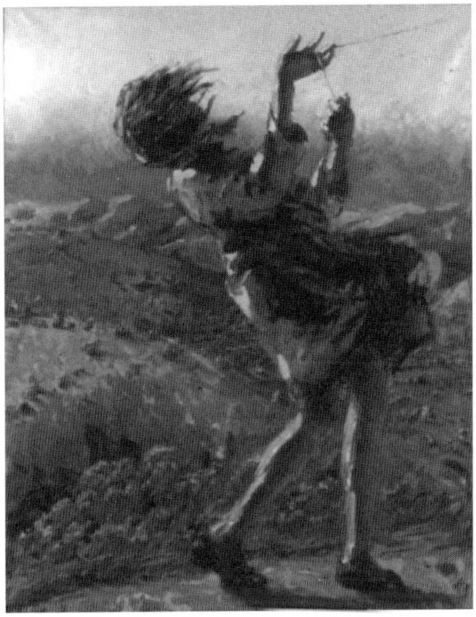

The Lost Romantic
oil on canvas, 185.5 x 152 cm
1994, coll: courtesy of Flowers East

I saw one of your paintings from that period, 'The Lost Romantic', used on the cover of a collection by Maura Dooley. And here in your 1996 Flowers East show Paintings from Wales, which also went to Copenhagen, you've used a quote from the poet Harri Webb:

> *I am old now, and lame,*
> *But I will go back, if I can,*
> *To the place whence I came,*
> *To walk where I once ran.*

Does that englyn help to explain why you've come back to Wales?
I mean by that 'where I once ran away from'. I had done that painting 'Running Away' before I knew the poem. I mean away from the smoke-filled skies. Since that final year at the RCA when I realised that I was a figurative artist I've always painted my immediate experiences, and now that I've returned to live in Wales it doesn't mean that I am automatically a Welsh painter; it's that I use the things I see and that are near to me as plastic elements in my work. After seeing the skaters at the Rockerfeller Centre I did paintings called 'Thin Ice'.

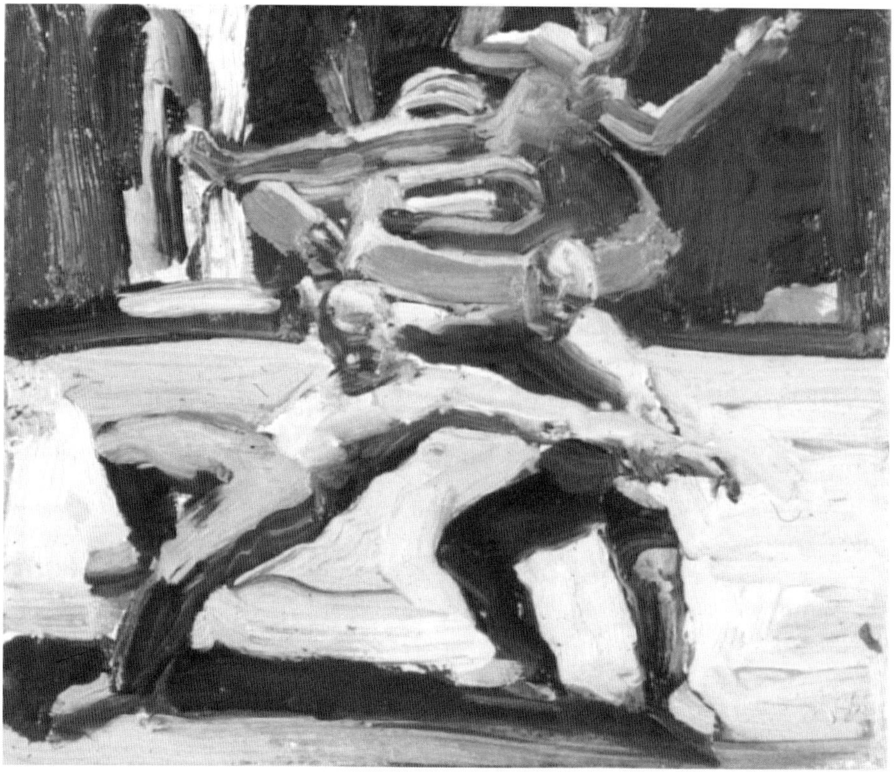

Thin Ice oil on board, 20 x 25 cm, 1987, private collection

But there is a reason for you choosing to come back to Wales and these Paintings from Wales are not of your present surroundings and experiences, are they? Your paintings are works of memory and imagination.

Yes, there's always some symbolic input. The paintings I did of New York were about thin ice, about the risks of capitalism, and the same thing applies in my paintings of south Wales now. Some of them are things I simply see, like people hanging their washing out, but others like 'The Artist in Retreat' paintings are about me retreating to Wales from a phase in my career when my head was in bright lights, I suppose, a retreat from success in some ways. It's not that I've been that successful, there was a short period in the late Eighties when we had enough to live well, but it was only short-lived.

People think that when an artist sells a painting they get the money, but it's more complicated than that, with galleries and expenses. Even quite successful artists do some teaching.

You have to sell a lot in order to make what a primary school teacher makes. You'd be surprised how many actors and entertainers are out of work for a period and struggling.

In your painting 'The Artist in Retreat' this young man looks like he's gone

out to paint the landscape and failed.[see colour plate] Is the title saying something about your return to Wales?
Well, we didn't return with a skip in our step. In the painting the weather, the landscape, the culture, the mood, whatever it is came into the painting as I did it. I begin a canvas with little sense of the meaning. Meanings attach themselves as the painting develops. The longer the painting went on the more it became consolidated to me as precisely that. It's not only retreating from the adverse elements, it's also the traditional artist being put back stage, in retreat from the fashion of the day – installation, conceptual art. He's got an easel on his back, not a video camera.

And he's in the landscape, which some people would say is a dead form for the modern artist.
Let me show you the study, which I still have.

But there's another figure in this version, which you've cut out of the final painting.
It's mysterious, a mentor from the past. Because ultimately my paintings are about paintings not about me. I left the figure out for compositional reasons.

That figure is somewhat androgynous and adds several possibilities – is he walking from a girl, is he walking from a parental figure or a mentor? It's not part of your job to explain that, is it?
If it was a real person then I'd say it. But I have never been concerned about how my paintings are interpreted. Once they've left the studio and are on someone's wall that's another aspect of their life.

You have to sell because you are a professional painter and that's an honourable thing to do. But are there some paintings which you would not sell? Like that key early painting which you've shown me?
I'm very emotionally attached to that picture. It's a good question which I've never asked myself before. There are several pictures like that. And this one which I'm working on now may be another.

Because it's to do with this new house – the autumn leaves and the wheelbarrow in the trees behind us?
It's to do with something that happened, a mishap with the dog: we inherited a Rottweiler with this building which we took on as a guard-dog. It mauled some sheep. The dog is in the wheel-barrow and I'm taking him to be buried. My father-in-law is also there pulling at the rope attached to the barrow as I push up the slope. This is 'The Funeral', a good title. It's going to be a painting I started with a literal idea.

So that's the exception that proves your rule.
Yes, and because it's so odd I expect it not to sell and I'll put it up here as a memento for my wife and myself.

The titles of your paintings are very important, but the moment you call that

'The Funeral' or 'Funeral of a Rottweiler' it completely changes the meaning of the picture.

It almost gives it a German Romantic effect. Rottweilers are named after the town in which they were raised. My pictures have a kind of Bavarian air about them since this incident. I don't know why there have not been more paintings in Wales, apart from Richard Wilson, that have that German Romantic sense about the landscape. I suppose Kyffin has that.

You mean the landscape as drama, as opera, Wagner?

I mean pre-Wagner, Caspar David Friedrich: spiritual landscape rather than simply hay-wain landscape. Because there's height and sky and heaven and church in the hills.

Like Wordsworth ascending Snowdon and being changed spiritually where "Nature lodg'd/The soul, the Imagination of the whole."

I want to do that and put a figure in there as well. Though there is a landscape in my recent show in Cardiff at Martin Tinney's which has only a small figure in the middle distance. They should always be the figure coming out as the most important element. In a great artist you can find a figure put in rather awkwardly for purposes of scale, whereas pre-naturalism, eighteenth century as opposed to nineteenth century you have landscape playing a supporting role around the figure. I see that as a role worth occupying with my work.

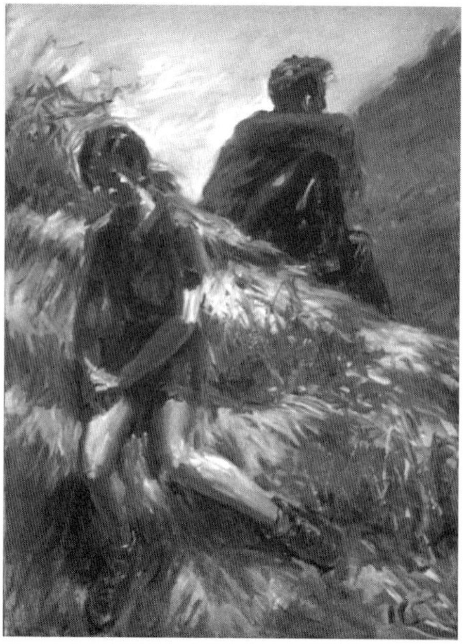

The Break
oil on canvas, 144 x 110 cm, 1997
coll: the artist

When you have landscapes with figures in them or figures in landscapes, you are celebrating God, or recording the despoilation of man, or that interaction. We are in the world and one of the things that painters do extremely well is

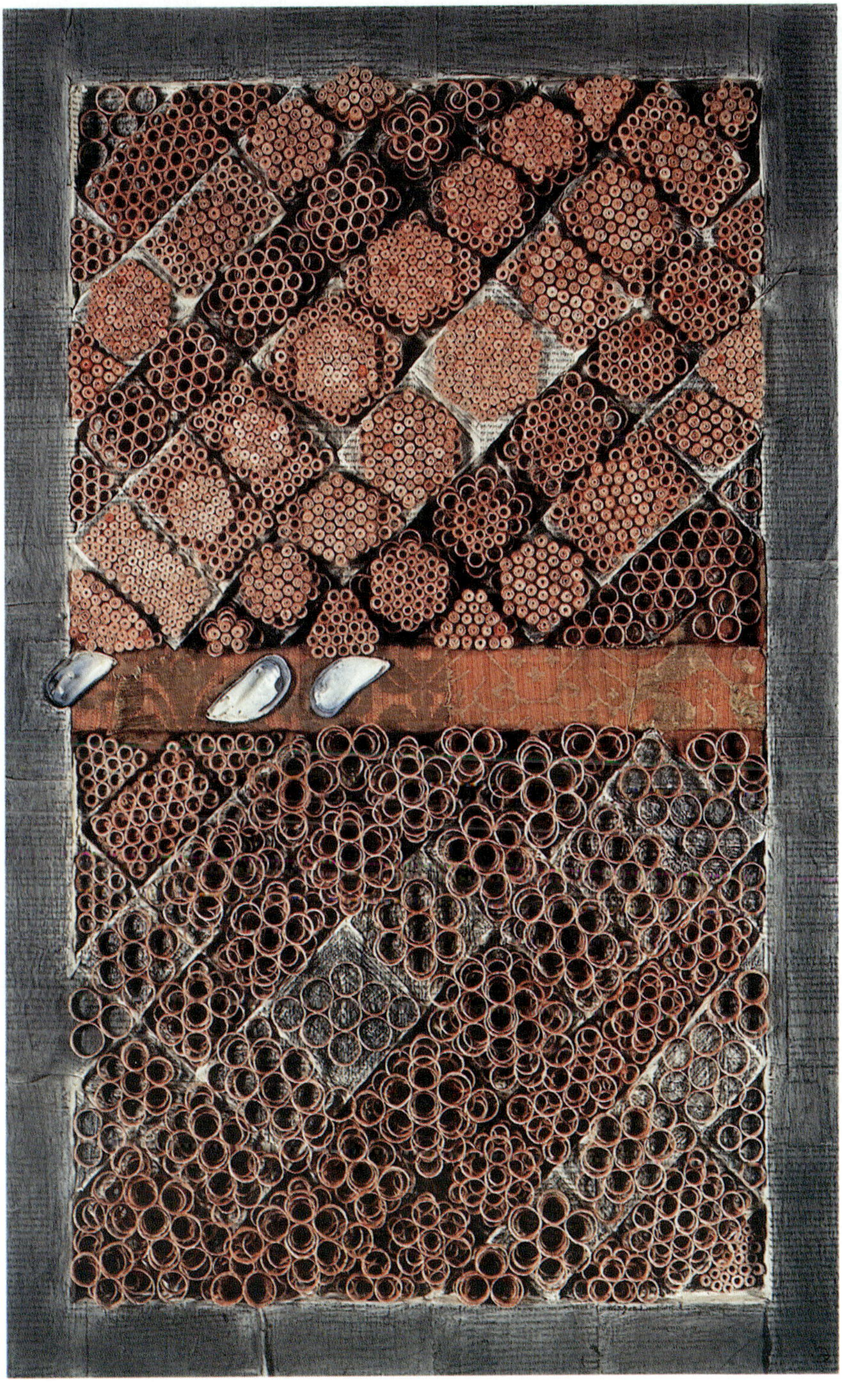

Arthur Giardelli: At the Sea's Edge
paper and shells, 94 x 61 cm, 1980, coll: the artist

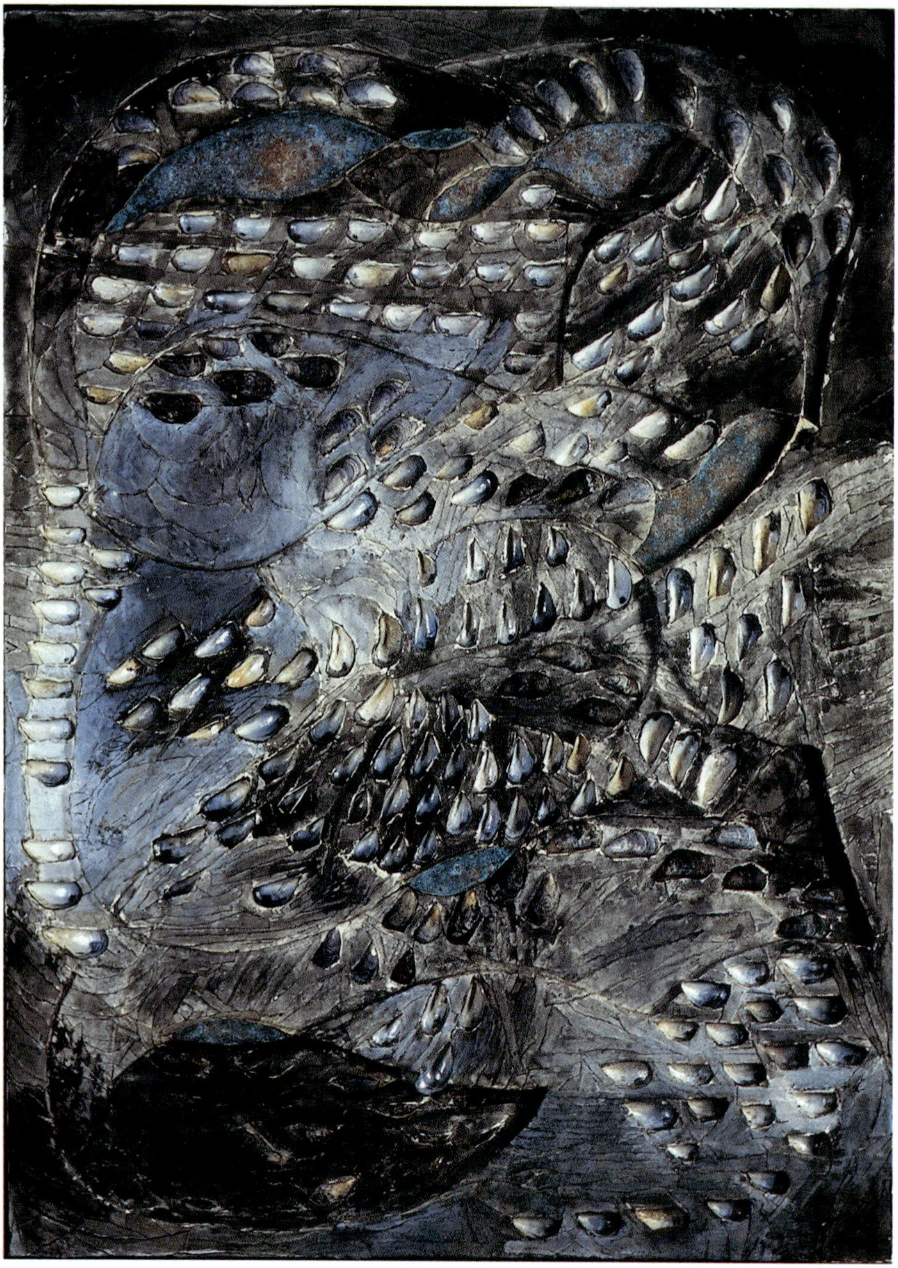

Arthur Giardelli: The Sea Has Many Voices
shells, paper, watch parts, 110.75 x 91.5 cm, 1990, coll: the artist

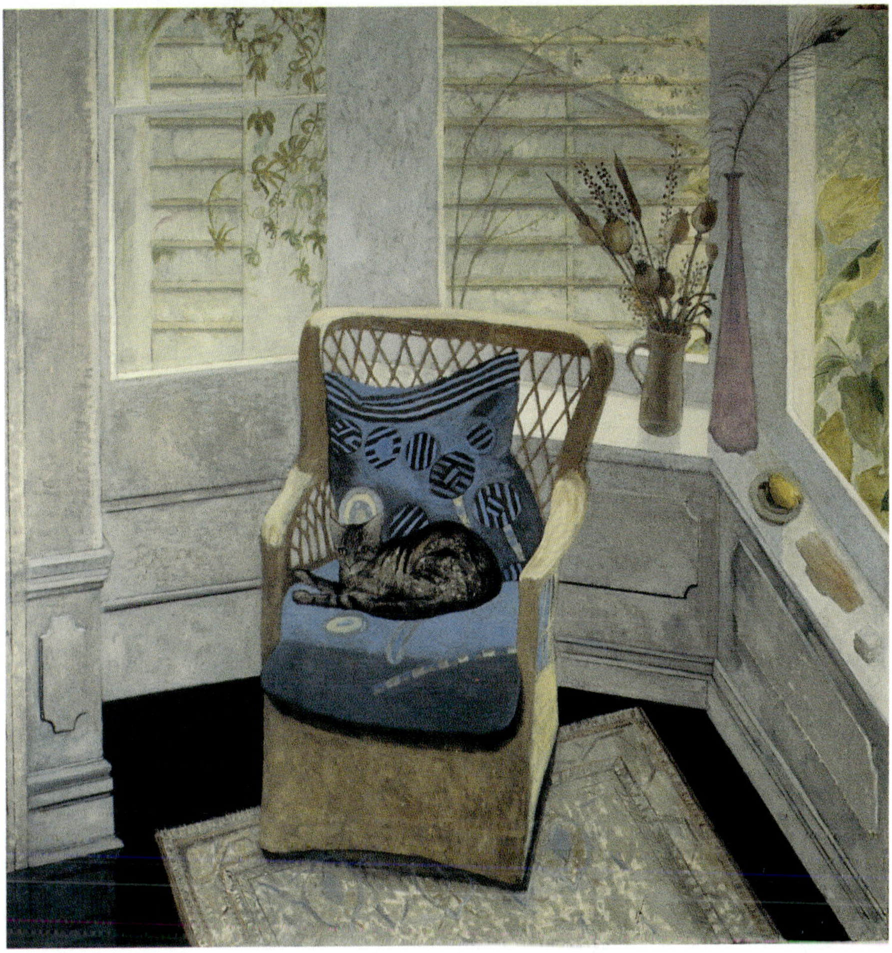

Charles Burton: Cat on a Chair
oil on canvas, 183 x 183 cm, 1981, private collection

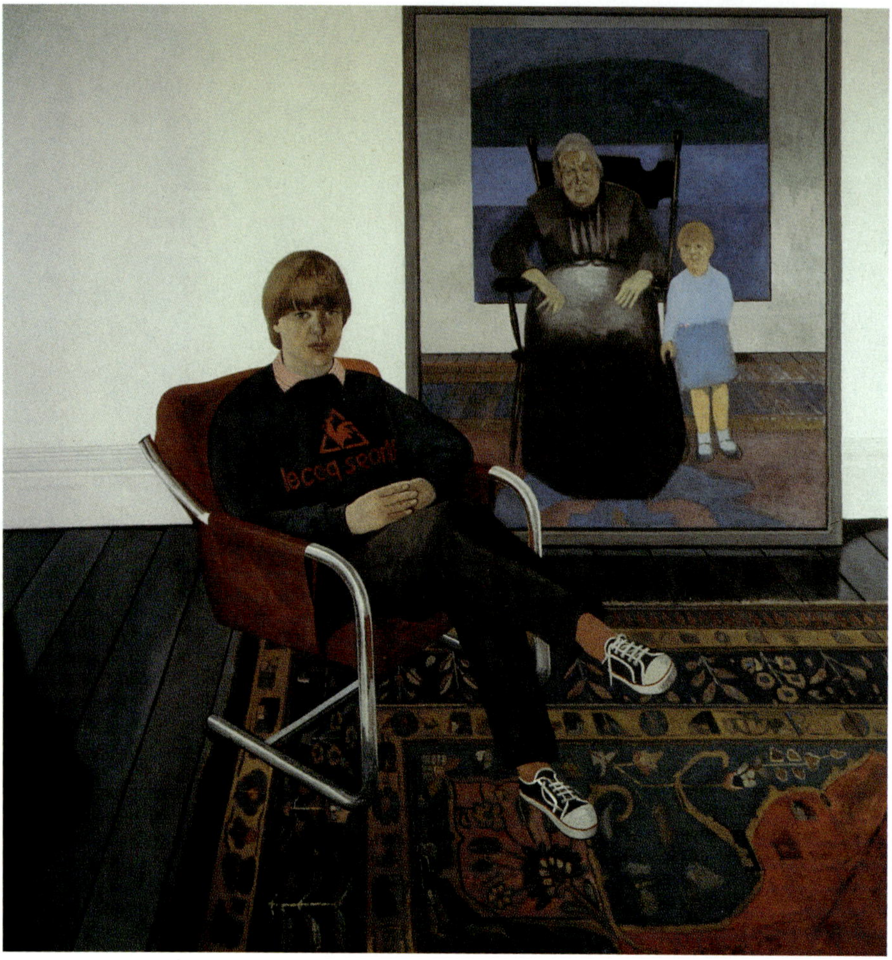

Charles Burton: Branwen
gouache on canvas, 183 x 183 cm, 1981, coll: the artist

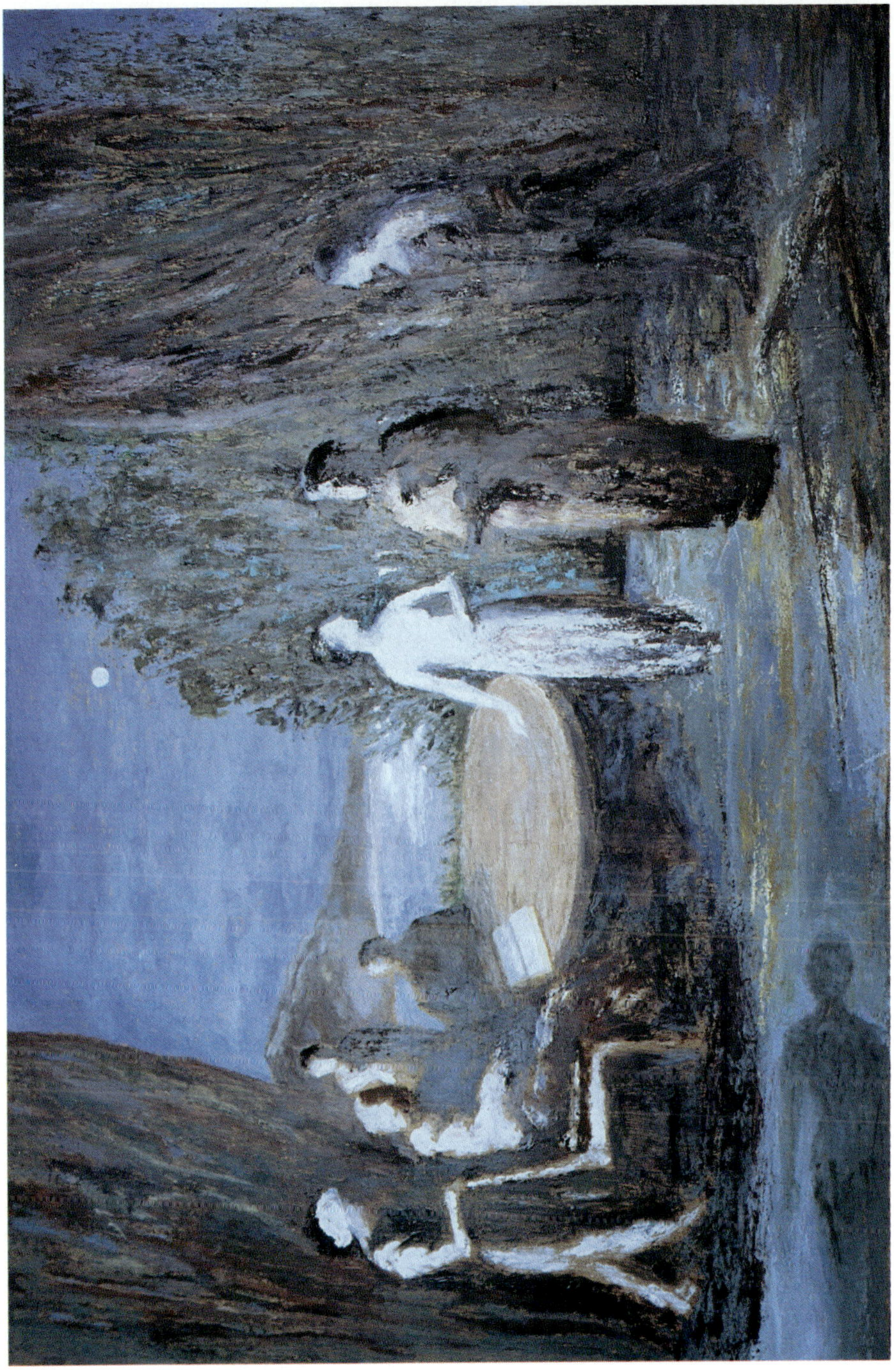

Felicity Charlton: The Ceremony
oil on board, 61 x 94 cm, 1997, coll: the artist

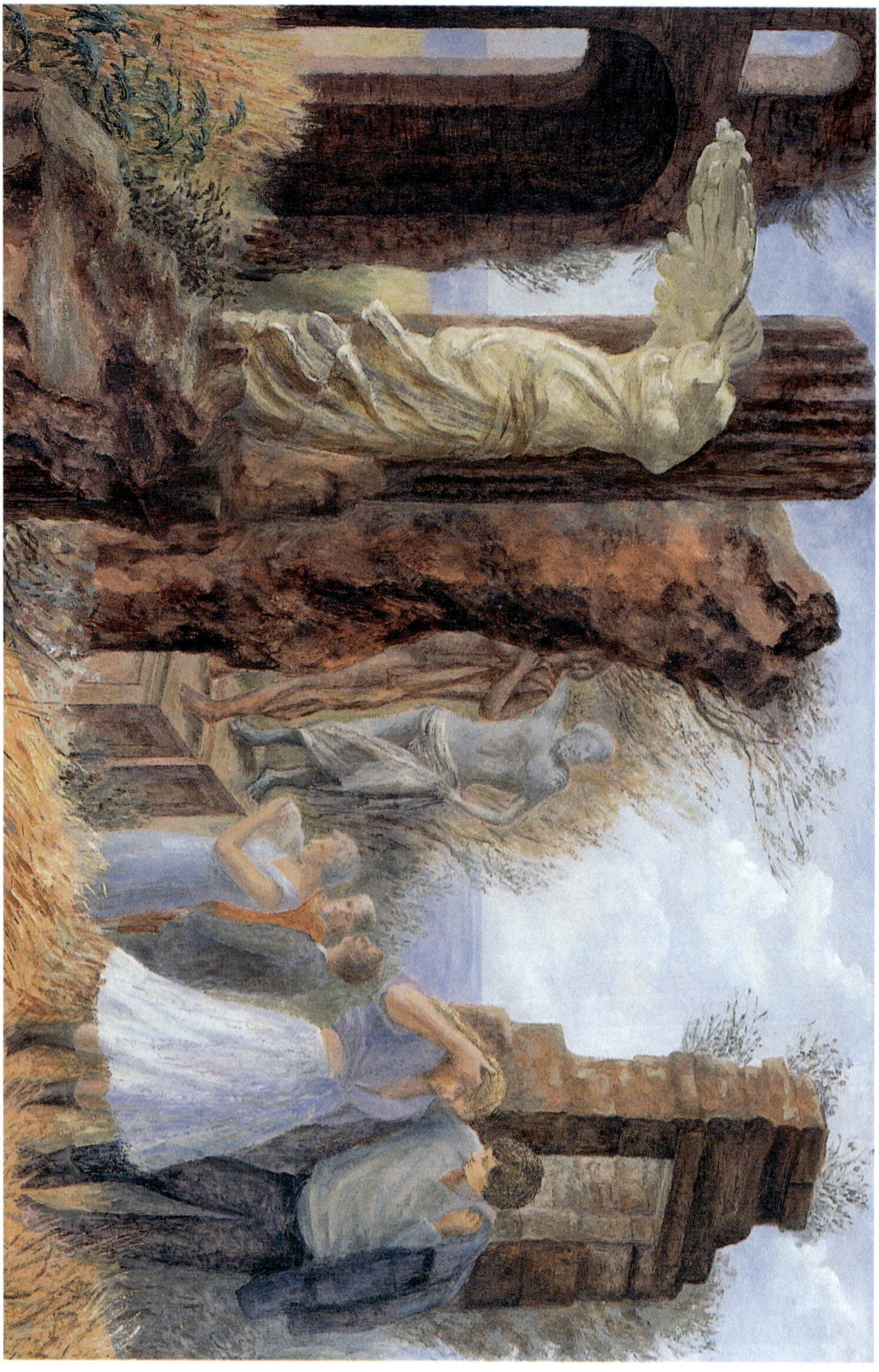

Felicity Charlton: The Island Excursion
oil on board, 61 x 91.5 cm, 1989, coll: the artist

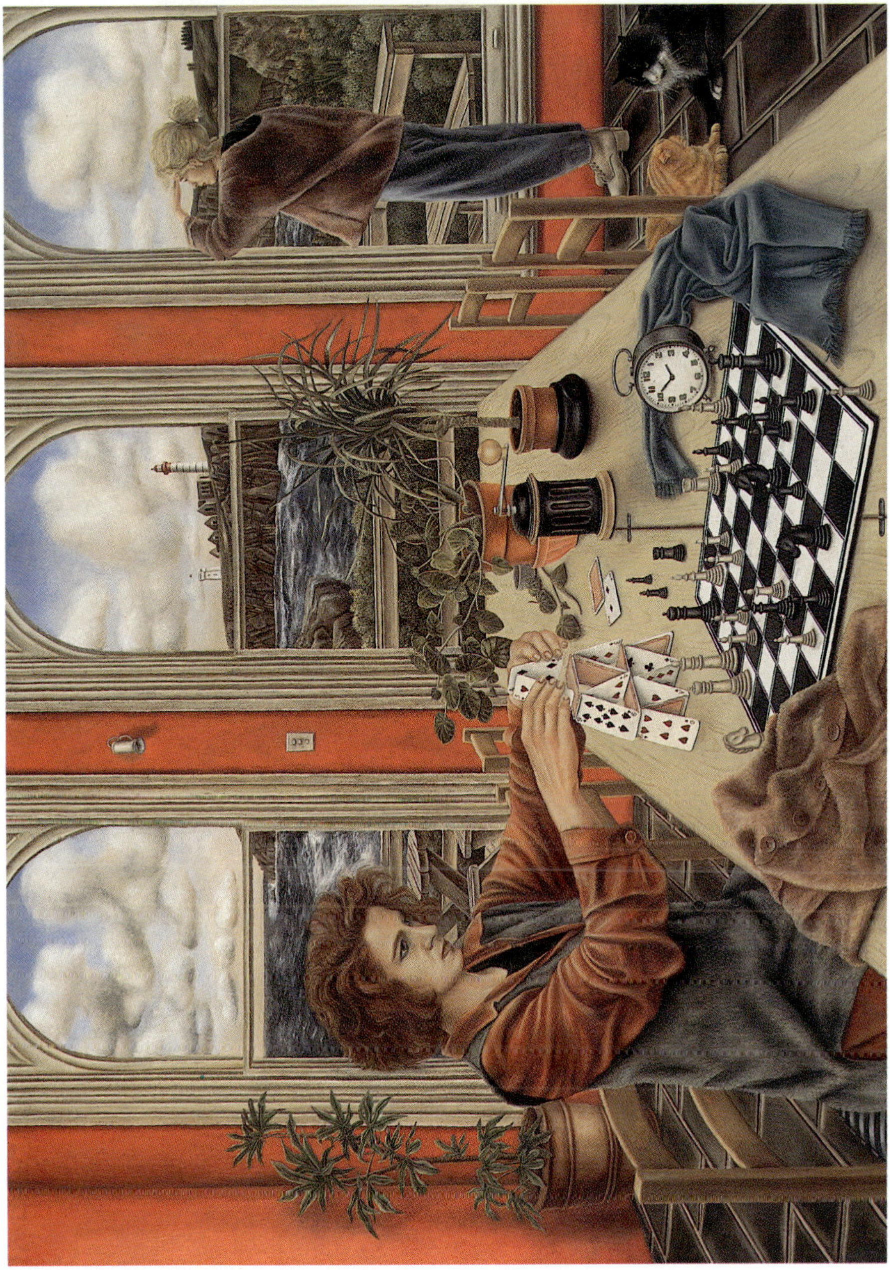

Sally Moore: House of Cards
oil on panel, 127 x 91.5 cm, 1994, private collection

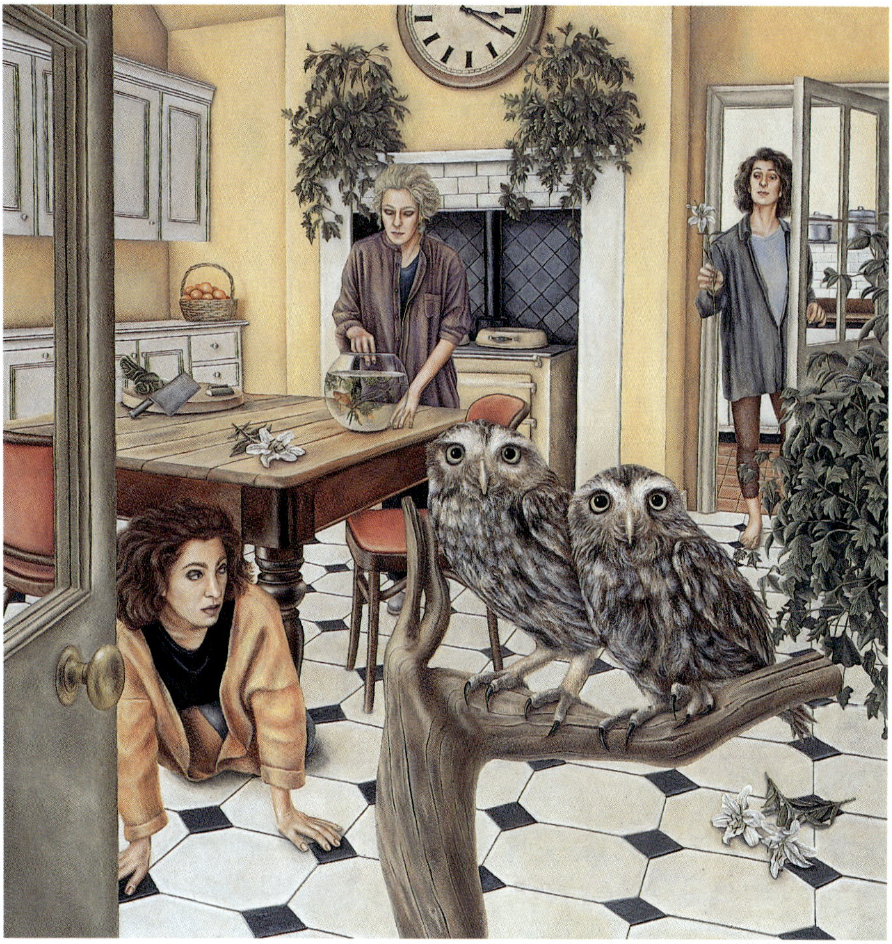

Sally Moore: The Visitor
oil on panel, 101.5 x 101.5 cm, 1994, private collection

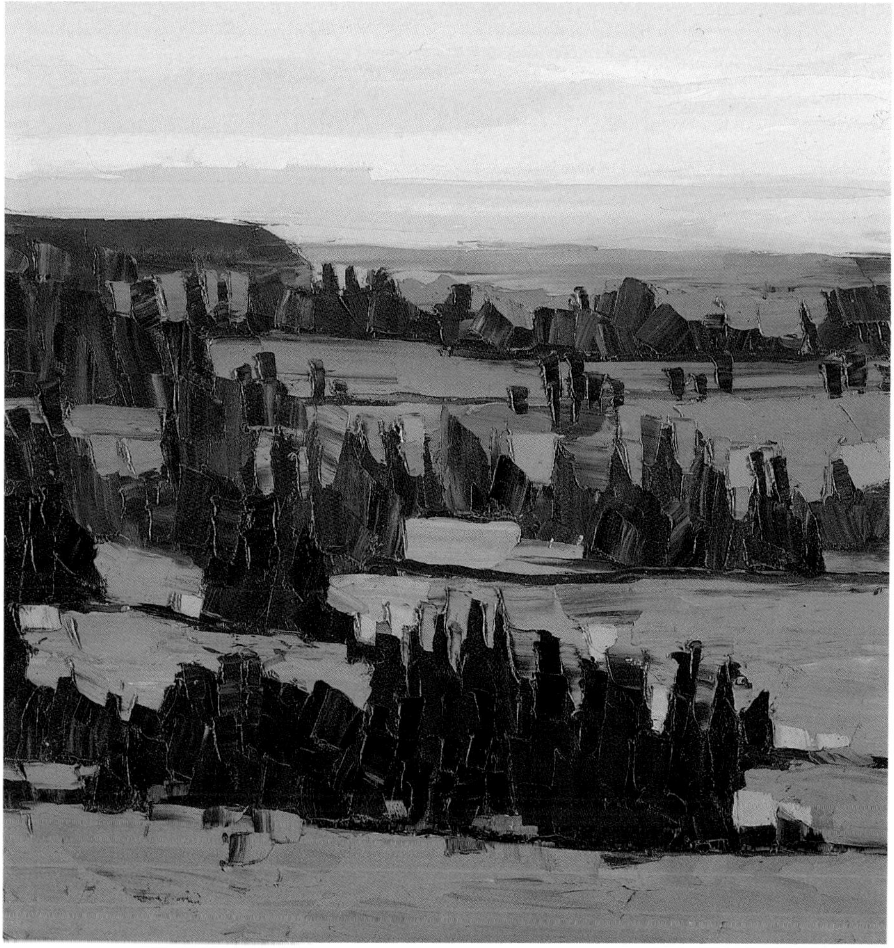

Kyffin Williams: Dyffryn Camwy, Patagonia
oil on canvas, 121.3 x 121.3 cm, 1970, coll: National Museums & Galleries of Wales

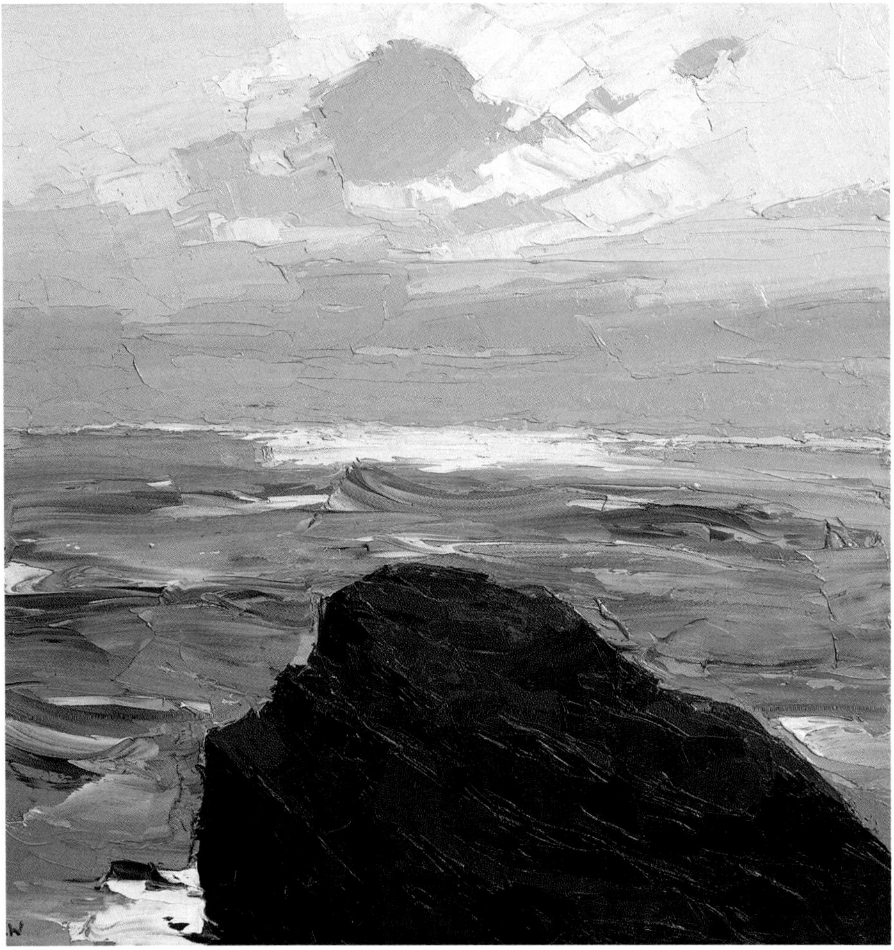

Kyffin Williams: Evening, South Stack
oil on canvas, 76 x 76 cm, 1992, coll: Prof. D.Z. Phillips

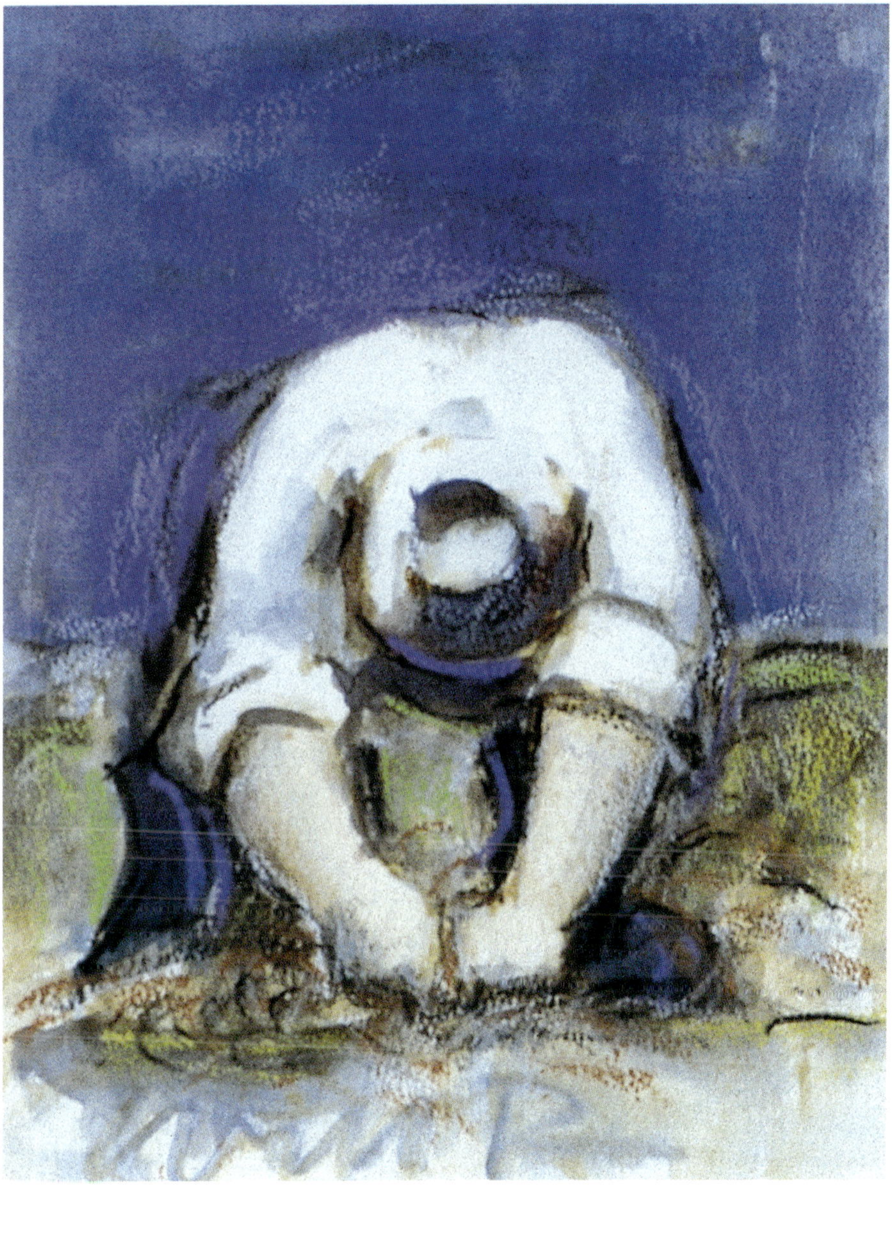

Will Roberts: Planting
Pastel and watercolour on paper, 35.5 x 28 cm, 1997, coll: Prof & Mrs Curtis

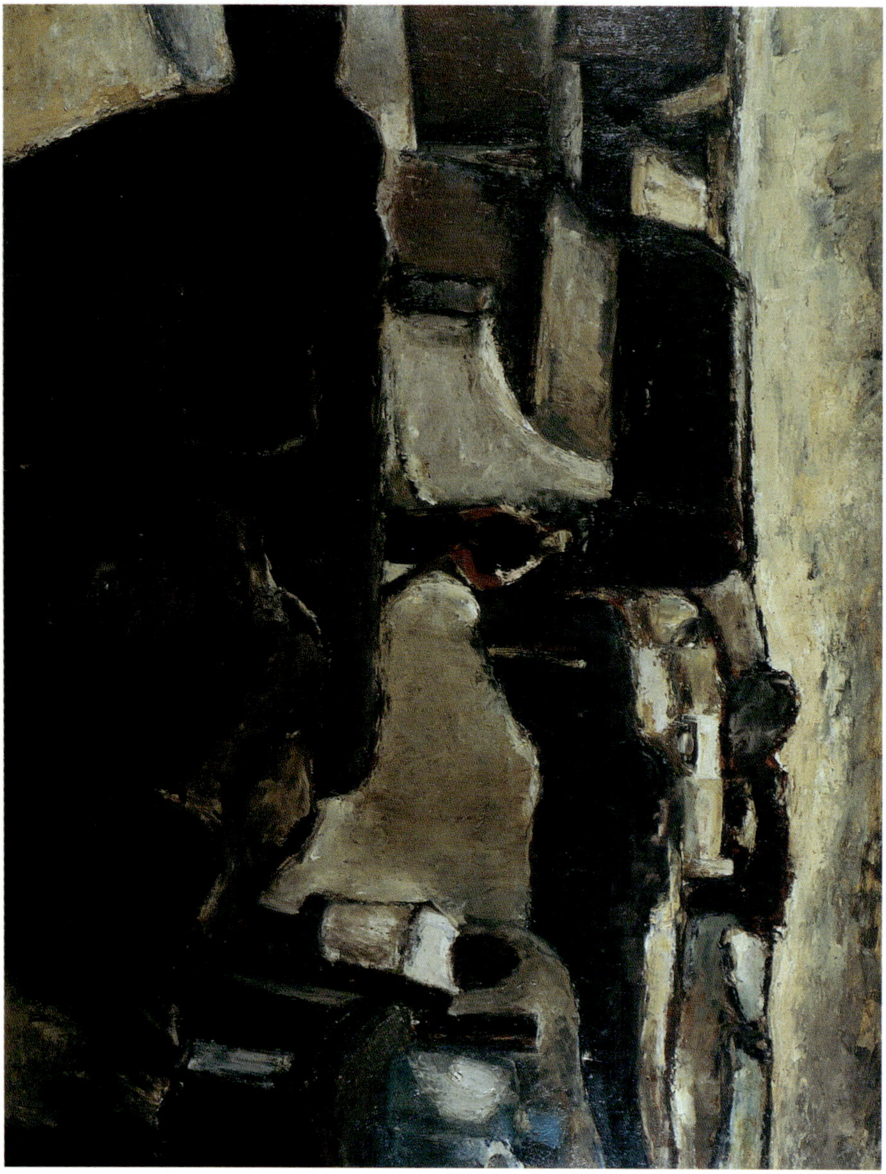

Will Roberts: Farm at Cimla
oil on hardboard, 91.6 x 122.1 cm, 1962, coll: National Museums & Galleries of Wales

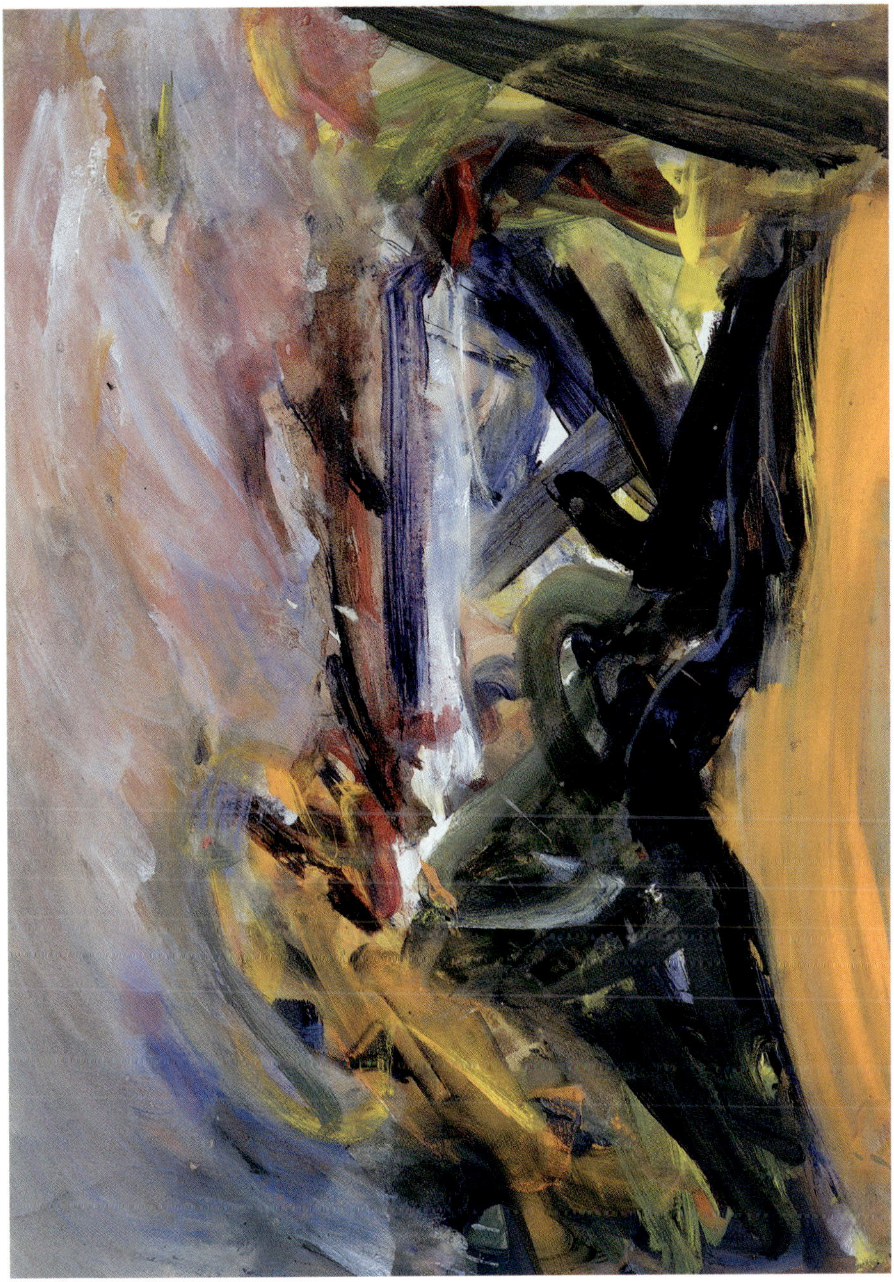

Peter Prendergast: Tal-y-Bont – Orange
watercolour on paper, 51 x 76 cm, 1996, coll: Agnews

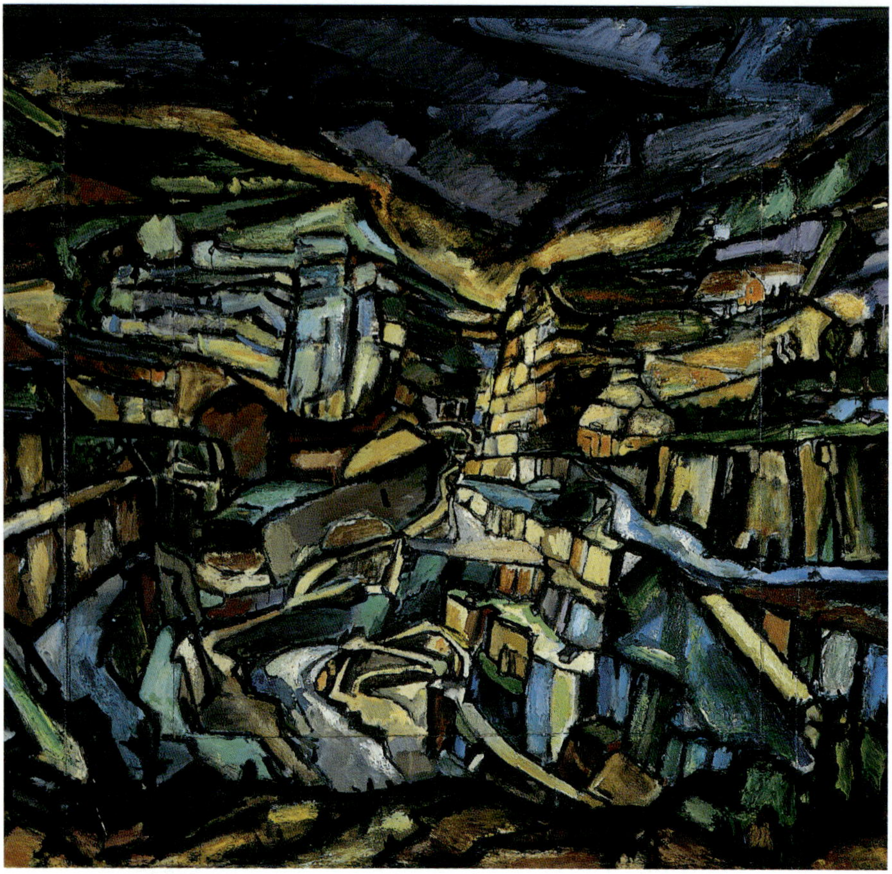

Peter Prendergast: Bethesda Quarry 1980-81
oil on hardboard, 166.4 x 192.6 cm, 1981, coll: Tate Gallery

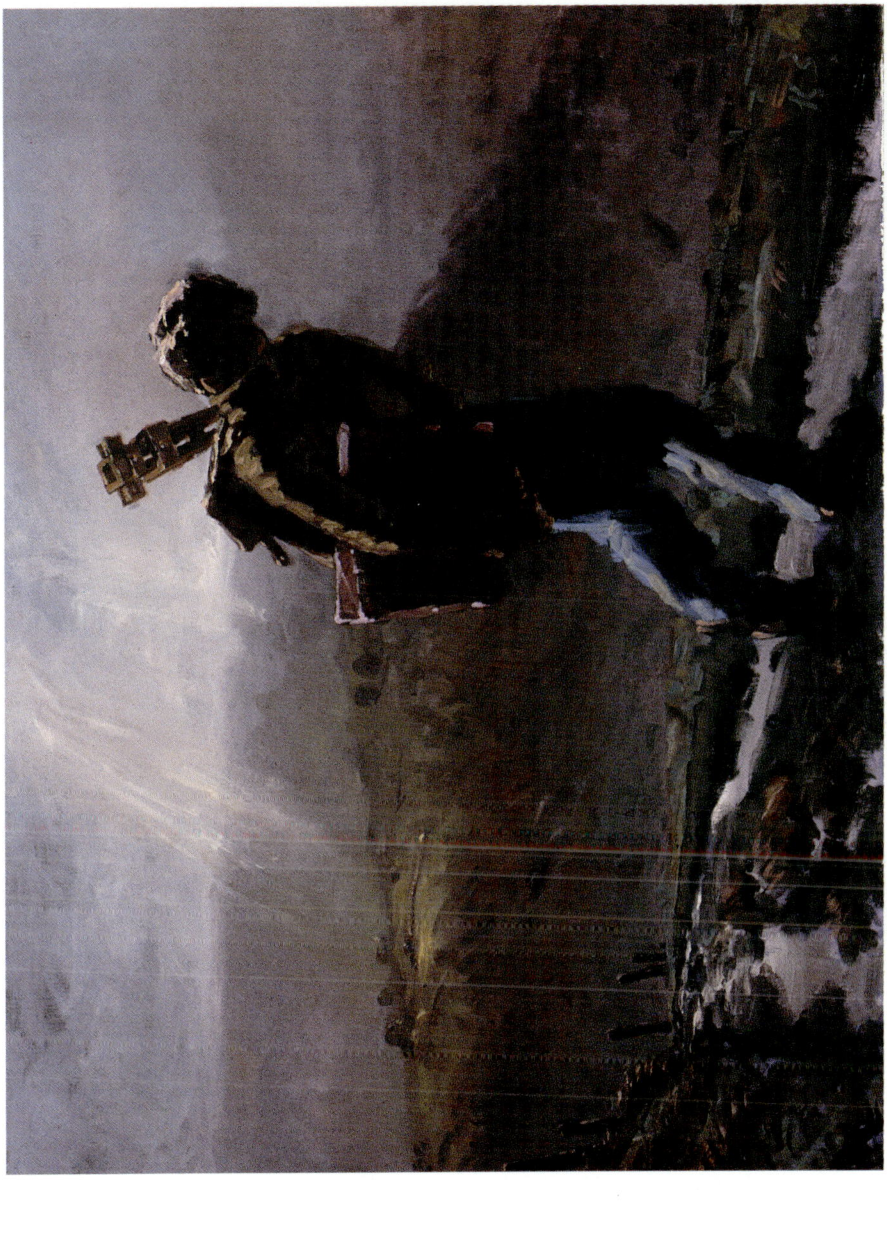

Kevin Sinnott: The Artist in Retreat
oil on canvas, 110 x 143 cm, 1995, coll: courtesy of Flowers East

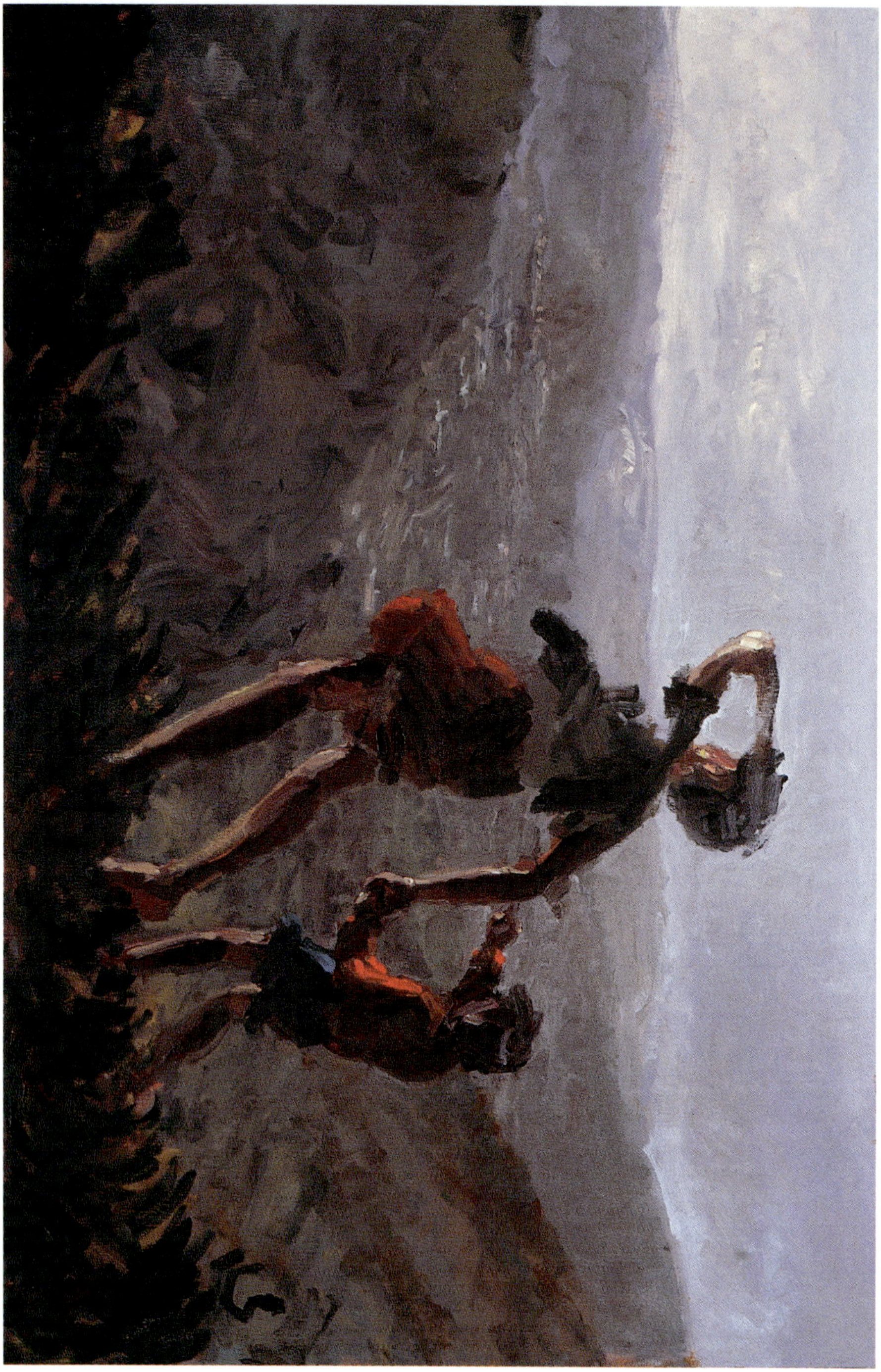

Kevin Sinnott: Into the Future
oil on canvas, 110 x 167 cm, 1995, coll: Robert Oliver

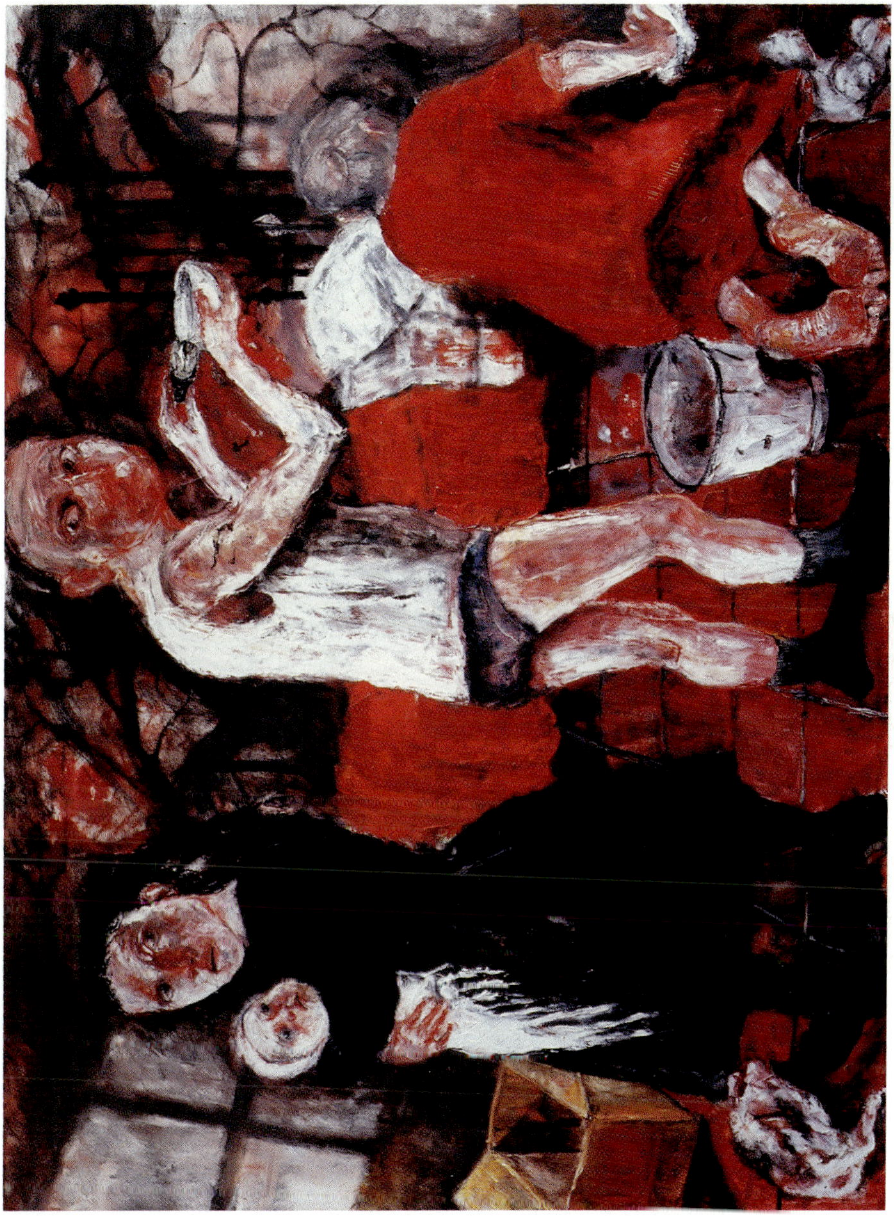

Shani Rhys James: Morning Shave
oil on canvas, 172.5 x 203 cm, 1993, coll: Contemporary Art Society of Wales on loan to Newport Museum & Art Gallery

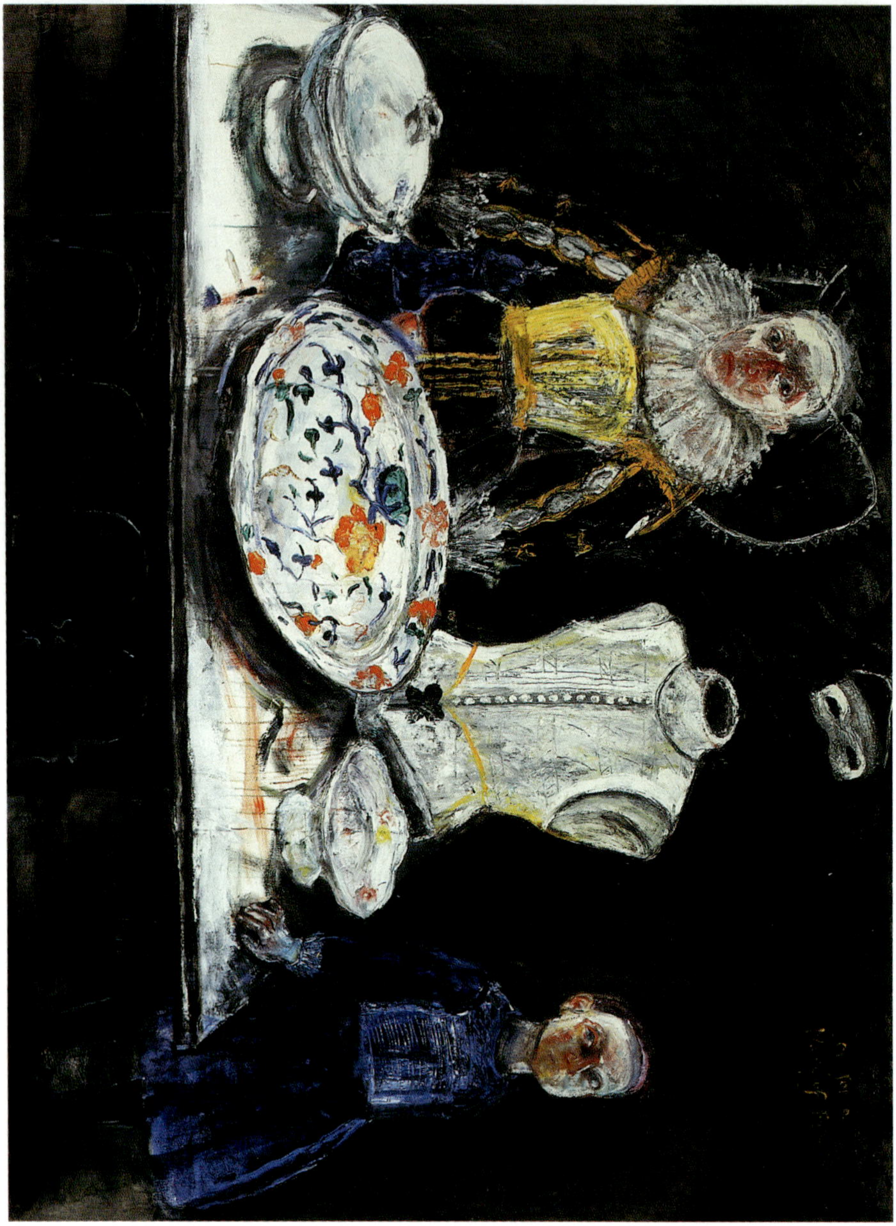

Shani Rhys James: Oh for a Muse of Fire
oil on canvas, 183 x 244 cm, 1994, private collection

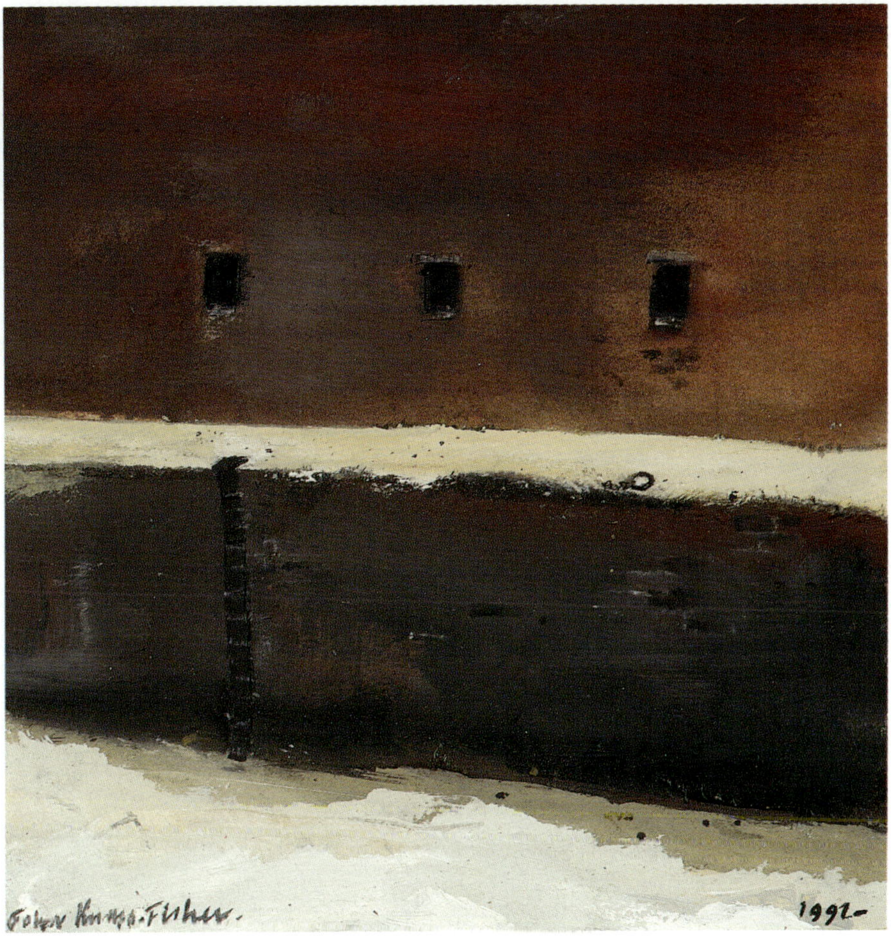

John Knapp-Fisher: Porthgain
oil on canvas, 21 x 21 cm, 1992, coll: the artist

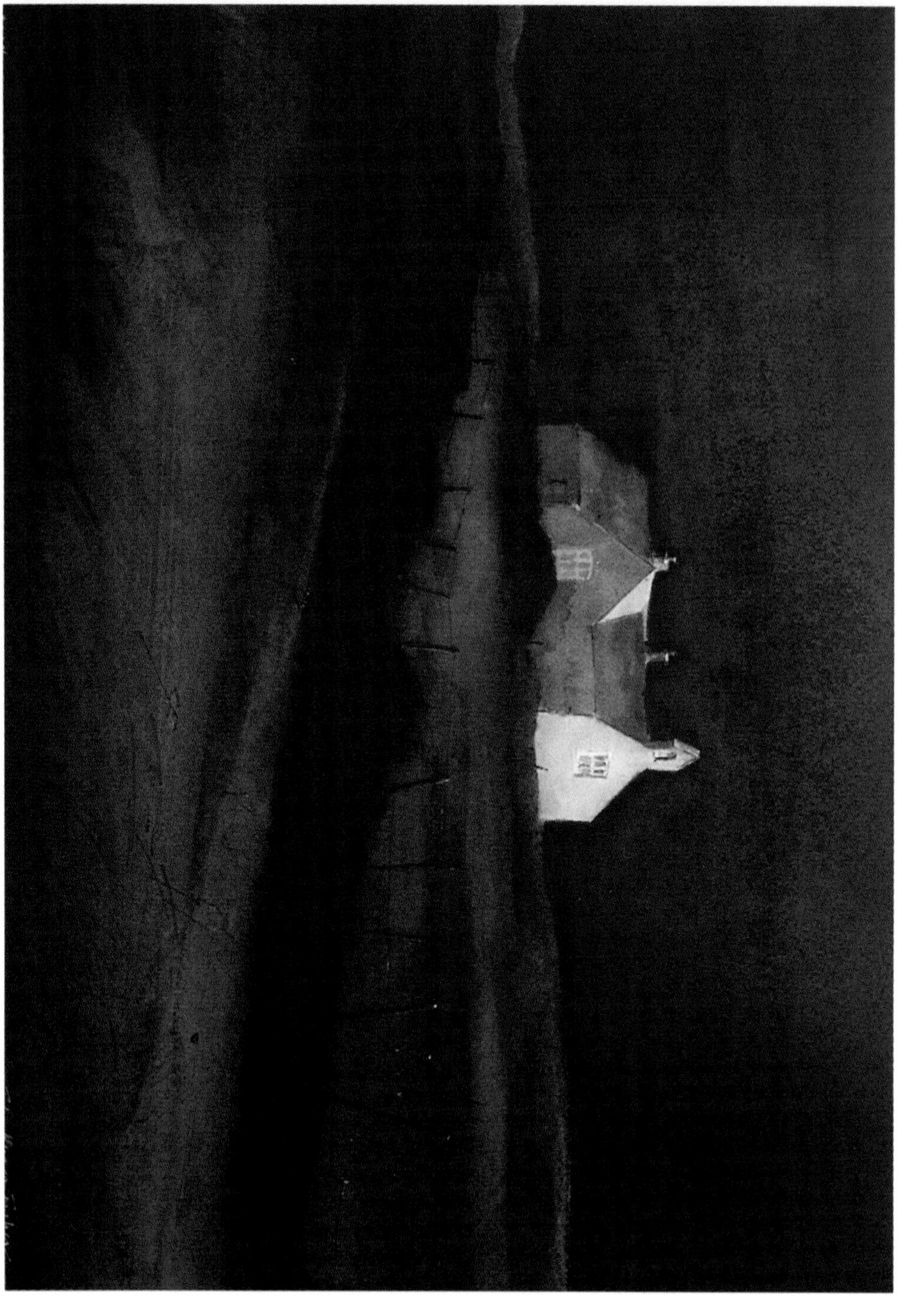

John Knapp-Fisher: Schoolhouse at Llanwrda
ink and watercolour, 30.5 x 51 cm, 1995, private collection

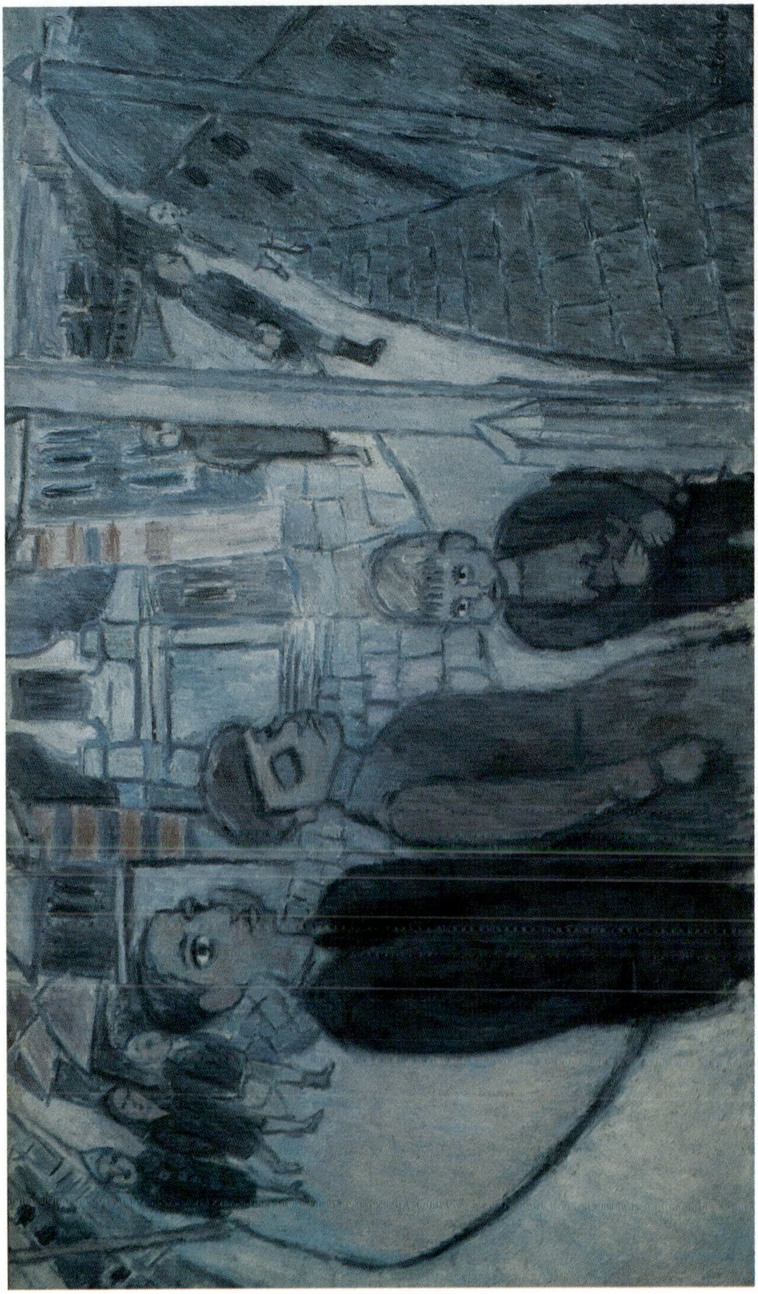

Ernest Zobole: The Family, 1961
oil on canvas, 91.5 x 152.5 cm, 1961, coll: the artist

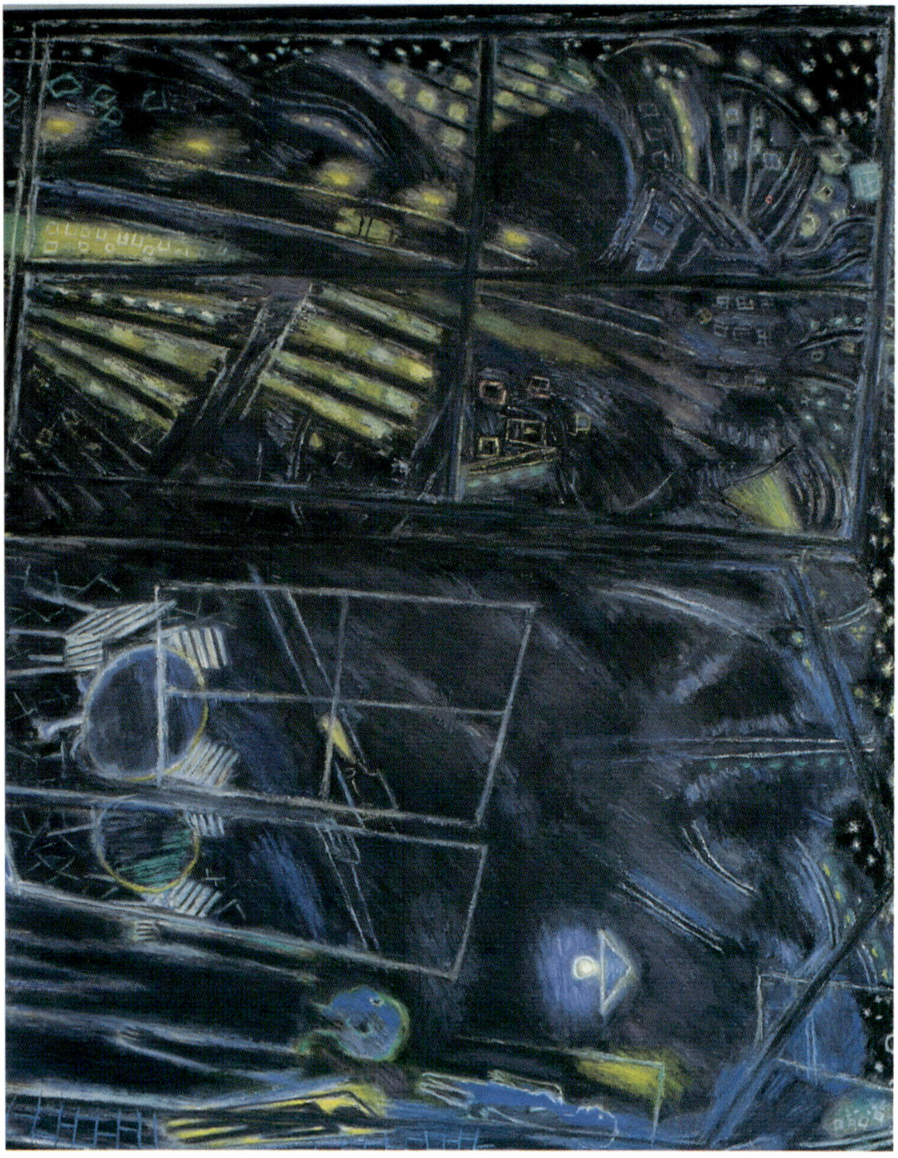

Ernest Zobole: From Inside No. 2
oil on canvas, 122 x 152.5 cm, 1991, coll: the artist

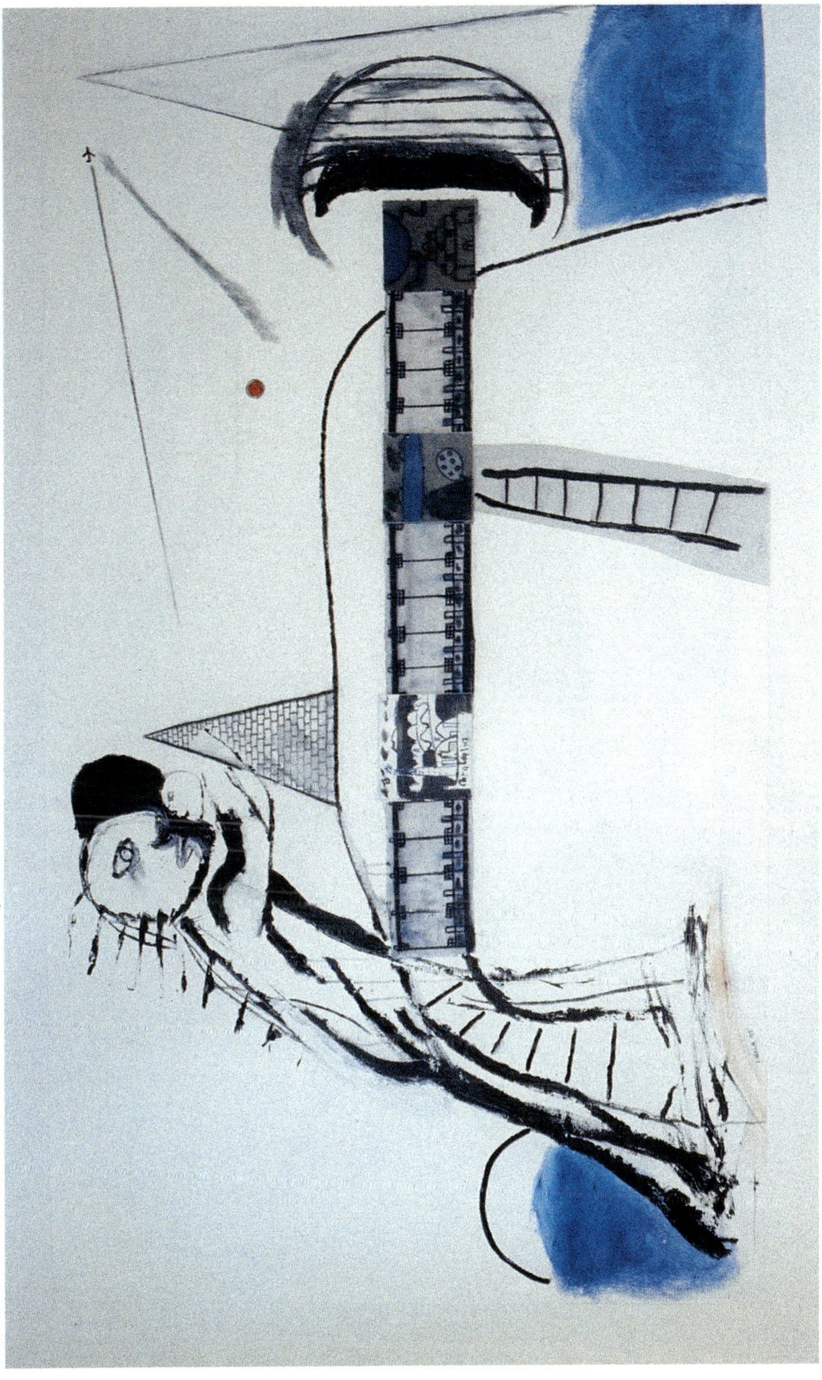

Iwan Bala: Haunted by Ancient Gods (True as History)
mixed media on board-mounted canvas, 122 x 213.5 cm, 1997, coll: the artist

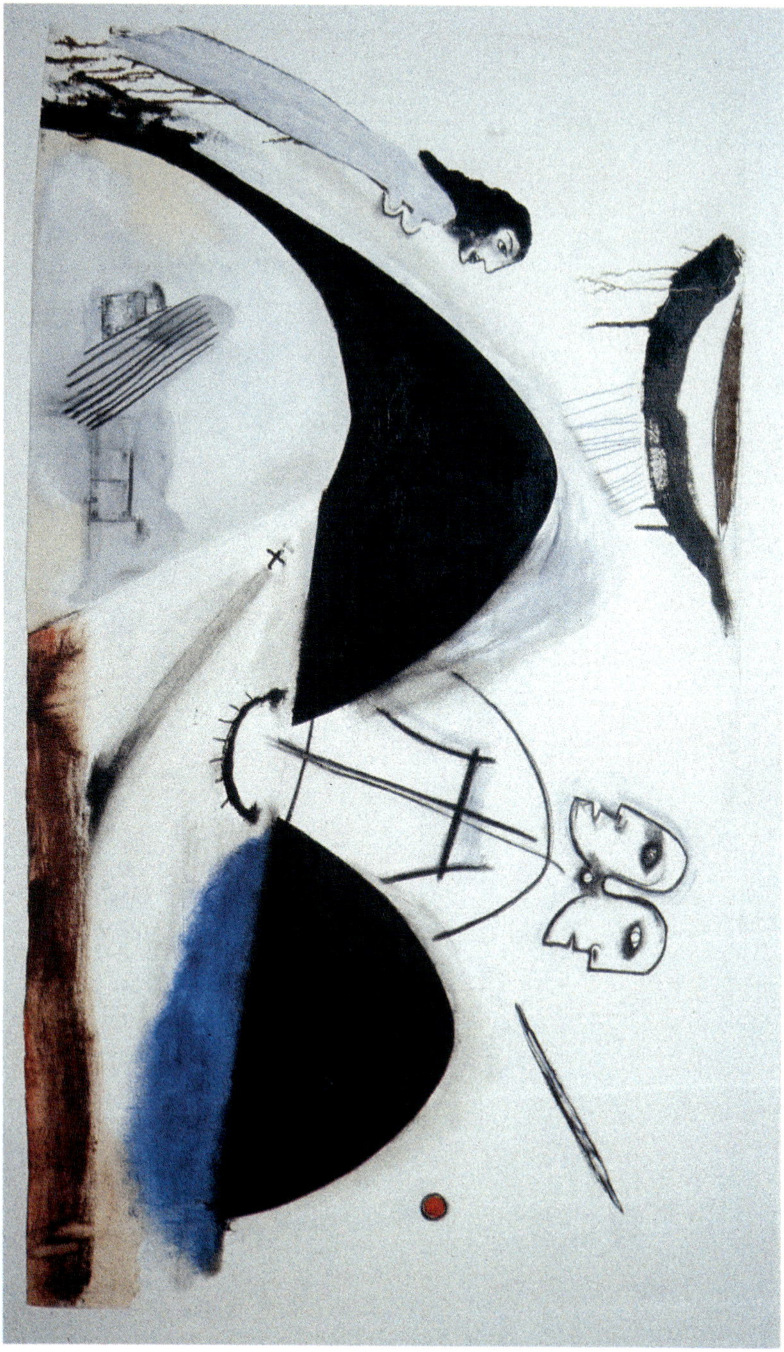

Iwan Bala: Haunted by Ancient Gods (Figure in a Landscape)
mixed media on board-mounted canvas, 122 x 213.5 cm, 1997, coll: the artist

to celebrate the world around them and us. And isn't there always something awesome about that? Not to do that is to miss the point of why we are here, isn't it? And you've come back to Wales to paint Wales, actual, remembered, whatever?

Well, at the moment I'm in a phase where there's still a lot of new experiences flooding in so they are getting painted. I've been back here for about three years, but I have been in this place for only a year and there are still experiences coming in. Most of this time I have been busy building this place, so I am still crazy with ideas about the woods and the trees.

Is all that practical work taking from the painting or adding something to it?

The practice of building has been a distraction. But ultimately it will be fed in.

But all that effort is being put in because this is going to be a great place to paint.

Inside this is going to be a great place to paint, and outside will be a great place to look. The principle work produced since I came here is the commission I undertook for the church painting at Dowlais. St. Illtyd's Catholic Church wanted to have a painting to commemorate their one hundred and fiftieth anniversary last year. I started to execute that commission when I began this place and I didn't know what to do. But isn't that interesting in the light of your question – about the practical work of building and it was from that work that I got the idea to do a rather secular subject for a Catholic church where the climax of the composition is a plasterer re-pointing the base of the cross.

But he is taking the pose of a rather arty plasterer – Tony Hancock in Paris – it is almost like a palette, that awk he's holding. All he needs is a beret and a striped top. How did the commission come about?

Well, the fact that I was a Catholic returning to Wales got around on the grapevine. St. Illtyd's did a lot of things, improving things. The priest there, Father Nick James is an extremely cultured, erudite, enlightened young priest from Bridgend and he has a small art collection himself. He had this extraordinary idea to commission a work of art.

But he didn't want another crucifix, so how specific was he?

He wasn't specific and I did a number of maquettes, small paintings, slightly more religious, but Father James and a group of parishioners chose this one.

There's something very medieval about this one – the craftsman at his work.

It's just an ordinary, humble parish church, not a cathedral asking Epstein to do something. They just had this inspired idea to commission a work of art.

You break all the safety regulations with your composition of the children on the scaffolding. Though it is an ascent into adulthood.

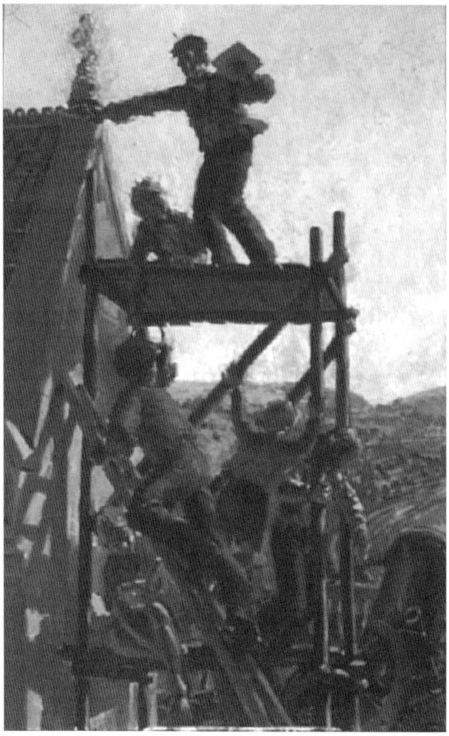

To My Children's Children
oil on canvas, 259 x 183 cm, 1996
coll: St Illtyd's Church, Dowlais

Yes, when the workmen came along to hang it, because it's a heavy painting – nine foot by six – they said, "Well, you wouldn't have anyone on the scaffolding". "But it's symbolic," I said, "it's a painting."

It's clear to see why they chose this one from the ideas you showed them – I don't mean because it was 'ordinary' people, but there is a distinction between an informed view and that of the public, isn't there?

I'll show you one of the others – you see this one is more religious as there's a risen Christ in the sky hidden behind this sort of tree of life. And again we've got this information I was using – cement mixers and other things from the ruins of the steel works in Merthyr. It was left for decades strewn across the landscape, great big sides of open furnaces. Then there is a hod carrier climbing the base of a tree, which is really bizarre, surreal. There are children reading and so on.

And the Christ is almost like a Guy Fawkes stuck up there in the tree.

It would have been more fragmented, the Christ, I think; it is a difficult thing to do now, to have that amount of faith to paint Christ's figure, so I used this pictorial device to break up the figure. There's something that R.S. Thomas writes about Christ being necessarily hidden; it's not that he's not there, but that in modern terms he should be worked for. It lets us off the hook in a way.

It is interesting that Will Roberts has done some religious work, some specif-

ically for a church and others not with a specific church in mind. I sense that you would hold back from a commission specifically for a Christ or Madonna.

Yes, but I couldn't say no, it would not be an impossibility, but it would have to be a great painting; it would have to be very successful in artistic terms.

Born a Catholic and always a Catholic. Does that in any way give power to the things that you've done?

I've never regarded myself as a religious painter. But when the commission from Dowlais came I said yes, and it was such a success, such a good thing to have done. It is so much better there than being in a museum. You have a living audience there. It's very interesting putting art in this liturgical role, giving it this job to do within a greater whole than itself. It's in the community, but it's also done for the greater glory of a God; therefore art isn't too overly self-important, so you don't have these enormous claims of relevance.

It doesn't need to claim a relevance because its very context is its relevance.

It doesn't have to articulate anything other than itself. It is relieved, firstly, of an art for art's sake complex, and in addition to that it is relieved from being given too high a status in our lives.

There is certainly a sense that art is the new rock and roll. Nations and cities are queueing up to build new cathedrals to art; that the art gallery embodies national prestige, cultural power, even political power. And people go with a sense of hushed awe to galleries.

Yes, it's become like that. Prague and Warsaw, cities in the godless state of twentieth century communism.

And you've subverted it by this church commission which has this wonderful warm light coming through it. It's full of hope; it's about learning and progress and climbing higher. And even if at the pinnacle of that you have a mere craftsman labourer, who may or may not be a painter, there is the association with the Christ of physical labour, the practicalities of a carpenter's family. The other thing that strikes me is that the traditional, the obvious commission would be the wooden structure that holds the dying, but ironically rising figure, the crucifixion; and what you've got here is another kind of scaffolding performing a different function.

Yes, it was very difficult to avoid a whole number of religious allusions in this; people were talking about Jacob's Ladder, all kinds of things. Apparently there's a *bas-relief* in Assissi of St Francis re-building his church where he misinterpreted a vision he had of God telling him to "re-build My church". And he took it literally.

A mistake he shared with some recent American evangelists – "Help us get closer to God, send in your dollars for another brick".

But this composition of St Francis is, apparently, close to what I've done.

How productive are you, because that Flowers East show had a number of large paintings from 1995. And at the same time you've been involved in altering and moving into this house.
Well, I did that commission in 1996, but not a lot of painting last year; though after I had finished putting in this floor, around May, I worked non-stop to complete those pictures for my show at Martin Tinney's.

Do you need that deadline for an exhibition?
Yes, it's not that popular myth of the artist waiting for inspiration, because he can't afford that. After a little while you can get idle and it's a question for me now of getting into a routine, starting as early as I can, working my way through, making myself do it. A deadline is another reason for doing it. Normally, if I'm up painting then it's up here first thing after breakfast. Throughout the day I have to walk away at times because if you are close to the canvas too long you are not actually seeing what's happening. You think that you are seeing, but if you go off to lunch, or off to Pontycymmer for the newspaper you come back and say, "What a mess I've made of that".

But you have here in what was the roof of the church an enormous studio space. You can stand right back from the canvas, some thirty-five feet from it, as if it were a big gallery. Do you work on more than one thing at a time, putting things away and coming back to re-consider them?
Yes, I do. It's the great advantage of having this studio space, being able to work on a lot of canvases at once. The way I work now, I paint to block things in quite quickly and frantically and then put things aside to come back later, so that the paint is quite dry.

It's the same with poems: you have to put them aside and come back, perhaps months later, because you can get too excited about them and think they're good.
That's exactly the same with being too close to paintings. You can think a thing is finished when it isn't, so you need then to put it away even if it's just to come back a month later to say, "yes, it is finished".

Like Eliot's and Pound's famous quote from Mallarmé, "A poem is never finished, only abandoned". But you do know when a painting is finished – like the Dowlais picture, don't you?
Yes, I hope I do know when a painting is finished. Otherwise it would be like hedging your bets by saying that it isn't. It's also too romantic. I think that I should be able to bring something to a conclusion. I'm not a part of that scene, whatever it is – Experimental Art. I mean, you rehearse in order to perform; but to call something 'experimental art' and then put it on show as finished is wrong.

How has your painting changed since returning to Wales?
Well, I was working for an exhibition of what I called my 'beach' pictures when we moved so I continued working on them for six months

after coming here, even though when I began them in London they did evoke my childhood memories of beaches in Mid Glamorgan. So in a strange way there had been an artistic portent of the move. That series was successfully exhibited in Flowers as 'Shorelines'. After that the influences began, the weather, the landscape, the light. I became quite excited about placing my figures in a landscape, unlike, I felt, what much of Western art had done. In Turner and Constable figures are often a quite embarrassing supplement, often awkwardly positioned and not necessary for the composition. I started to feel that relationship between figure and landscape as an enhancement of my work and that was a direct result of my returning to Wales.

Can we talk about your painting 'Running Away with the Hairdresser' which the National Museum of Wales has just bought? There's a period feel to it; painted in 1995, but it looks like the Sixties at the moment when those kids realised that youth had legs, and could get away to a louder, brighter life, away from the cosiness but claustrophobia of the community and its terraced houses in the penned-in valleys.

That's more what the previous painting 'Running Away' was about. I wanted to make the next one more complex in order to make it a bigger painting and inadvertently I changed its meaning altogether. Because it's not running away from all that you described, but it's running away with the hairdresser, like leaving your wife for somebody else. That's what's implied in the title and in the fecklessness in the type of figure she is. He's not running away from her to go to university, that's for sure. Whereas in the earlier 'Running Away' that could be the case.

In the 'Hairdresser' painting it's also the sense that you are taking from the community a useful person and in some way despoiling that community. What is intriguing is the ambiguity: they aren't holding hands – and is she reaching forward, or is he reaching back? There's already a sense that he will be moving away from her: it's a bad choice. You are a narrative painter aren't you?

I know that. It's because I use my imagination. I don't simply portray things, use a nude model, and paint a house or a landscape or paint somebody in that landscape. They are doing something, and because I am painting something out of nothing there's a relationship figure to figure, and some meaning. Why are they moving away from each other. Why are they embracing? Why is someone flying a kite in a landscape? It's a romantic thing to do. It's like a modern Icarus.

And it's also the colloquialism, 'Oh, you're flying a kite'. So you're really interested in language too, like a poet.

Well, look at this one, 'Into the Future' [see colour plate]. This is two figures in a landscape – a mother and child. Now once you've got two figures actually doing something there will automatically be some meaning; and you can't get away from more meanings leeching on, crowding in.

They are like actors in a play. But halfway through the painting you aren't sure precisely how they will act?
No, I just let things happen. Then towards the end I may manipulate it, tease it a bit further.

And then the title comes in at the end.
That's when the poetry comes in. When a title has a life of its own, quite often it enhances the painting.

Yes, as in this new painting of your father-in-law working on a window in this house. The title is 'The Restorer'; but if you were to call it 'The Arch' or 'Through the Arch', or 'My Father-in-Law' then the painting would be charged with another meaning. It's so obvious, because you are living in a church, that there is something religious, sacramental about it. The awk is almost like an open book, a physical act of giving the sermon. How do you feel about living here?
I did wonder until quite recently whether it would be a good place for me. But the size is so good. And it's not so strange to live in a house with arched windows, the Victorians had those mock gothic places.

And as it was a Church in Wales building it wasn't one of those nonconformist fire and brimstone places. Was the altar where your lounge is going to be?
No, the altar was where we were eating.

Well, that has huge implications – the breaking of bread, and the wine we had! A lot of people would be spooked by that, not to mention the impracticality of the heating bills for this place. How does the family feel? Or is this simply Dad's indulgence as an artist?
Oh yes, living is a distraction for me. The doubts I had were whether it would function as a home. But we had a fantastic Christmas here, so it's proved itself.

Do you, like many other painters and writers, feel the need to get away from the house in order to work – a summer-house or shed? Because here you are committed to living below your work.
The last but one house in London was a big house and I started to work at home there. It's useful to be able to return to a work, after doing a little drawing at breakfast or something. Most of the time for me it's been an advantage. I like to leave a picture for a while, but having to drive, say, six miles home, you might be distracted and not return for days and then it's dry and it will be difficult to push it further.

But there will be family distractions.
But Sue is very supportive and I just have to put up with the kids.

You keep sketches and though some of them are quite small you do find them useful, don't you?
Yes, I use sketch books though quite often I will be dealing with a study on canvas or board without preparation. Though, since I work from my

imagination, this isn't an activity I have to do. It's a kind of note-taking, so that when I'm painting and I need to put something in an empty space I will look through, because the landscape plays a supporting role for the figure. So a sketch of my father-in-law was used in the Dowlais painting.

Can we talk about your Turkish Bath paintings, your first exhibition at Flowers East?

Yes, I still have some here.

They are so large, aren't they? A tumble of nude women.

The show was a flop but they do sell now.

Why Turkish Baths?

Well, they're based on Ingres's famous painting in the Louvre. I explain it in the notes to my catalogue for the exhibition which contains extracts from my journal at that time. This one called 'The Poet' is after Millais and his young Chatterton painting, though the title was suggested by someone who saw my painting and was reminded of Millais.

The nude is a tricky area, isn't it, in a Feminist or post-Feminist world? Are they odalisques in a way? They are available, voluptuous ladies.

But as an artist I am interested in the composition. And not to have painted in that way because of some mind police, some PC pressure, would have been wrong. It is about composing not looking at women. This one with Cézanne in it is playing with that humourously: is he looking at Mont Sante-Victoire in the background, or at the women? It is the artist and his motif, as opposed to his motive.

There is a terrific fleshy energy to them. We were talking about Freud earlier and his big nudes; they don't move you. They certainly make you feel uneasy, as if you ought not not be seeing this person.

There's no imagination in the artistry of the Freud work. They are simply voyeuristic, I think, in a redundant, indolent way. Though the Turkish Bath show was not a big success, critically or financially, my wife Susan, who is my shrewdest critic, thinks it the best of my exhibitions. It was a very intense period for me. My palette changed at this time to a cold light source, the cool end of the spectrum for the lit, bright and primary colours, whereas the shaded areas became warmer. There were lots of greens and blues rather than browns and reds. I painted like that for nearly two years. Now I may incorporate both approaches in one painting.

Would you do portraits?

I have done one notably, a family of five done in the summer of 1990. That was Terry Ellis of the Chrysalis record company. But it was such a large commission I had to do it. He had seen my work in New York and was adamant that I should do it. It was a big painting. I would do portrait commissions if it were more than a job, I would need to have a feeling for the subject. Handling someone's likeness in a painting tends to inhibit me. I would rather paint figures from my imagination. In many ways my work ends up looking quite naturalistic, but painting from life would, strangely, bring a woodenness to them.

You are a fiction writer really; in the way that a fictional character like a painted character is an amalgam of many others. Like coming to a new author, I've enjoyed meeting you and seeing your work.

Thank you. It's been interesting trawling back through my life like this. I haven't done it before. Did I say that I was the last of sixteen children? My oldest sister was born in 1925, that was another age. My first memories were of coming back to an empty house when everyone was out working, or had left. With crowded weekends and Christmases. I mean, what was it that made me succeed; did the family give me the energy to pick myself up? Now I'm back here I am asking these questions.

And what do you think the future holds for you as a painter?

Well, I work from one painting to the next and I'm always excited when I've finished a painting because it seems to suggest to me new ways of moving on. But whenever I look back on six months' work it always seems to be so similar. The euphoria I feel after each painting is just part of the process; I'm so relieved to have come to some sort of resolution, as if each one were the definitive work. But I always feel that I'm moving on to new things, though the movement is a fraction of an inch each time now.

SHANI RHYS JAMES

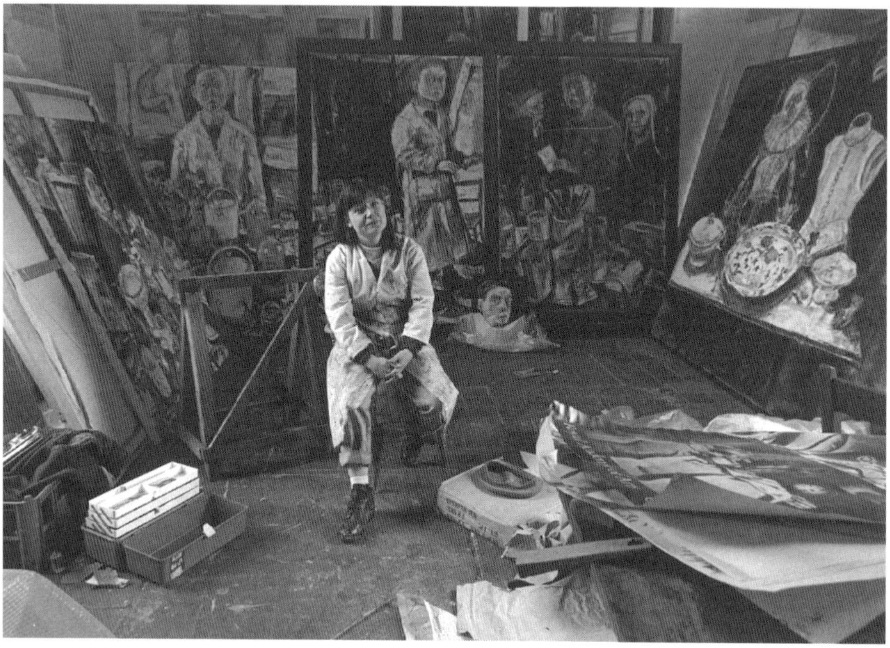

I spent a day talking to Shani Rhys James in November 1994 in the farmhouse where she, her husband Stephen and two sons live. It is reached by a lane off the main road to the west of Welshpool, a few miles from the town. Remote and full of character, the farm has a large outbuilding in which Shani and Stephen have studios. Shani's studio is as wonderfully chaotic as her paintings represent, with the bowls and other pottery, discarded gloves, mirror and masses of paints which provide the sets for her compelling works.

Your first father was a Welshman, but you were born in Australia; Shani, do you in any sense feel Australian?
I do feel Australian in so far as that sun, those open spaces, that bush, has had an effect on me. I was brought up in a miner's house from the age of four. That was not because we were poor, it was a romantic conception of my parents to live outside Melbourne in that way, with the dunny out the back and kerosene lamps; and my second father pulled down all the walls and made it an open space house.

So that experience gave me contact with the bush. And I did feel that excitement when I went back again. D.H. Lawrence talks about this feeling of going out into the bush in *Kangaroo* and there is a peculiar feeling, an excitement, it's almost that you feel the spirit of the thing. You don't get it in England, and that's why I can't do landscape in England, because it's been tamed, a pretty landscape, very beautiful. But there you get such extraordinary white, big trees and terrifying creatures. When you lift the toilet seat you have to be careful out in the country that there wouldn't be a redback spider under the seat. We had snakes often, and they would kill the cats. Wales has a certain wildness, one senses the spirit of the place; it's also true of Scotland where I have painted landscape.

The Australian landscape is still in your head, but it doesn't make its way on to the canvas very often, does it? The Blood Ties *show had a painting of you and your dad on the telephone and the background there is Australia, isn't it? But in 'Departure' I'm not clear whether that is an Australian landscape. Perhaps, it's not something that you want to go back to, in your paintings anyway.*
It's a memory really. My use of colour comes from that, because I do use striking colour, and the influences. My early years were living in a place where there were a lot of artists. My mother knew Sidney Nolan and Boyd, Charles Blackman and the Percivals. There were a lot of artists around – it's like Wales in a way. It's an enormous country, of course, but you all live in one spot, stuck in places that were no more than villages. There is suburbia, but there's not this sense of being able to live where you choose, because of the vast bush. I mixed with a lot of these artists. I think that spontaneity and that expressionism was instilled in me: the feeling of responding intuitively.

With that sort of background there was nothing odd in your becoming an actress or an artist. Unlike a working class kid who might be regarded as soft.
No, but the school where we lived was a country school and some kids were dismissive and narrow, because I was a bit of an outsider sometimes. I looked like a beatnik, I wasn't wearing pretty dresses.

Your parents started a theatre, so they created their own artistic context?
They converted a bakehouse into a theatre. It was an intimate theatre, whereas everywhere else was doing drawing-room comedies, so there was that sense of idealistic dream. It's interesting that people like Branagh and Redgrave are doing it now, being entrepreneurs, if you like. But my father had his dream then. He went to art school, then drama school. He was very good at bringing up other people. My mother had a talent which he brought out, and his son has become quite a well-known Australian painter, John Money. He was a brilliant teacher, he supported his own theatre by working in the day as an art teacher; my mother was an art teacher too. It meant that there was the concept of thinking of a whole production like *The Doll's House*: he would be painting the backdrops, directing it, playing Dr Rank, making papier maché furniture; my mother making the costumes and playing Nora. I was given the idea of being creative in every sphere of the theatre. Of course, that all changed when we left Australia without him. And that started a whole new chapter of our life.

Often I hated it, there was lot of hanging about; but there was something good about just sitting there watching my parents rehearse, watching the words come out, watching relationships between people on the stage and the pathos and the bathos.

Even something very adult and heavy which you couldn't understand at the time? This was the period when you were between four and nine.
I think children are underestimated, because I did know what was happening. I was watching my mother play Nora when I was two, and they did children's theatre as well. I do remember thinking very clearly from the age of two or three about visual things. Like remembering how a drawing was conceived when I was doing it. I think that the essence of a person is there, you are formed, but it may take a lifetime to bring it out.

Was this the proscenium arch stage? Because, in a way, looking at your parents in that square of lit theatre space is almost like a canvas. Or is that being too clever in hindsight?
I suppose it was. But I always felt there it wasn't for me to be on that stage. I always felt intimidated – that they were like gods, if you like, that it was their thing, with me as the onlooker. I was never incorporated into productions; although other people would see potential in me and take me off for photographs in magazines or this little film that I did.

Did you think that was intrusive, or did you enjoy that attention?
Oh, I was quite a good actress. I got very involved with it. And in the school things that I did later on. In London years later I had to re-live this scene of saying goodbye to your father as a drama idea. Of course, I had to say goodbye to all my family when we left Australia – my grandmother, my uncles and cousins. What you don't realise is that they literally could have all died, because that's what happens; it's that cutting off of any connection with those people. The extraordinary thing is that when you go through something like that you feel absolutely numb, dead inside. And when I came over the England I didn't express, I didn't cry, not a glimmer of emotion.

The sea journey must have taken some time in those days, and that must have been a very odd limbo.
It was very strange. My mother had a friend, and she talked incessantly to my mother, so I didn't even have my mother to myself. I didn't mix really with anyone; I had this crazy doll which I hated. I'd left everything. This whole thing was brought out when I did this production at school where I just literally lived the part and that was my first feeling of theatre, being taken over by a sensation, a method, a feeling which all-consumes you. I wish my mother had been there to see that.

So the drama was an insight, a way of dealing with things. And the painting is a way of dealing with things.
A cathartic thing, yes. It's usually best when it is to do with something which is very near the bone. But, of course, you get removed a bit because there it does change in the execution and it becomes what it wants to become. And you yourself don't know what was important about the experience: you think you know what's affected you, but when you do it there are other elements which are important to you which you didn't know about. Painting is a sense of discovery. It's just that animals need to express themselves.

But isn't that what distinguishes us from animals?
Some birds do. Lyre birds do.

But human beings have always wanted to leave a mark, whether it's the Lascaux Caves or a prisoner scratching on a cell wall. And in western Europe painting has developed into the most sophisticated way of leaving a mark.
But who needs a painting? You can't justify it; it's not a life or death thing.

Well, I do. I need images around me, and as I can't draw a thing, I have to acquire the products of other people's talent. A lot of people obviously make do with the moving pictures of television. Would you agree that it's so basic to human beings that, for example, if there were no shows or galleries taking your work, you would still work?
It's a discipline, you have a choice. If I had three or four lives I would

like to live one life painting, in another life I'd like to be an actress, in another life I'd be a writer, in another a film-maker. Having chosen painting, that's a discipline which I stick with for my life; like a journey I've decided on. But it's like when you write a poem; the poem has a different way of expressing the nuances which you couldn't possibly have in a painting. You can interpret a painting, but language is more specific. It has a weight about it which can express something very immediate. Sometimes in the middle of paintings I will write a burst of poems or start writing about my childhood, or start writing a comedy. I wrote about doing out houses when the children were little – almost like an Adrian Mole diary, or a country living.

Have you ever thought about doing anything with these writings?
I'm not good enough as a writer; the discipline would have to be far more thorough before I would show it to anyone. Poetry moves me and music moves me and I would say that there is a connection between poetry and my work. Gerard Manley Hopkins's poems – "Despair, despair, despair!" – have an extraordinary effect and the Bible and *Coriolanus*.

Are there occasions when the painting comes directly from words? Rather than the painting being completed and then a title being put on to it?
When I write poetry I am a visual poet, and when I read poems I get a strong visual sense. Some of the best ones seem to come into my head complete. You get a sense of feeling coming through the poetry which you can't define; I want to get that poetic strength into my paintings.

Yes, the sciences are about reducing things to an equals sign, while the arts cross out that sign and trace arrows of connection between things apparently unconnected.

Let's pick up your story from the move to London. How difficult was it?
Well, my mother was a talented actress and she learned on the boat coming over that she had won Best Actress Award in Australia. Leaving was a bad career move. But she did get work in England, in London and at the Liverpool Playhouse and acted with Philip Madoc and was Berkoff's mother in *Metamorphosis*. Then at the point when she was breaking through she decided that painting was what she wanted to do. I mean, it's very difficult as a woman, because at a certain age there's no interesting parts. Look at *Hamlet* – who would want to play Ophelia? Women are always trailing after the heroes. The real human being in the play is the man. You get the intimacy of Hamlet's mind.

In the theatre of your paintings you've reversed that, haven't you? They work to foreground the woman. There are very few men in your paintings.
Well, I'm a woman, that's the first thing, and I can only paint from my feelings. I do think that men are very different animals, because women are much more liable to express their emotions. I do think that they are

more in touch with their feelings. Throughout history they have been painted as odalisques and as oddities, voluptuous things to gratify man, and not the human element of them. The fact that they are feeling, thinking, responsible, thoughtful beings is not dealt with, because it is often men painting women.

So the woman is maker when you paint, and the woman as maker is your subject?

Being a woman is relevant, but Rembrandt painted himself. I just see myself as a person, I'm not obsessed with the fact that I'm a woman.

And quite often you portray yourself in a non-gender overall. Not exactly androgynous.

No, not androgynous. You could say that Charles II in a portrait is androgynous. It's not really important: I think it's just a person painting their strong feelings. I do come from a line of very strong women. My mother has given me a role model of needing to fulfil yourself. Leaving Australia was very brave of her as well as a bit silly.

But men are important in your life – you live with three of them – your husband and two sons.

Yes, well, I love them dearly and feel protective towards them.

They're not in the paintings are they? Though in 'Morning Shave' you have Stephen, your husband, don't you?

No, that's my father.

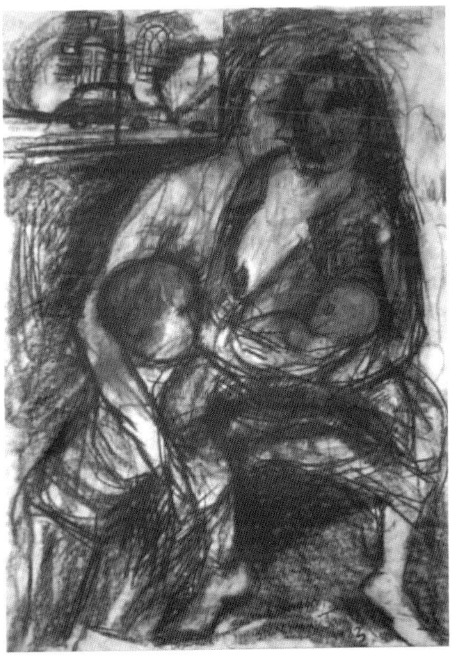

Departure from East London
charcoal on paper, 30 x 22 inches
1983, coll: Prof. & Mrs Curtis

But Stephen and your two sons are in that drawing which I have –

'Departure from East London'.

Yes, I did many drawings of them as babies, changing nappies, fighting each other and so on. But I had an exhibition in London and they didn't like seeing themselves on the wall. And I thought – wait a minute, I'm being voyeuristic here, I'm painting them, I'm not painting me. So all these self-confrontational paintings began. Me as a child as opposed to them as children. I was actually painting about myself through them. It's been a revelation having boys. There's an openness, an innocence and a great energy and excitement about guns and fighting and physicality. You realise that this goes right back to our beginnings. I feel they should get it out of their system when they're young. The guilt of Christianity has caused a lot of problems.

Have you got a religion? You said when we spoke earlier that you and your husband had looked at Buddhism.

No, I haven't got a religion. I was open to Buddhism when I was a student. I have had visions in Buddhism and mystical experiences without drugs or any of that paraphernalia. It was interesting in the squat where I was living as a poor student; in London everybody was Buddhist or a potter – it was a very constructive environment. We had a housing association and I lived with eighteen incredible, energising people – one was Henry Pim, a famous potter now, and Cullen the painter. At that time it was a politic thing to squat, a stance – this was 1973-76.

In the Disclosure(s) *catalogue you are reported as saying that you felt a little beleaguered at art college, everything around you seemed trendy and abstract.*

But I went deliberately to St Martin's, which was an abstract school, as a figurative painter. So I was throwing myself to the wolves. Because I did not want to end up as a stereotypical English figurative painter. And that's why a lot of people think I'm quite primitive in many ways. They say, "That's not finished," because the quality I want in my painting is the element of abstraction, the energy of colour, the chance element coming in. I want everything. But I did not want to end up as a Sladey girl or a Camberwell figurative painter – stultifying! The figurative art schools are the most stultifying, the kiss of death. The idea in England is that as a figurative painter you have to be Coldstream, measuring one thing after another, and I've been through all that.

You sound as if you thought hard about it and knew more than most kids applying for college.

Well, I had a year off and worked hard on my foundation course at Loughborough. I was determined not to end up in the provinces. I had three enormous portfolios of work that year. I put on three stone in weight so that no tutors would be attracted to me, because that's what happened in art school. I had problems with such tutors being attracted. They chose you for your looks. They say that fat is a feminist issue!

I chose St Martin's because it seemed the most exciting and vital place. The painting school was at its peak. We had tutors like Jenny Durrant, Ken Kiff, Gillian Ayres – there were wonderful painters who were abstract, and abstraction seemed like the most wonderful childlike exuberance which they seemed to enjoy, also Patrick Heron and John Hoyland, and I was not going to be denied that, the physicality, the enjoyment of paint. I wanted that feeling that you could create a mess, I wanted to get into the paint, up to my elbows in paint. I wanted to express myself through paint. I didn't want to do a tired old dead copy of realism. I felt a vocation to painting since I was eight. I made a pact with God, if you like, that I would dedicate myself to paint.

When I went to art school I thought that they would all be sincere. But many were there for a career and were interested in Cork Street and success. I thought that they were idealists, like van Gogh, but a lot of them were very smart cookies, career movers.

Of course that was the seventies and the international art market – art was popular, art was Pop, America. There was the whole Pollock thing. And I found out at art school was that it was so much decoration. And what I wanted was Soutine, the quality of the best painters. If you look at a Rembrandt, it's actually about paint; it's not about the illustration of a woman in a room. It's about physicality, lifting up that white chemise. I wanted the living paint, and this is my quest. I'm getting there: sometimes paintings work, sometimes not.

Because of the hours you spend in that studio across the courtyard from here, you must get a great physical pleasure from painting as well as a great visual and emotional charge. And that comes through in the paintings of your studio – it's a hell of a messy place isn't it?

Well, it's created, nurtured in a way into that mess. I clear it all and in two weeks it comes up again – the gloves litter the floor – the gloves are because of the danger.

Would you describe yourself as 'painterly'? Do you want the viewer to be aware of brushstrokes?

It's like language, like words being an enigma. You've got the paint which is becoming the object. It's almost like creating a Golem out of nothing, so it can't but be painterly, it's about paint.

But I see the paint as the vocabulary; though the language of the painter, just as in the way written language works, is also to do with custom and practice and the context – the Bible and Shakespeare – determines meaning. Whether we know that or not we are using words from that context, with all those associations. And when you paint you must be aware that others have painted and that there is a history there.

Absolutely.

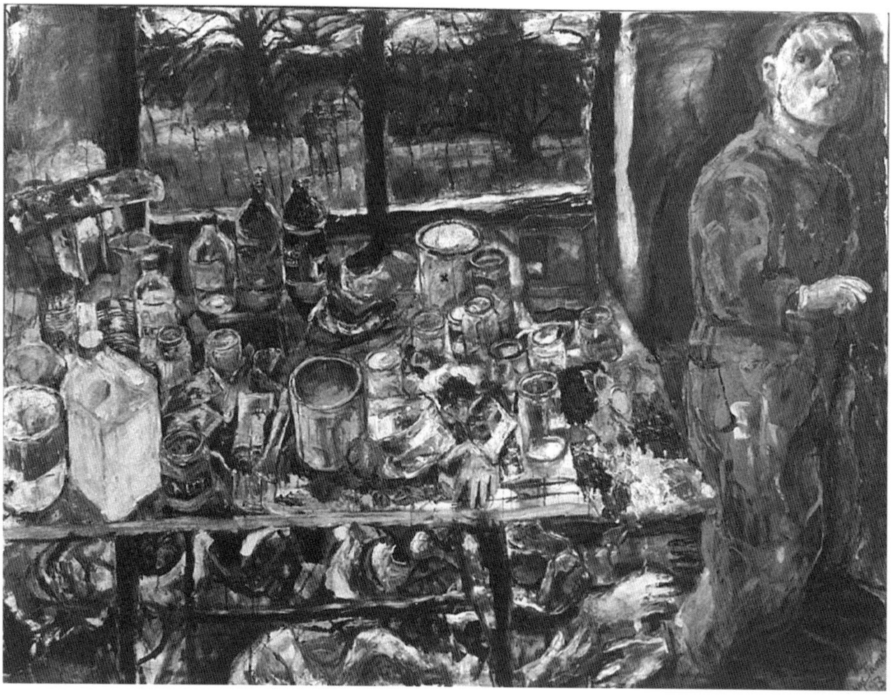

Studio oil on canvas, 183 x 213.5 cm, 1993, coll: Newport Museum & Art Gallery

Of course, Oriel Mostyn must have worked from that premise in commissioning yourself and six other artists to work on the Disclosure(s) *exhibition; by encouraging you to go in the museum and react to the tradition. Why did you choose the Sir Thomas and Lady Mansel painting and the Katherine of Berain? Was it the woman which drew you to those, the constraint of their costumes and that potential for metaphor?*

The Katherine portrait was done a hundred years later than the British painting, but, because it was Netherlandish, it was much more sophisticated. I was interested at first by the simple and decorative qualities of the Mansel double portrait, because of the simplicity of the black background, something which I've started to introduce in my work as a means of simplifying. Paintings which had been so cluttered in the studio. I've had very cluttered paintings and very undecorative paintings, apart from the Alice paintings, of course, and I was attracted to the stylisation of the two figures. And the writing on the side that you get in the Katherine of Berain, which immediately flattens and mixes the two dimensions. But I think it was also the stage element: you get two figures on the stage and the dramatic use of black and white which I like – the waistcoat which he's wearing, the little white buttons, the gold brocade.

In the course of working from these images in the National Museum I discovered that what I was interested in were the Courbet painting of the little girl with the doll there, and the enormous keys of Harlech castle which I've used. Also Daumier's work. But what interested me when I started the painting was the way in which I did her corset, the strokes; it was like she was in a cage. Both men and women were corsetted, they couldn't dress themselves, or even bend down. They were dressed like mannequins, like dolls, so there was a helplessness about these figures. They could be fine linguists and have brilliant minds, the Welsh aristocracy, but there is the idea of the fettering of the female, with her pushed to one side leaving him centre stage. I talked to Emyr Jenkins's wife and she told me that, under Welsh law, women had the right to keep their own property before the twelfth century. I wanted to show the strength of women, the strength of the matriarchy in Wales. They had to be strong; often they'd have ten or twelve children. So in the Katherine of Berain painting there's a skull and she's old. She has a gold chain around her waist which makes her appear as if she were bound, in chains, like someone in hell, or someone's property. But in fact she was her own boss, she had three husbands and had strong connections and she secured property for her children.

So you did a considerable amount of research, beyond simply looking at the paintings?

Yes, I was fascinated and intrigued by these images. Katherine was a kind of Hamlet. She had beside her a skull on which her hand rested – she was touching death.

That was a stock pose, wasn't it? One thinks of John Donne the poet being painted in his shroud. You've been, in a sense, theatrically dressing yourself in parts in your paintings, but now an interest in costume itself is emerging in your work. Will you push that further?

I'm a little frightened by the departure with it. It has unleashed a whole lot of skeletons, a whole lot of memories of my childhood and the theatre. There is one painting of a little girl in high heels. That room is one from our house in my memory, but there is poetic licence within that painting. There was very little furniture in that old miner's house and so the red chair is significant. It may even have been there when we moved in. I remember once my father sitting in that chair and a snake coming between his legs and him falling back in surprise.

Psychologists would have a field day with that.

Well, I may use that one day. And I used to play with finger puppets, a man and a woman. You have to be so careful that you don't get too sentimental in dealing with such material.

One of the paintings in your studio at the moment has a puppet theatre in it. And there's a not very benign god-like presence over it. You say you used a torch-light shining up at your face for that image; it's quite frightening and threatening.

It's that mask thing of the theatre, the lead paint on the face and the wig – the disguise you go through. Actors wait in a limbo state between productions, waiting at the end of the phone.

As a child of actors you were also a bit isolated?

I was a person who was quite introspective, although I was very sociable. As an only child you can be anything, there's no brother or sister to tell you what you are. It's always been very important for me to fulfil to the best of my ability, my potential. And I feel that I have a lot to say. I get affected by words and music and films. I often have music on when I paint as a way of getting to things subconsciously. Last week I was listening to John Lee Hooker and that had a rawness and gutsiness about it, so unpretentious and so poignant. I was listening to a lot of Bach recently, but there you are working to a tradition which they are working from and that can sometimes get in the way. I listen to Mozart's 'Requiem Mass': the music can be like a chant or a mantra.

Is there a sense in which you can create a theatrically-dressed space for yourself to paint in? Is there a Bach painting or a Hooker painting?

No, it's quite paradoxical at times. I play each piece over and over so it becomes a mantra. I don't always listen to it closely. It's way of shutting off the conscious head, the pre-conceptions. Each painting evolves very slowly and you have to be patient in teasing it out. People may think that my paintings are quite rough, but I wouldn't want them to be smooth: late Rembrandts are quite rough and early Cézannes have a rawness about them. Manet had a wonderful facility with paint, but it was like very good handwriting. I admire the rawness of Soutine and van Gogh, they had a passion about them. Picasso too. Whereas Matisse had a facility of decoration, an aestheticism, to the point where at the end he hardly made a mark, but the colour and line were wonderful.

I think you go through periods when you feel excited by a phase and you take it as far as you can go. The National Museum of Wales influences were good, but I would not have done anything simply for commission.

Do you not see yourself in a position where you would accept a commission from a subject?

In a way it was good for me to come only second in the National Portrait competition. I didn't have to do the commission. That's a craft; one has to accommodate the subject.

Not an art? But what about Freud? He is a great painter of the human body and the human face, but he is not a portrait painter, is he?

Yes, he does his own people. My ideal is to paint like Bacon and Freud mixed together. But I'm a woman as well, so I don't have that male harshness. I hate violence of any kind and it upsets me to paint it; so if I am dealing with violence I will put a shaving brush in the hand instead of a scalpel.

You are referring to 'Morning Shave' [see colour plate]; so is that painting a way of dealing with it? You've found what T.S. Eliot called the "objective correlative", something that will match and hold the emotion without being too specific. As a poet I'm very interested in narrative and metaphor. I think you as a painter have those two qualities as well. The viewer of the painting is challenged to make sense of and complete the story. If there were a razor in 'Morning Shave' it would be easier to understand, too easy perhaps. I thought that the earlier study for that was very effective too.

Yes, that was me in my mother's arms. Though, obviously, I can't remember that.

Although the male figure is centre-stage, you've given him a John Major whimpishness, you've put him in his place in those pathetic Steve Bell underpants.

But there's also a sense of Lorca's 'Blood Wedding'.

Even though you concentrate on each painting intensely, is there a sense in which you are aware of an exhibition and so are thinking of the conjunction of things, each piece resonating and taking its place in a larger narrative.

Yes, it's also very important to know the exhibition space and to have that in your head.

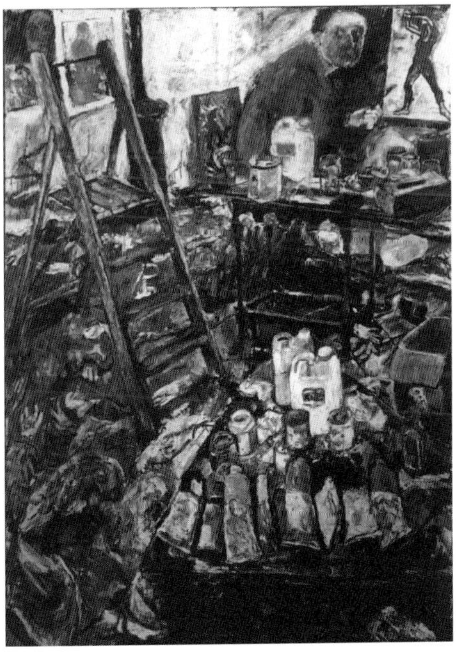

Studio with Gloves
oil on canvas, 213.5 x 152.5 cm
1993, private collection

When one walks into your studio there is a sense of one painting working off another. The one which you're working on at the moment is literally the backdrop to other things, it's almost as if one is walking onto a set. They're very big. Do you feel bereft when they go off to an exhibition?

I feed off them and when I'm left with an empty studio it feels as if you've lost them. But once they go you can start a whole new way of thinking. The paintings I'm really pleased with I can get upset to lose.

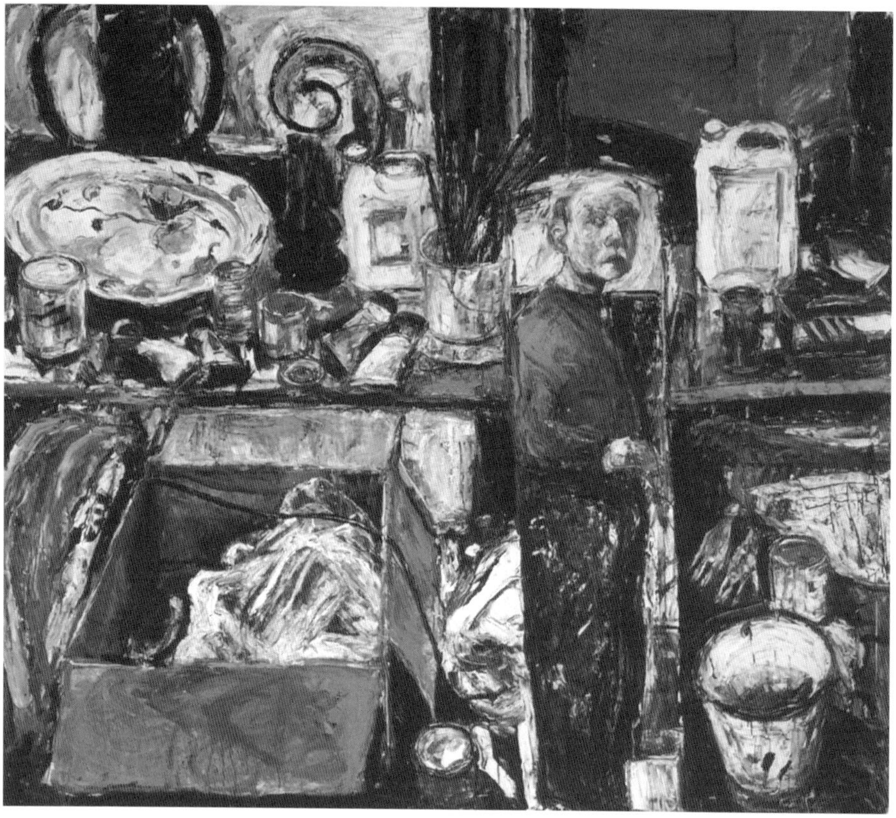

Caught in a Mirror oil on canvas, 72 x 84 inches, 1995, private collection

Yes, but they are getting bigger. Who can keep them, do you know?
Not really, except the ones which have really got it. They tend to be the big ones anyway, because of the movement and gesture you can get. A painting which is small is usually me cutting it down in concept. Naturally I think on a bigger scale – about six foot by seven – you can really get something in there.

The size makes them dramatic, but they won't fit in anyone's dining room, so isn't there a dilemma here? You are making personal statements, involving the position of women and women in history, but at the same time they are, very personal to you; and, because of their size and cost, you may be making a public art.
Yes, I like people to see them, but when they are in someone's house, in a private collection, who sees them? The Contemporary Art Society for Wales have bought 'Morning Shave', and the Red Self-Portrait is in

the National Museum in Cardiff. But a painting like 'Red Living Room' is locked into someone's house, they took out a window to get it in, and now I can't get it out for exhibitions.

You like exhibitions, don't you, the imperative of a deadline?
Yes, I rise to the occasion with a deadline. The *Disclosure(s)* show I did over four months.

Reading Alice in Wonderland *to your sons sparked off a number of ideas, didn't it?*
I thought that I must deal with that. Alice says, "As for you!" and just whips the tablecloth off; I like the whole idea of everything smashing, but they don't really break because it's a dream. As to the idea of the Red Queen turning into the size of a pepper-pot, it's wonderful for children to have adults tangible and small enough to be dealt with in such a way that they are not these big ogres.

The canvas is a wonderland in which you can do what you like. Your painting in terms of canvas size, and what you do to perspective, is a manipulation of size as well, isn't it?
Size is a way of making things important. People make too much of my size, it's very irritating. As Queen Elizabeth said, "I may have the body of a woman, but inside I have the heart of a king".

Have you taught art?
I taught for seven years – life drawing and so on – I don't now, though a lot of students come to me with their thesis ideas about me. I enjoy

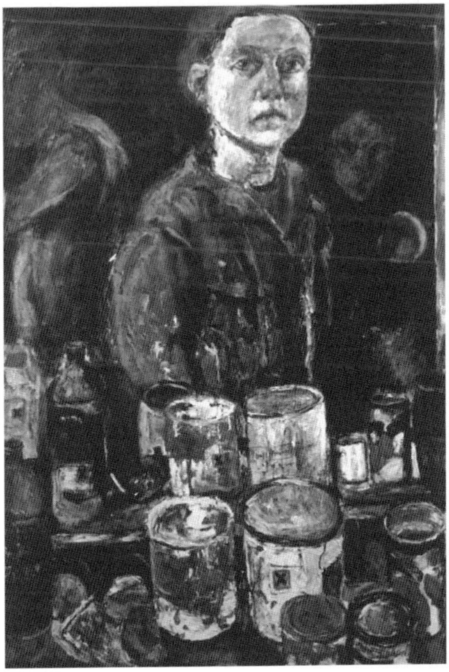

Self-portrait with Shadows
oil on canvas, 183 x 122 cm, 1993
private collection

visiting colleges as a guest lecturer. Painting is in such a bad state of regard, and I've had students saying that I've brought back a belief in it for them. Sometimes I feel a mission to teach painting again, but it takes everything out of you.

You must know that although you paint for yourself, you are also painting for other women.

I'm painting about the human condition, so the gender is irrelevant. So I'm painting for men as well; it's important for men to see women as strong. We have lots of women artists now who are very powerful painters – Maggie Hambling, Amanda Faulkner, Paula Rego. This is at a time when we have a *fin de siècle* atmosphere, the fetish, art is becoming masturbatory – people taking pints of blood out of their body and freezing it. Damien Hirst is gimmicky, it's just about novelty. That's what I faced in St Martin's: when I painted people, they said, "That's been done before. Can't you do something different?" Their whole attitude was to be new, to turn your body into a novelty. Things are becoming so extreme that you could end up with snuff movies. Art is into experimentation, of course, but you need a discipline. I could take the whole of my studio and place it in a gallery: Bethan Huws did that. There's an arrogance in doing that.

Yes, I was in Vienna last summer and went to the Secession House where the painting exhibition consisted of an empty room with the windows left open by the artist who, apparently, invited one to look at the view. I paid four quid to get in! Without wishing to sound like a tabloid journalist, there are some things which one ought to shout about.

You seem to be very settled and happy here in Wales and you've had several people suggest that you paint what is around you here in the Welshpool area. Yet most of your paintings are set in rooms and are about being enclosed. Might there be landscapes in the future?

The landscape here is very beautiful, so I might paint a contemporary idea of us being in a landscape, although the scale wouldn't be big enough, because I do like to do things to their full scale. It is beautiful here, a sort of sanctuary. I'm here because I can be receptive to everything, although there is sometimes a sense of loneliness. The landscape is now about all the terrible things that we've been fleeing from – which is the high rise blocks, the pylons. If you think of all those landscapes by Monet and van Gogh and Courbet, how could you avoid doing all those things that come in, they're like giant trees – beautiful in a way.

Do you know that Stephen Spender poem 'Pylons' which celebrates the first appearance of pylons in the thirties? They were so taken up by modernity; he did another one about an aerodrome and Auden, famously, produced 'Night Mail'.

Yes, I know the Futurists and the Vorticists and the films of Eisenstein and *Metropolis*. It was a romantic departure, in a sense. But now it is a living nightmare; we are left with an awful legacy.

Peter Prendergast has had that fascination and commitment to the huge, gouged structure of Bethesda quarry, and Ernie Zobole paints his idea of the Rhondda over and over. Do you see yourself ever being drawn to something like that?

I can see how that could happen; but that's about something personal as well. I had a strange experience at the *Blood Ties* exhibition: some people from this area came and said that they knew it was about Dolpebyll, they felt the spirit of the place. I do feel a strong sense of something in this place. But the room is most important. I'm very interested in writers who use the room – Beckett in *Malone Dies* – and the edges of the room with Winnie buried, planted outside. I like the possibility of floating, the womb, the refuge.

The awful pollution and pressure of London comes through in the threat of the London streets in that drawing 'Departure from East London' and you are far away from that here.

In London so many things are bombarding your eyes that you censor and there's a numbing effect, you cut yourself off from your visible stimulus. As a child I used to go on a bus and a train and a walk to school and I would see crowds of isolated people. It was like Eliot's 'Waste Land'. I was looking at things in a way or a Hogarth way.

In that drawing you and Stephen are shielding, protecting the boys from the city outside. If you hadn't had your sons, would you have put up with it for your own sake?

Yes, I would have stayed, for Stephen's career; but for me it had to be Wales or Australia. My mother moved here and I kept on visiting and I found that it reminded me of Australia, that openness. The people were receptive to new people and ideas.

I'm interested to hear that, because so often Wales is seen as a place which artists – Turner, Wordsworth – visited and reacted to and then went away again.

I do feel that I am not exploiting the place, I hope that I am contributing to Wales. And Stephen, in the gallery in Aberystwyth, and now in Wrexham, is very much involved in promoting Welsh art. I sometimes wonder whether I'm getting enough stimulus in Wales. Though in a microcosm you can create a macrocosm. I was flattered that Oriel Mostyn involved me in the *Disclosure(s)* project.

I like to keep in touch with the exhibitions in London, but I do admire some of the artists in Wales, as I do the Scottish artists, there's passion there. The world is so small now that you can travel anywhere. It is healthy that people come into Wales.

Do you have a political life, is there an agenda?

Politically, I'm a socialist. Because I believe that the distribution of wealth is absurd. And there is a parasitic way in which the royals and the aristocracy feed off us. I paint things big because they are for the public. Paintings became things to acquire with the rise of the middle classes, the Dutch particularly.

Yes, they became possessions which celebrate social positions and possessions. Your paintings deal with relationships and situations, rather than objects and possessions, don't they? Though you are bringing ceramics that you own into recent paintings.
Often painters will do that, both Matisse and Cézanne used pieces that resonate.

It adds a dimension. There's a picture within the picture when you include a pot.
They are a contrast to the clutter and paraphernalia of the studio. I have to overcome Manet and Cézanne who have used bowls and pots. People have compared the studio mess to Bratby and the Kitchen Sink thing, which I hate, though he was a good painter in the beginning. My paintings deal with the patina that builds up in the studio. There are paintings behind other paintings.

The post-modernist angle of painting about painting. Do you start a painting before finishing the last?
Yes, I try to for that security of mind. I am waiting for the paintings, particularly the three big studio pieces, to come back from *Blood Ties* to remind me where I was. And then I can go forward.

JOHN KNAPP-FISHER

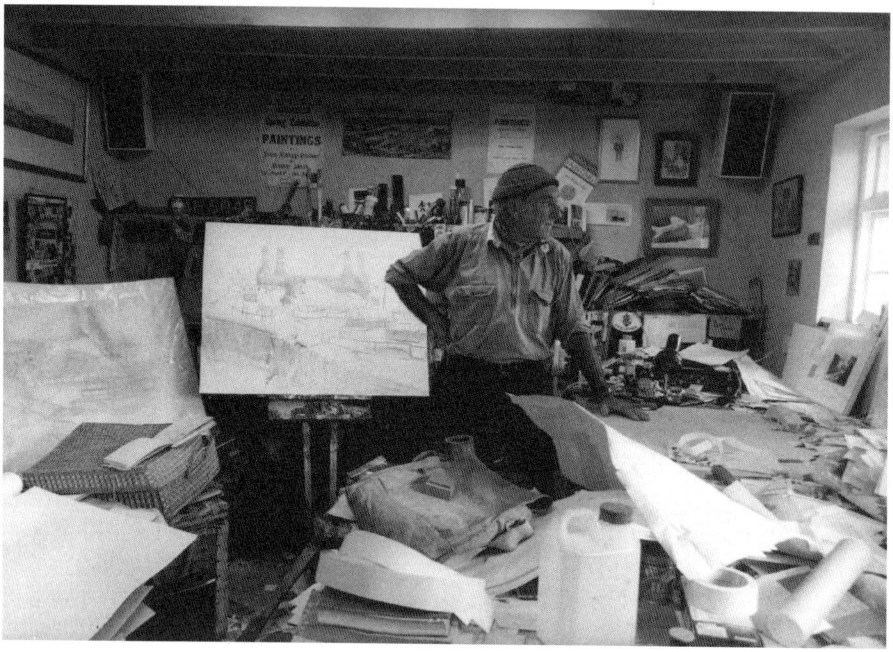
PAINTINGS

John Knapp-Fisher's cottage studio and gallery in Trevigan near St David's is a regular port of call when we go to Pembrokeshire. The first interview took place in October 1992, but I have visited John several times since. Of all the artists in this book, he may be said to live fully at his place of work and income for his front room is the gallery and office, and his outhouse building his studio.

At a time when the pound has slumped, Europe is in the throes of economic and political crises, people are dying in what was Yugoslavia, the average visitor to your gallery could be forgiven for thinking that all of this was very peripheral. to your work. Here you are painting watercolours at a time in your life and at a time in history when such a thing might be seen to be of very little moment, very little consequence.

I think that this has existed throughout history. If artists had worried about that, then no-one would ever have done anything. Occasionally you get somebody – and in Wales it's usually someone with a Welsh nationalist approach – who'll say, "Okay you are painting landscape, but you are not saying anything about Wales, about the Welsh language". They really want you to be a propagandist and not an artist. In my view, the artist is apolitical and doesn't concern himself with pushing forward an idea as such. I don't, and I think that's the wrong approach.

Are you intimidated? Here you are an Englishman, a foreigner, living in Pembrokeshire, I mean, it's only been twenty-seven years hasn't it? Isn't there a sort of milieu of Pembrokeshire incomers, latecomers, craftspeople seeing in the very remoteness of Pembrokeshire a rather fashionable place to put down roots.

Well, of course I dislike that sort of influx thing. It's like Cornwall; it became very interesting as an art centre in the years between the wars and just after, and then the influx of rather bad artists spoiled it. I'm not concerned where artists come from as long as they do it well, adding something to the life of the area.

We are a few miles north of St David's and, of course, north of the Landsker, that traditional line which distinguishes the Welsh Pembrokeshire from that strange, hybrid settlement area in the south. How would you respond to someone who said, "Well you've been here, running the gallery for twenty-seven years, but you are still just looking at Pembrokeshire through a glass – you don't speak the language, you're not Welsh. To what extent have you assimilated the Welshness of this area?" How would you respond to that?

I would say that I do speak the language, if not in terms of the spoken language, but in terms of understanding the area and the people. I was involved with the farmers initially when I moved to Wales – to Carmarthenshire. I worked on the farms, and with the fishermen when I came here. I was accepted by them and still am. Obviously, there are some who resent certain aspects of what one has done. There's a sort of jealousy factor, which applies to the successful Welsh too.

I remember when I first arrived one or two people had a go, but they stopped it soon afterwards. I've been around the world, and, like you, I have a mixed background, half-Scottish half-English. I don't know – where are my roots? – they must be somewhere. I'm an artist, a painter, and if I worried about everybody's views I wouldn't do anything. I happen to be a bit self-absorbed and remain too concerned about such things. I mean, the present international situation, one has a concern about it, but I can't do anything about it. I should have gone into politics for that. I do the best I can in what I do, and that's art. And in a way that does help. It's remarkable the effects and influence that art does have on people. In fact, more than I sometimes think it should do. It gives an enormous pleasure. People come back to visit the gallery and say, "That painting we bought twenty years ago is our most precious possession". That makes it all worthwhile.

And in a sense, you've given over twenty-five years of commitment to a particular area, a particular landscape and those are your roots. The paintings around us in this gallery, and the fact that you live in your gallery, it's also your house, is an unequivocal statement that your roots are now here.

My worksheds or studios have always been important to me. Here in Croesgoch I have adapted the original cowshed. I put skylights in the corrugated roof and installed electric lighting. At first I set up a rough plank table and used oil paints, brushes, watercolour boxes, sketch books and papers which I brought with me from England. There was an organic rightness about the place that I liked. You see, I have to be honest and say that the art comes before the locality. I mean I've been dealing with the locality by virtue of the fact I've been here for more than twenty-five years, much of my landscape is based on this area of Pembrokeshire. That's interesting, but above all I'm a painter, I can work elsewhere. When I travel to South Africa and Europe I still paint and my priority is painting good pictures, not being too concerned with the area. That is, the quality of painting and drawing must have a technical value regardless of the subject matter.

I am here in this place because all those years ago when I was exploring the north west Pembrokeshire peninsula I discovered the little harbour of Porthgain. I have always been interested in boats, and had been living on one exploring the coasts and river estuaries of the south and east of England. So when I saw this little quarry harbour I decided I must live as close as I could to it and moor my boat here within its protective brick walls.

Do you have moments when you feel trapped by this landscape? If you look out of the window it's there; if you don't look out of the window, it's there because it's encoded, it's framed on your walls as well.

It shouldn't become too obsessional. It just happens that this is a particularly good area with so much variety. I have to watch out for the cliché which one gets known for. And I have to say to myself, "Well, I'd better not keep on doing that".

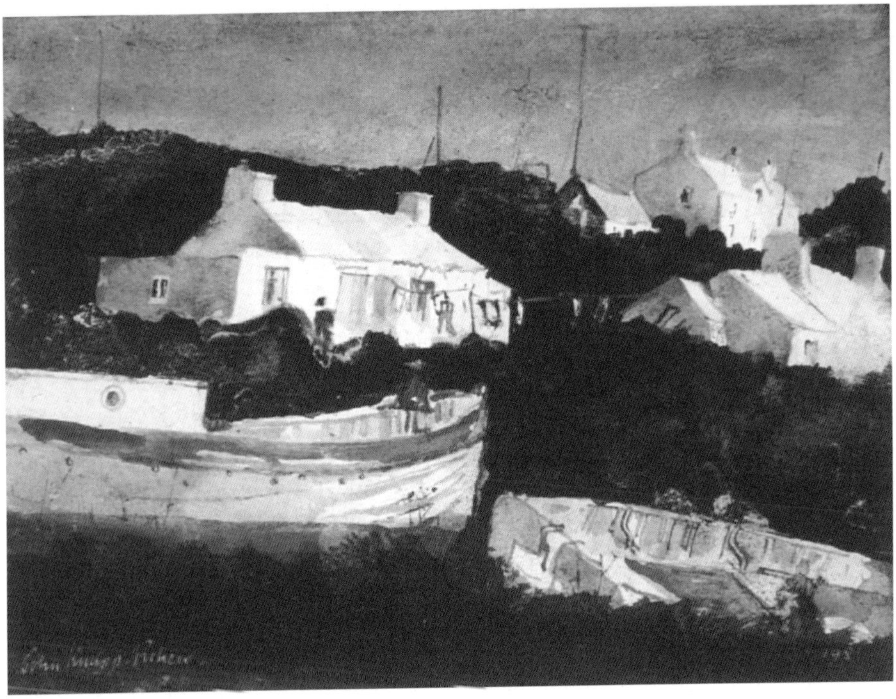

Porthgain with boat ink and watercolour, 15.25 x 23 cm, 1981, private collection

Let's talk about your methods, then. Do you go out to paint in that sort of traditional, gentleman watercolourist way?

No, not in quite that way. Though working in the environment, the landscape is very important, because art is not in any way about photographing or copying, it's about absorbing and feeling. I know that it sounds a bit precious to go on about feeling because we don't know how it works, but something does get through if you feel strongly enough about something. Even if you do appear to be making a pig's ear of what you are doing, something will get through. And often the best and most truthful things are the sketches done very quickly, on the spot, and you think that's a failure. Then you get back to base and you see there's a truth in it, far more than if you'd taken a photograph or sat there all day doing a very structured picture. So the little notes and sketches done at the time are never thrown away, and some turn out to be very important. The advantage of painting over photography is that one can carry over an image in one's mind and recreate – exaggerate if you like – at a later time.

What is a working day for you, John? Do you paint most days?

With my work I tend to concentrate on small areas, very often within walking distance of this cottage. I go out in all lights and weather making notes and sketches. Sometimes I will almost finish a smaller picture on the spot. Early on in my painting life in Pembrokeshire I indulged more in what I might call my 'reacting' involvement with landscape. I would work in snowy or freezing conditions, in gales or rain, allowing the elements to play a part in the painting. Once or twice I walked some twenty miles over the Preselis. I must have completed ten lightning sketches on the way. In recent years I prefer to work from notes and drawings done on the spot and then completed back in the comfort of the studio. That way I can create a more considered and structured picture. One can concentrate more on selected passages of what one saw and put down in the actual location.

I would say that one's art is in one's mind every day in some respect. It may not take the form of painting and drawing, although that does happen most days, and in certain periods of time I will do that every day and for most of the working day. I always feel slightly guilty if I should have done something and haven't. Though it's much better to go out and work on your boat and get covered in tar, as I have been doing for the past week, and then suddenly things get into perspective again. You can get very bogged down in your work and you can become precious and get things out of proportion. Somehow, doing that more basic job gets you back to what painting is about.

Like Churchill doing his bricklaying? I suppose that's one of the distinctions between a visual artist and a writer, because you are making an object, albeit within certain parameters, and when you're painting a boat you are making another sort of object.

Yes, there's a curious connection between the structure of the boat, or painting a house, and the painting of pictures; it allows you to get away from the precious detail of creativity. But it's all part of the same stuff. It gives you a sort of breadth of handling paint – even painting a room – there is a connection. I started off painting for the theatre. That's sometimes very boring, I mean back-cloths, flats, but it was working on this broad scale and having structured work to do that actually helped me in my other art. All the training I had, such as it was, was in the applied arts, in graphic design and book-binding. There's a graphic quality in what I do and those disciplines all play a part. So many things play a part, almost everything that happens plays a part.

I find, when you are in the business of teaching people to be creative, or encouraging them in a college context, that's what they find difficult to grasp, that everything is grist to the mill.

Yes, that's why taking a break between school and university is a way of getting things into perspective. Being an eternal student is an incestuous process. My son Buzz, who was at St Martin's School of Art, has handled agricultural machinery and learned about welding and it all comes into his sculpture. All those things are now becoming allied to the creative side, the ideas side of what he does.

You are very practical, aren't you? You built a boat and sailed it around Wales. What was that about?

That was my other interest, the sea, boats – I lived in a boat for five years. I built my first boat when I was thirteen or something. It was a coracle, which is interesting because I'd never heard of the Welsh coracle. There might have been something in my background that knew about this. I just thought, what would float on water? And I built this sort of basket and covered it in canvas. It wasn't until years later that I realised it was a coracle. People say, oh, you're an artist, why haven't you got long, delicate fingers? It's not like that, it's a very practical thing – I mean Henry Moore came from a mining family, didn't he? A very physical training, working-class origins, his family working with their hands and I think that practicality is important.

In 1968 I built my boat *Viking*, launched her at Porthgain and used her for fishing for several years. It was mostly mackerel and pollock I caught. I'd sell these from the cottage to supplement our income. I also took out people on fishing trips, which helped to pay for the boat. And each year I painted fish that I caught. I love boats and I have painted and drawn many of the local fishing boats from Cardigan Bay to the Milford Haven. It is important that they look right as boats, but also right as pictures. The bones of drawing must be sound as should compositional, tonal and colour values. And also when I paint the sea and beaches with figures I don't want them to be weak or sentimental.

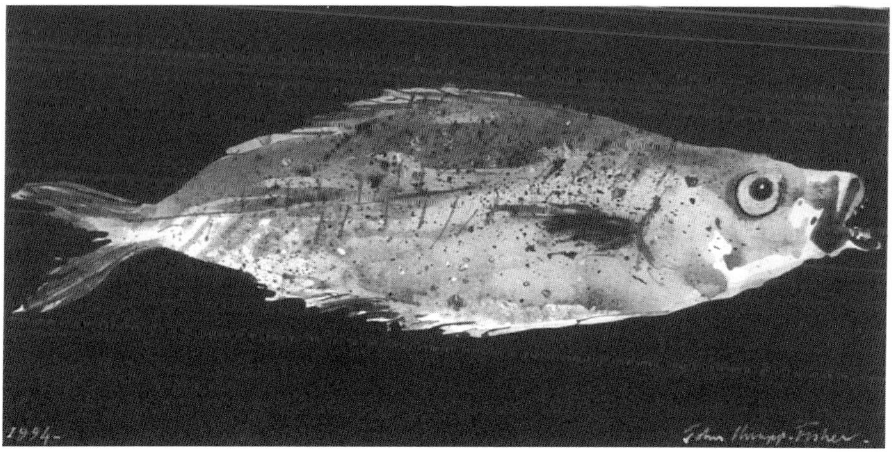

Pollock ink and watercolour, 18 x 30.5 cm, 1994, private collection

As a painter, in a way, you are working, late-comer though you may be, in a sort of ambassadorial role. People take back a part of Pembrokeshire in their cars. These people who come back to the gallery and say we treasure

that painting. I certainly treasure the Pembrokeshire cottage that I got some eight or nine years ago, after that poetry reading I did here with John Tripp. This is one of the memories and images of Pembrokeshire that I go back to. One can't discount the anecdotal in art, in my art. I work from localities. I want to be involved in my experience of landscape and paint it in a largely figuratively way, as opposed to going into realms of total make-believe.

You regard abstract art in those terms, do you?

I think pure abstract art is a waste of time. But I think that the abstract qualities of painting which are arrived at through nature, one's eyes, are worthwhile. The 'minimal' or 'abstract' in nature does then interest me, and I have recently returned to my trees, sky, sun and water themes 'disassembling' my subject. After all, one is born with a brain and eyes, so let's use them and marry up all things.

So the paintings are recognisably of a hill, a farmhouse at night, but some of your paintings are dealing, almost as Rothko does, with slabbed contrasts, rather than great splashes of colour, aren't they?

To that extent I am interested in the colour-field paintings of Rothko, but it's not enough for me to be simply in the studio making these effects. I like to use what they get with those very exciting things, but connect it with my idea of what I want to do. I do take in all sorts of other movements of art – Cubist to Surrealist to certain Abstraction – I am interested in those things, but I don't want to do it solely in those ways.

So they are in the brain, but not in the front of the brain. They are informing, not directing.

I do understand the approach to abstract art; and people may say, you are restricting yourself, shackling yourself to this anecdotal thing, what you see. And of course it is a dilemma. It is so much easier to chuck it all away and start again, and paint, just have the quality of paint. But for me that's not enough. I've got to get both.

But you use watercolour predominantly. Do you get frustrated by the thinness of it? It seems from recent exhibits that you have started using some oils, gouache and other media.

Watercolour has this image of a Victorian lady working away under her parasol, and it is a very beautiful medium. But I don't really differentiate; I now mix it up so much that no-one really knows what I'm doing – oil, watercolour, ink, drawings or mixed-media – I paint the same way. I've always broken the rules of watercolour. I keep unfinished or unsatisfactory things for years sometimes and I can go back to them and re-work them. Although I do understand the rules – translucent washes, the excitement of this – but I tend to think not in pure watercolour. I think painting the picture is important and the media is only secondary. I've got to use something. I like breaking the rules and restrictions of 'modern' watercolour method; often I will scrub on and hose off colour. Really, the only difference between watercolour and oil colour is that one is diluted with water and the other with turpentine. Now I'm tending to use oil, but painting in much the same way as for watercolour. In fact, in the gallery people can't tell the difference. Most of the oils have been sold from this present exhibition.

Of course, this is your living. And it's a commitment, a real response to your art if people put their hands in their pockets.

There's nothing wrong with that. Half the excitement is to do both – to be involved in creativity, to do something important, and then to sell it. But you have to be careful not to paint more of the same thing because it's sold well; that would be cheapening your art. Each picture has to be a voyage of discovery in itself. But I know from experience that if I only paint pure hedges and fields in a more abstract way, without figures, then people wouldn't buy them. But having said that, look at that tree though the window – that is the basis of a painting in the studio which everyone is going mad about. It's one of those almost colour-field paintings, a curious turquoise sky and this tree. In a sense, that has nothing in it. You can be wrong – anything may work or not work.

The validity of what you do is the feeling you get, not the selling?

Well, you get a name for a certain sort of thing; my buildings pictures have got a name. Subjects come along, but you do have to consciously set yourself to do – you can't be totally naïve about these matters. The important thing is that it's done well. I am also concerned with the whole presentation of my work, including the mounting and framing. I make most of my own mounts, hand-cutting with a Stanley knife and heavy straight-edge. I use where possible very good acid-free off-white board, building up my mounts into perfectly proportioned triple or double layers – as little as an eighth of an inch can be crucial, and I adjust masking boards to get the detail and composition exactly right. I am prepared to crop a picture severely if I feel it doesn't work or isn't balanced as a whole. I used to make my own frames using a tenon saw and mitre block. In those early days I also stripped Victorian and Edwardian frames from junk shops. I would paint or scrub them to get a finish that suited my oils well. I liked to use the old sparkling mercury glass. I will still use that when a suitable frame turns up. I find that limed oak frames work well with some pictures, but I always avoid coloured mounts and brown or black mouldings. A painting should stand on its own as a work of art, regardless of the locality that inspired it, but the way it is presented is an essential part of its effect.

Many of your paintings are small in format, aren't they?

Well, the format of my work varies from the long thin 'letterbox' shape, to the upright square; from tiny two-inch squares to three foot by four foot rectangles. I have also produced composites of various sizes. The

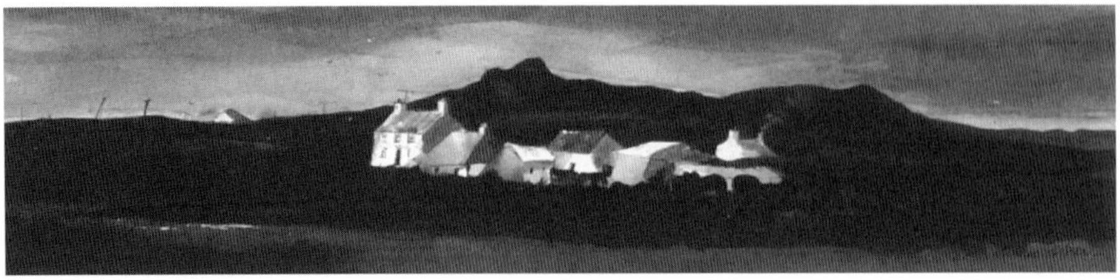

Pembrokeshire Farm ink and watercolour, 12.5 x 51 cm, 1993, private collection

first and largest of these was called 'Aspects of Pembrokeshire' and hangs in Withybush Hospital in Haverfordwest. That is four feet square and has individual pictures six by seven inches, the whole thing set out in a two level checkerboard format. I've also produced smaller composites, generally sixteen or seventeen inches overall with very small windows for the pictures.

What effect are you aiming for in these works?

I want to suggest an almost Op Art appearance when they are viewed from a distance and a mini exhibition when examined closely. They allow me to incorporate very abstract passages of landscape with the occasional figurative counterpoint. There can be bizarre juxtapositions. I enjoy the scope this offers and it's fun to do.

How do you respond if people coming into the gallery say, "There are very few people in these paintings, why is that?" Is that part of the appeal of Pembrokeshire? Ironically, I think, that's why thousands of people come down here every year – to get away from each other.

I don't think that's a valid criticism. I don't have, like Stanley Spencer, masses of people rising out of graves. I have gravitated to lonely spots before – I was in East Anglia living on a boat in the marshes. I spent weeks painting just sky, marsh and water; there was nothing else there. I did hundreds of them. It got rather boring in a way. It became an obsessive, almost abstract feeling.

I do include figures in the composition. Either because humans are an essential ingredient or because they help and give life to the message of the work. I like my figures to be an integral part of the scene, as I want their dwellings to be in sympathy with the landscape. A landscape painter working in a farming area such as this is bound to reflect this in his paintings. Not only the farm buildings but the crops, machinery and animals. These things appear in my paintings, not in an illustrative sense but because they are part of the natural evolution of this landscape. As with the sea, the abstract qualities of such things interest me. The sudden splash of yellow rape-seed, the blue of linseed, the geometric patterns of a plough, the emerald green pasture and the lonely tractor. Sheep can look like sculptures on a hillside. I have painted the remains of the industrial past and present too: quarries, refineries and mills.

Some are like relics or gaunt shells, like the Blue Lagoon slate quarry, which closed at the turn of the century, and Porthgain brickworks and the granite crushing plant which closed in 1931. I have painted Middle Mill stone quarry too. And, of course, the Milford Haven refineries.

Yes, Pembrokeshire is a mixture of natural beauty and solitude and bustling industry, especially the tourist trade. This gallery and house and the studio where you work at your pictures of that landscape is by quite a busy thoroughfare.

Yes, I moved here from Carmarthenshire and a lonely farmhouse called Ffynnon Ceisiad on the slopes of Garn Wen above Hebron on the border with Pembrokeshire. It was isolated and the only person I saw for weeks was the postman climbing over fences to get to me. But nice though that was, I do need people as well.

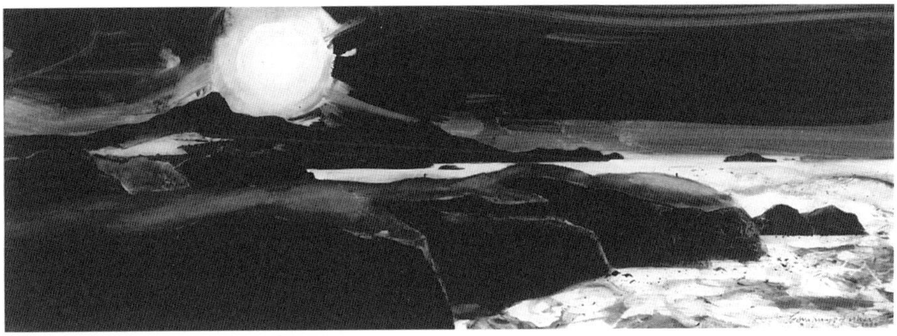

North West Pembrokeshire Coast watercolour and ink, 35.5 x 96.5 cm, 1989, private coll.

And there are artists around you here – the Giardellis work here, and David Tress, the Rosenthals and Ozi Ozmond, they have worked in the area – you have some of their pictures hanging with your own. Is there a sense of an artistic community down here?

No, I think not. People have tried to make out that there's a sort of Pembrokeshire school, simply because some of us got together and exhibited. I don't think there is at all, not to the extent that there was a Cornish School where there was a cross-fertilisation of ideas which can be perceived, between artists as far apart as Ben Nicholson and Alfred Wallis. They did communicate with each other and use each other's ideas. There's no doubt that I have influenced a number of artists in Pembrokeshire – some admit to it and some don't. Of course there can be bad influences as well as good. I suppose it's the same in writing?

Yes, especially when you are starting off. You want to publish or exhibit, then you gauge the market; and the market is determined by other people working in geographically and thematically the same area. Though we're in Pembrokeshire we are only two hours drive from the centre of Cardiff and another two hours on the train from central London. Do you still keep in touch with things in the city galleries? You also travel to South Africa, don't you?

Yes, I still go to shows in London and little things work to influence me. I wouldn't choose to go to South Africa, but connections from my ex-wife and Gill, my present partner, take me there. I do paint there and have done a tremendous amount of painting there since I first went about seventeen years ago, and have had several exhibitions there. I don't now, because of the economic problems, there is an historical reason for those things. We thought recently that things would improve substantially, but then Ciskei happens and it all goes back. I just wish they'd sort themselves out. But that's just the artist in me not wanting to get too political. I suppose writers get more political because it's a more political medium.

It's less oblique. In a way, politics is about hot air and words. Though you could argue that televisual images is what politics is about now – the image and the sound-bite. It's difficult to get people to sit down and talk about, say, the real situation in South Africa, and what one might do about that.

Yes, when visual art gets involved in politics in regimes like Nazi Germany or Communist Russia the artists are subverted into doing what the authorities wanted them to do – heroes driving tractors, or such rubbish.

In this village there's a Baptist chapel which John Piper included in his Welsh Chapels, and in 1990 you collaborated with Michael Fitzgerald on a book of Pembrokeshire churches which is selling widely through the county. Do people often commission you?

I refuse to be commissioned in a way that would restrict me. I've taken note of certain people's interests and then explored them. I mean, this business about the lack of colour: if they don't like what I do then that's fine. I work within my own range of colour and can express myself within that. It's up to people who buy the work: you have to ask them what the pictures say to them: do they express for them this curious light you get in Pembrokeshire, usually in a stormy sky in the evenings, with the low sun beating against the buildings? You don't see it all the time. I have that idea in my head and I tend to use this imagery again and again. A lot of what you do is based on what you see and absorb and it cannot be done at the time. It has to go into the mercury of the brain and come out later. It would be a psychological fallacy to think that I am dark and brooding because my paintings are dark.

Isn't there a vibrancy, a sort of theatre involved in living at the gallery? The passing trade calls in and discovers not only that there are no twee pictures of the area, but also that the artist is showing them round. You must draw an energy from that?

It can be a real surprise for people. And we have had over a hundred people coming in on some days in the summer. That's good, but it can also be a distraction. I still have to go out into the fields, to go out and get an idea, come back and make notes that allow me to turn it into a picture – perhaps one of the big, significant pictures.

ERNEST ZOBOLE

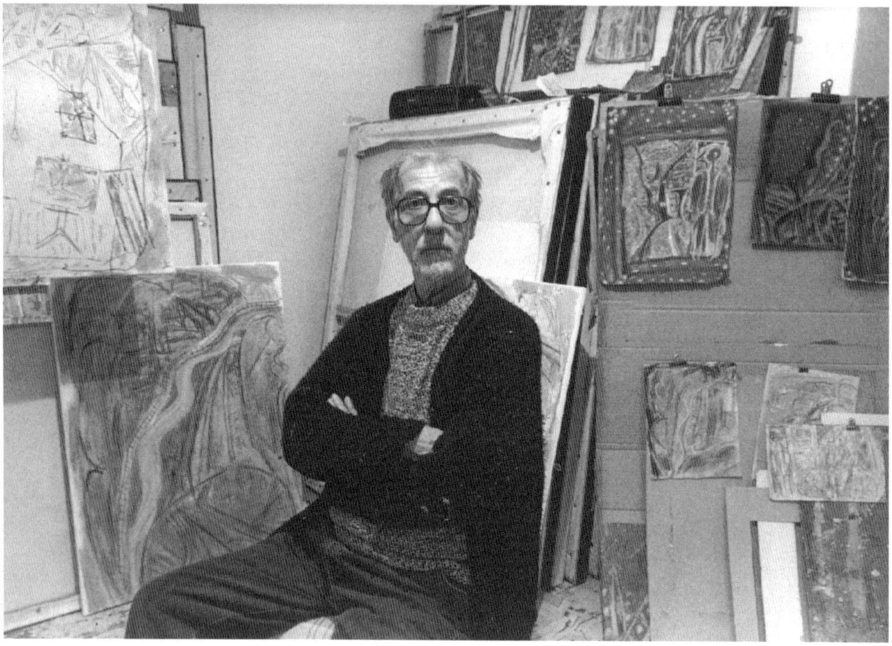

Ernest Zobole lives in a Victorian vicarage at the foot of the Penrhys Hill in the Rhondda. I visited him there in January 1997. He paints mainly in upstairs rooms, though not necessarily those facing down the valley which he has continued to paint for more than thirty years.

At times since the war it must have been difficult for a painter to find exhibitions and to reach a public in Wales.

Well, this is why the groups came along, like the 56 Group of which I was one of the founder members. David Tinker, Eric Malthouse and Arthur Giardelli started it off – the first two were the originators, I think. There were ten or twelve members after a while. They thought that having a group of, not like minds, but minds of a certain kind could exhibit their work together, giving it a stronger pull, making a stronger statement by exhibiting in a group. The Arts Council worked well too at that time, because they held annual shows and everyone was invited to submit, it was a bit of a hotch potch, but nevertheless things were going. And of course, directly after the war it was a good time; there was a state of euphoria in that there was a new Socialist government and things were looking up, there were mental fireworks, or at least something to look at, a display of anticipation. So the Arts Council did things and there was a Pictures for Schools exhibition that Nan Youngman used to run. Looking back, it seemed an active time. Things were happening.

When you say that you were involved in the start of the 56 Group what did you mean? Was there a meeting, or were you written to at your school?

I was written to and I assume that others were too. I was in Anglesey teaching at Llangefni so I must have sent a picture down to them. It became an annual show and sometimes a few members within the Group would put on a show themselves. There was nothing dictatorial about the selection. Just that one or two people might look good together. Arthur, of course, was energetic, as he's always been, acquiring sites for exhibiting and negotiating and making things happen.

There was also that aim to get the work from Wales to travel, especially to Europe.

That was later. Earlier on the work went to England and then Washington D.C. I remember having meetings to discuss what the group was for, grinding meetings, they were. It was not suggested that we have a manifesto or anything like that. We were painters doing some work and getting together.

I suppose that writers and artists at some point inevitably get together in some pressure group, or political group, a manifesto group, but you've always got to protect the space where you do your work. A lot of energy can be dissipated into this promotional stuff.

Yes, at times we would agree that we were an educational group. The old thing about the visual arts being secluded in museums and galleries that people are shy of; we thought perhaps we could fit in here somewhere. But it wasn't anything that we could come to any conclusions about. You felt that you were doing something worthwhile, but when you saw it written down you denied it.

You were in Anglesey because you were teaching; it was your first job after leaving college in Cardiff. And you had gone to Cardiff School of Art straight from school here in the Rhondda. So school teaching was the natural thing to do, was it?

Yes, but having come from art college it seemed to me the unnatural thing to do, but nevertheless because of the numbers that did it, it appeared normal. Though inwardly you screamed and skidded and shouted and tried to stop this terrible slide into teaching. But you went, quite docile. You see, coming out of the army and art college and going into school you almost became a pupil yourself.

So you were in the army?

Yes, and I had rheumatic fever which set me back a year at school. By the time I came out of school I went straight to do National Service. I was sent to Palestine. The vast open spaces there made it very strange for me when I got back home. The streets were tiny, everything looked so small and compact.

So when you left school National Service was for you, as many other people, an annoying interruption to your plans. Because you wanted to go to art college didn't you?

Oh, yes. When I left school there were local scholarships. I was at Porth Grammar, it had a good reputation. I was going to go on to college.

Did you paint or sketch anything in Palestine?

Not really. We enjoyed the sun and the sea, the oranges and melons. When I came home I went straight into Cardiff School of Art. We were a lot of ex-service people who came out with an army grant, which was more than you got with a local scholarship. You could survive quite well on that.

Well, there's nothing for art students now, on their foundation year. Charlie Burton says that you all caught the train down to Cardiff together. And that was the famous Rhondda Group, all of you catching the train of necessity.

Yes, we had a grand time. This was our extra-curricula, extra-mural studies. On the way down we talked about painting, we showed our paintings to each other, criticised each other. There was Charlie and Nigel Flower, there was David Mainwaring, Gwyn Evans and Bob Thomas the sculptor. He and Charlie went off to the Royal College. Tom Hughes used to come down with us, and then there were younger members later on. It was an enjoyable and instructive time. Of course Charlie was the senior man, two years ahead of us.

Academics and critics are always looking to tidy things up and put people into groups and periods. But was there a sense that you were going down to Cardiff – which was a long way in those days, taking over an hour – in order to learn something, or were you becoming empowered to paint the valleys, your bit of Wales?
There was a desire to paint; but, yes, you are probably right, the Welsh bit came into it, being here, living here. I think, again, that it was something to do with coming back from the army. I didn't want to go anywhere, digs or anything, I wanted to stay home. That was the reaction for me. Tom was ex-service as well; he'd been in Europe in tanks. So there was a Welsh feeling – a feeling of belonging somewhere, a source of energy which I felt very strongly.

It sounds like a Hollywood movie, a John Ford production – 'van Gogh of the Valleys'!
It was a crazy time, it was a little bit wild, but gently wild, you know. We took over the train compartment, spreading our things around and making it look full so no-one else could come in. We needed the space to do our work, our interest was intense and extremely enjoyable – unbelievably so, something we looked forward to each day.

And then people went their separate ways. But then the next generation, like Peter Prendergast, still had to make their way out. You had to leave that camaraderie at college to get a job; your first post was in Anglesey, so what took you there?
Well, you tried for jobs anywhere – I even tried for a job in Buckinghamshire!

That would have changed your paintings a bit, wouldn't it?
What a crazy place to have gone to. And there was one in Durham. I just saw the adverts and somehow went to Llangefni.

Where there is now a good art gallery, Oriel Ynys Môn. But there wasn't anywhere then.
Oh God. It was so windy and desolate, but people lived there. And the only mountains you had were the ones on the mainland, but you could only see them in the distance like postcards.

Yes, Anglesey can be rather featureless. But did you go into Snowdonia to paint at all? After all, you were there for over three years.
No. I simply got myself a job there, and was a bit slow perhaps in trying for a post elsewhere. Of course Kyffin Williams was nearby and I had some contact with him through Lord and Lady Anglesey when he came back to visit from London. And Gwilym Pritchard and Claudia Williams. Gwilym taught at Llangefni too. There were some social contacts, but the rest was all wind and chapel. It crackled with conformity. It was starchy. I don't speak Welsh so that was a barrier and there were things and some occasions which I couldn't join.

So you left to teach back in south Wales?

Yes, I came down first to a Church in Wales school in Aberdare. Two years there and then two years up in Treorchy with Percy Griffiths, a little school which is now a comprehensive. And from there I went to lecture in Newport in '63.

What was Newport College like then? Because I knew well someone who taught there in the Seventies who said that the traditional skills were being replaced by video and performance.

Yes, late in the Seventies there were changes. Now things have to change, of course. But I felt that a lot of it was chasing whatever the current trend or fashion was; and there was an essence that was being dissipated in all of this.

You would expect shifts in an art college, by its very nature. But things lost their way didn't they?

Yes. At one time there was a degree equivalent that art colleges felt they had to have in order to add some kudos to their position. This degree in fine art brought visiting committees to sanction your course. And it was supposed to raise your status. You had to make art justifiable to people who didn't know about it. It was almost as if you had to make it acceptable to civil servants. So that they would give money to it.

So painters such as yourself and Jack Crabtree and John Selway became uncomfortable?

I certainly didn't like it. You see, this creative thing, whatever form it takes, must be encouraged of course, but at bottom all you can do is encourage and talk about the relevant technical things.

You can't teach talent, you can only develop someone's technique or direct it in some way.

But this new approach seemed to assume that painting had come to an end, or at least it was relegated to a low position. An end of painting – this thought has been in the air for some time; it suggests a lack of ideas. And they said it in the nineteenth century when photography came along. The interesting thing is that now it's the photography that is being replaced by a more manufactured photography that isn't just recording, but doing other things.

But further than that you have computer-generated images. That's the next step, so that conventional photography, light falling on sensitive paper, sounds like old hat. It's not recording in the way that people thought it would to replace painting as a record. Are your paintings recording? Do people come along expecting that and see your work and say, "It's all blue!" Is this your Blue Period?

Blue is indicative of space, something not solid. It allows me to move about in the space of the painting. If a painting describes something literally, then the colour has to go along with it, and if you don't describe literally, and you draw your idea of a thing, rather than the thing itself, then some other non-objective colour has to be used, colour which relates to your idea – and since this thing that you are making in a painting is not a real object at all, I use this blue. The blue we usually see naturally is nothing at all, it is a void, a space, due to conditions of atmosphere or whatever. Since blue reminds us of that, I use it in organising the space in a painting, where I am free to move as I wish.

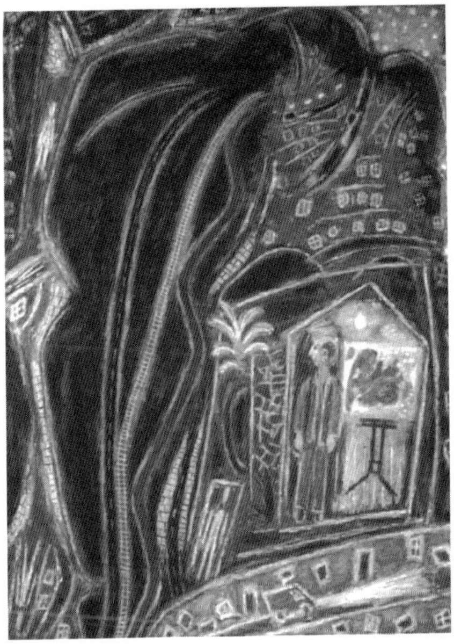

Painting about a Rhondda Landscape
oil on canvas, 122 x 91.5 cm, 1993
coll: BBC Wales

Your painting is not an illusion, it alludes to three dimensional things, but it does not pretend to be the view from your window. It's given up on Renaissance perspective, it doesn't want to do that.
It's more pre-Renaissance, or this century. There is a similarity between the two; there is a real space, and the space in a painting; the Renaissance system depicted space as a three dimensional illusion penetrating beyond the picture surface, whereas previously more emphasis was given to the picture surface itself. Work of this century has been more like this.

It's an encoding. T.S. Eliot talks about Shakespeare needing to find the "objective correlative" for his feelings; getting those feelings out through a character. Your paintings from the Rhondda are about your being here and your feelings about being here.
It's a mixture really. One imagines a feeling as some cloudy nebulous thing in your head. You can't say much about it except that you are probably directed by it. Being in the landscape, you become aware of your position in the middle of your subject matter. You respond to this, and you make your visual statement. There is always the difference

between what you see and what you paint. All painting is never just descriptive. There are other reasons for making a painting. You can dictate what happens. You make a picture space where things can happen. It's how you manage to remake three dimensions on a two dimensional surface, and what sort of form you come up with. It's the development of this form that keeps the process of working alive. Because the space can change in a painting, you can dictate that. Space isn't constant and scale needn't be constant. Time can be inferred: everything isn't done at the same point in time like a snapshot. It goes through a process of time; there's a kind of sequential thing about it. The fact that in a painting this is a piece of sky, that is a piece of land, are images that you base on reality, but possibly taken at different times. When you are out anywhere and look about you, move, turn your head, move your eyes, taking things in as you walk about, it can all build up to a kind of visual statement. I try to make painting about this sort of thing, not of some view.

Talking about it always seems inadequate, because what can you say about colour – well it's green, or it's red – but that's all you can say. You can't sense its mood without looking at the painting first hand.

But colour shifts depending what's next to it.

Yes, you can base colour on what you can see: there are lots of distant misty areas here because of the atmosphere, and it's blueish. You can get stark sunlight as well, but mostly it's this soft atmospheric colour. All right, you can base your colour on that generally, but the kind of colour you actually use is for a technical reason not a descriptive one. Some of my earlier work is essentially monochromatic, mostly of a grey blue

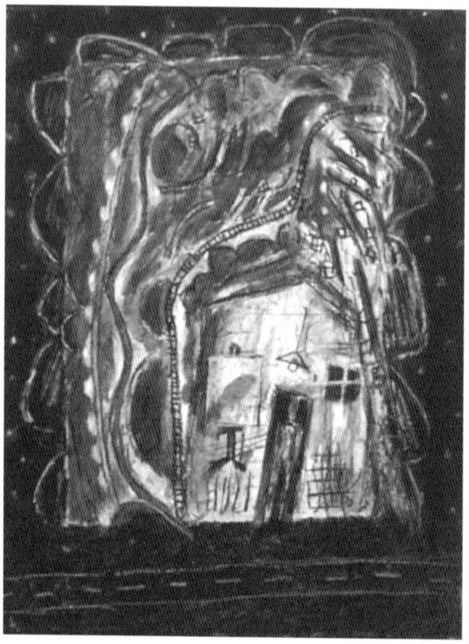

Painting about Tyntyla '94
mixed media on paper, 33 x 25.5 cm
1994, coll: Prof & Mrs Curtis

colour. It had to be that way for me then because I was concerned with trying to find a form to work with, and colour would have got in the way.

As you say, a lot of the work now has this horizon not just at the top of the picture but going right round.

Which is based on reality. The mountains dominate. They surround you. As you turn 360 degrees, the mountains give a continuous encompassing skyline, just as a vast flat area would give, except of course, there is a suggestion of more intimacy, because the skyline is nearer. The surrounding skyline, the northerly, southerly direction the valley takes, the rounded coal mounds or tips left from mining, all become part of the painting.

And in your paintings one does get that sense of being drawn into a closed world; which is what you say it is in reality anyway.

Yes, and because the sea's not far away, the sea comes into it as well.

But you can't see the sea from here.

In fact, from the top of Penrhys hill you can see it on a clear day. You can see the Channel glinting in the sunlight. There's a housing estate up there now, so I don't know where that spot might be. Being able to see the sea – it's a small country really. I remember thinking of the narrator in some of the tales of the *Mabinogion*, as taking an aerial point of view, describing things as if airborne, hovering over the country and seemingly reducing it to a human scale.

It seems to me that is where Iwan Bala is going now. In the late '80s he was using oil paint to explore the myths of Wales; but now he's using a diagrammatic version of what he feels it is to be Welsh and what it's like to live in Wales. His work has become more diagrammatic than yours even.

I was very interested in visiting the Vatican last year and going to the map room where there were paintings of maps, partly pictorial in the Fourteenth, Fifteenth Century style. And I thought that was a nice idea. It hasn't come through yet, but there is some evidence of it in the sea around the edge of some of the recent painting, and there's a map-like shape there too.

What those early map artists didn't know they made up. But in a sense your earth is flat as well. If you fall out of the valley then you fall into sea.

Yes, if you want to fall. It's a curious thing. I think of myself as moving about the landscape in making my painting, going from one place to another, trying to find a way of putting in more than you can see from a single viewpoint – a suggestion of movement in the making of a work. Yet I regard the finished thing as something static.

You met and were influenced by Heinz Koppel.

The first time I saw him was when he came down to the Art School in Cardiff. He was working on some terracotta figures which he intended to complete with paint. I never saw them finished.

Those settlements are mentioned as being important by a number of people.
Yes, we used to call there sometime after college. We used to talk a bit and do a bit of painting, Bill Austin a fellow student and I. It was a large hut with a converted stable where Heinz and his wife lived. Adults used to attend this art centre. I saw Heinz's painting up there and was very impressed. Charlie Burton and I went up in the daytime once. It was terrific and I was bowled over by it. I thought at the time Heinz's painting reminded me of Bonnard, but with a harder Germanic bite to it, and also, a touch of Mexican.

Things that you had seen only in books, because there wasn't that much opportunity to see such work in Cardiff, was there?
There is a quality to Heinz's work that you don't see often. As for seeing other work of quality, there was the National Museum, of course, and the Davies' Bequest there, and visiting exhibitions that were put on from time to time.

Were these paintings by Koppel of the valleys?
That came into it. I remember seeing a painting that he did of his wife Renata. But to say that he did a painting of his wife doesn't convey anything. This painting was a huge thing, ceiling-high. I remember all you saw was the top part of a head. The eye was huge. The painting was limpid, surreal, strong, the paint vigorously applied, almost raw. It was good to meet a painter of this quality. Along with Heinz Koppel, the painters I liked were people like Chagall, nearer home there was Ceri Richards. I liked painters who weren't imprisoned by perspective, the pre-Renaissance painters, Spencer as well, who also followed this great tradition. All these things stimulated me. That's the big thing – not that we talked that much, but seeing the things by Koppel, that's what mattered, seeing them.

Was that a road to Damascus conversion, or did it seep into your work?
It was an addition, but I was very excited at the time.

With hindsight it is easy to construct an argument that brought together the European influences of Martin Bloch, Josef Herman and Heinz Koppel; and there was Frederick Konecamp earlier in Pembrokeshire. These people who had come over under threat from the Nazis, if they could draw from the landscape then that was empowering you. All these things opened up native Welsh painters to wider approaches.
Yes, Josef Herman's work was very powerful. Though I met him later at an Arts Council meeting, I didn't really know him. There was this great feeling of returning after an absence, and belonging to a place, and then there were these painters from abroad who painted that landscape, giving that subject matter an extra importance. But it wasn't so much a pointer as an addition. I remember looking at a picture by Josef Herman

and feeling very moved by a piece of red, a piece of red paint. Apart from performing its function in the painting, it could be enjoyed for its own sake. Painting is about this sort of thing. You have to look at painting; see it; experience it.

I recently visited him in his London studio to involve him in another book. He is a wonderfully warm man. He still had drawings from the 1950s of miners, which we are using in my anthology of mining. Josef Herman was a big influence on Will Roberts, of course, and his reputation has needed to emerge from that association in critics' minds.

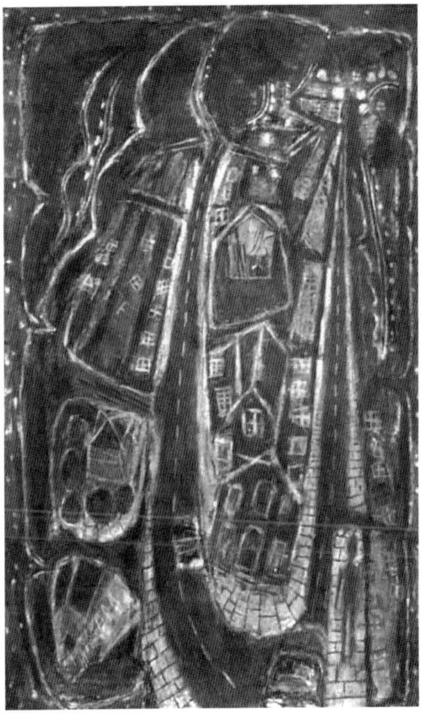

Penrhys Road and Tyntyla Road
mixed media on paper, 51 x 30.5 cm
1994, private collection

You've lived here in this house since 1973. A lot has happened since then – the mines have gone and the community has changed greatly. And the Penrhys estate has been built above you.

The idea is crazy, building a town on a mountain top. I'm sure that some bright spark came back from holiday in Italy and thought we'll have one of those lovely towns in the mountains.

Well, I came up here for the first time a year ago to play golf at the Rhondda Club which is just across the road from the estate. And from up there the view down both valleys was stunning. I thought at the time that a Welshman made good, like Tom Jones, might well have built a mansion up there if the estate hadn't been in place. The situation itself is wonderful.

Yes, there used to be an old farmhouse there which could have been made into something for the community. There is a changed atmosphere now. The old mining community has gone. The older, working people were role models for the young; people had things to do and were part of a society. I used to go up that road outside and up onto the Penrhys mountain.

People forget that mining communities were often close to the country. It came as a shock to me when I taught in Maltby in the West Riding coalfield – the kids were as much country children with seasonal pursuits, ferrets, harvesting and so on, as they were part of an industrial town.
Yes, I remember in our student days going up that mountain and drawing. You couldn't do that directly from the road now – you'd have to go around the intervening housing estates.

Your paintings are not just landscape, are they? They include landscape, they are really about the scheme of things. You are mapping something. There are lots of houses, the boundaries of the horizon, the sea as a route to somewhere else; there are streetlights and traffic. But you get an impression of an impacting of the houses in a claustrophobic way. And there are few people evident. Is that a reflection of the major changes to the valleys' society? There is always a person who may or may not be you.
Yes, it is meant to be myself. The people are not there and yet the whole landscape has always been made by people. The industry that was here. All the rounded shapes are from the tips that were, you grew up with them, the waste from the tips; you played on them and they were part of the life. It shaped the landscape and it shaped the people's lives as well, I mean the way that they thought, politically. You can't help being touched by it, the social struggle people went through, the deprivation, the continuous fight for some kind of justice. My father was a miner, though the family came over in about 1910 from Italy.

Of course, the Italian contribution to the valleys was famously in their coffee shops which became places to meet and talk politics.
It is strange to visit Italy and go into one of those traditional places late at night to have coffee and liqueurs. But the astonishing thing was that they looked just like an Italian Bracchi's in south Wales, only a grander version.

Yes, there's that mystique around coffee, the steaming like a locomotive, even in the juke-box places we had in Carmarthen in the Fifties. It was a kind of social lubricant. Your memories are earlier, of course,
Yes, the Bracchi at that time was an important place socially, people gathered there, met and talked. The fact that it was a shop seemed to take second place. My father worked 'on top' later on, continuing to supplement the shop. We never became a Forte.

So where did the art come from? Not that it needs to come from anywhere.
Well, there was nothing there; they were very concerned with day to day

living. Everyone in Wales was going to be a teacher and you had to live in Slough or wherever. People thought that you were doing well if you worked in England somewhere – Reading seemed favourite.

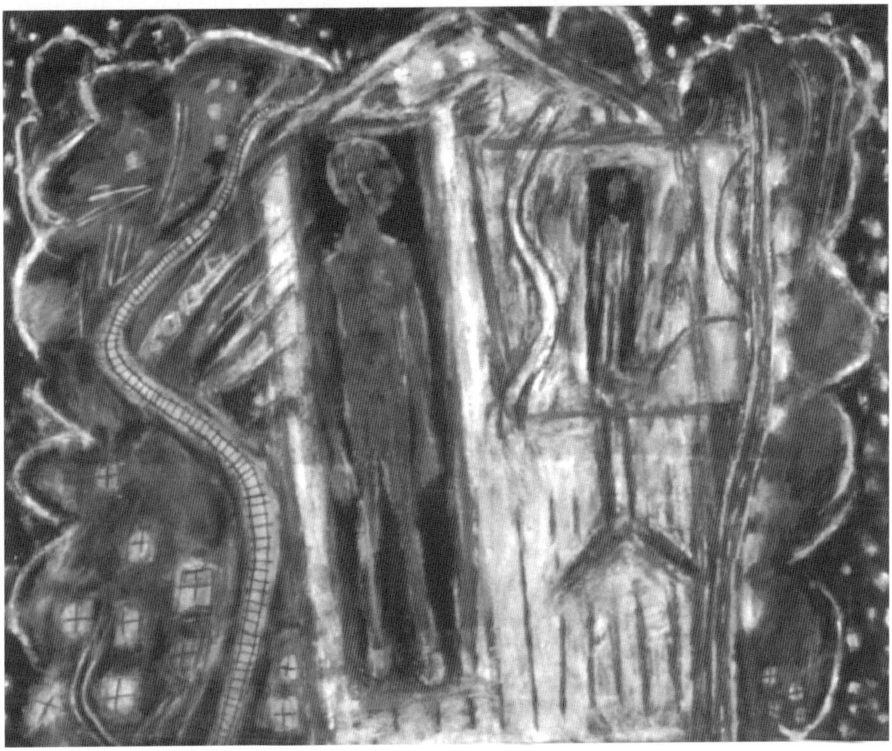

Night Painting No. 2 mixed media on paper, 25.5 x 33 cm, 1994, coll: Mrs S. James

The solitary you, that figure in the paintings, is often in a doorway, or is it a coffin?
Well, one has thoughts when you get to a certain age. It's the thing that governs all that we do. We leave some registration of our presence – that's why we work at all.

Yes, even a prisoner in a cell makes marks on the wall. Essentially that is what art and writing is. For God's sake make a mark; even graffiti is a desperate attempt to do that. The paintings that you are working on at the moment have people on or in roads, almost like a Chagall or Superman. Are they going somewhere?
I have used pavements and roads a lot. Probably it is because in a place which is lean 'architecturally', to say the least, there are noticeable areas, the tracks we walk and drive about on. Figures are placed on these roads and pavements, and that's it, they belong there.

Dai Smith, in a catalogue of your work for your exhibition in 1992, says that your people are "socially unformed" in the sense that they're not talking

to anyone, they are isolated; looking out, looking in – who knows?
Yes, well we are isolated aren't we? When we come to the crunch, we are alone. Apart perhaps from suggesting this being alone, I am not trying to say anything. The figures are simply placed in the landscape they helped shape. I don't attach any meaning to them at all.

But people are going to take things from you and put their own meaning to them. We all end up in a single bed, don't we?
You see that figure in the doorway – I think of that as being the door at the back, the back kitchen, and I think of that as that door only. And from there you can see the sky, that bit of it, even though the sky is elsewhere again in the picture. Though that's from another viewpoint. They are formal considerations all the time, not considerations that have meaning that I am trying to convey. I don't know what 'meaning' is.

You have achieved the freedom from perspective.
In Sienna, the city gallery there, which is better than the Uffizi as far as I am concerned, is full of beautiful thirteenth and fourteenth century stuff, and in those paintings things go where they are meant to go in the painting, they have their own perspective. There aren't any qualms about what size or scale things are. The later perspective is a tyranny. That is an imposition of outside rules.

Many of your landscapes are at night, benighted even.
Looking at night, the lit up parts only are visible, scattered in a dark blue background, and this has suggested the form the painting could take.

In a sense, the paintings are seeing from memory.
Partly by working in this way I'm not asking you to fill up the gaps; I'm using this as a formal method for putting things where I want. They don't have to be architecturally correct or whatever. I like the idea of your moving about the picture, moving about space.

Dai Smith talks a lot about Space and Time in your work. Space and Time are where we live, but in our imagination we can escape, reconstruct or recreate space and time, or space in time, or time in space. That all sounds abstract in expression.
Well, it sounds complicated when you put it like that. I have said that when working, I have tried to move about, as it were, in the painting, instead of taking a single viewpoint. Scale varies, size varies, memory comes into it, different systems of drawing are used. To me this suggests some kind of continuity rather than an instant of time, and I think that working like this is more real and natural; it is what happens when we look at things; this is the process we use – and of course all this is quite traditional. It is the single viewpoint or snapshot idea that's unnatural, unreal.

Sometimes you are there in this house with your easel; one's not quite sure whether something has been started, or you're halfway through a picture.

There is a potential between the figure and the easel. And then there's the dog. He's there because you like him and pets are part of the character of many owners. The problem is that whether you want it or not the viewer is tempted to make clear correlations between what is there in the canvas and what isn't. There are crosses in what appears to be the graveyard. Quite often, the door that the figure appears in, because it is detached from the house, does look boxed in. There's a sense of mortality here. You don't object to that, do you?
No. I've heard people say that it looks like a coffin. I can't remember whether I thought about that when I was doing it or not.

Are you saying that the ideas follow the paintings, not the paintings following through a pre-set idea?
Yes. Having done a number of paintings I reach an idea, naturally from working. To have an idea and try and work from it, seems to me the wrong way round. The idea evolves from working, it is contained in the medium.

Many novelists will say that if they knew where the book was going they wouldn't do it. The novel is the way of getting to an as yet unrealised destination. And the painting is also like that journey. People may say that the canvases are all pretty much the same; but it's all part of that journey, isn't it? The paintings are not here for you to talk about them and perhaps this interview is an intrusion. The painting is a conversation piece isn't it? And that's not an insulting thing to say about art; it should make people talk, in the home or in the gallery.
Of course. There's nothing explained in this talk we've had this morning. I can't explain why I do things. I'm talking around them. After the event, when you've made a drawing or a painting it arrives at some kind of end, somehow, independently of what you wanted to do. I don't mean that you don't know where the hell you are with it, but you realise that if you do this thing and that thing then it's over. Or perhaps you don't know what else to do. You might put it aside, leave it, work on it at a later date – it's quite possible the painting might finish itself.

So the meaning can change and you need to live with them for a while. But are there some that you don't want to let go?
You want to keep them in order to do more to them, but as to hanging on to them when they're finished, no. I think it's meaningless to do so. You know, I wonder sometimes whether the last stages of a painting are seen by anyone other than the painter who did it. Though after a number of years it's interesting to see what you've done. Someone has a painting of mine from the 1950s and sent me a photograph of it in colour. I was startled by it.

At what point did your paintings become the way they are now, based on a personal iconography?

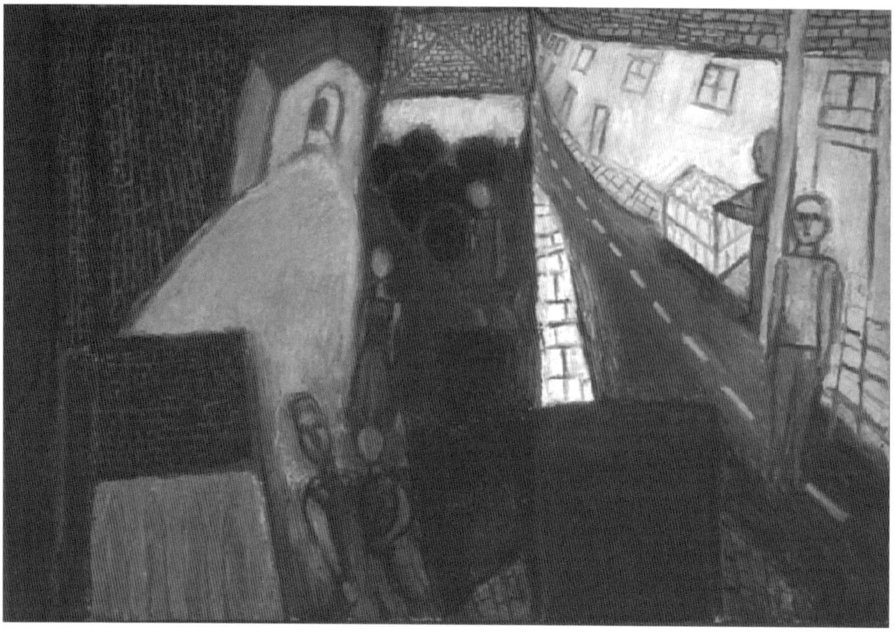

Ystrad People No. 6 oil on hardboard, 122 x 183 cm, 1959, coll: the artist

It developed over years. And, of course, the development of the form used in making the painting is what matters – it keeps the whole business alive and ongoing. In this sense, the change is in oneself and not the object – it's a gradual process.

And although the world within the paintings is an enclosed one, there is a lot of movement going on, there is energy. Although the person appears to be a static observer, there's a sense of things going on in the houses and the ships, the world sailing by. It's where the lines go. And there's this pampas grass which appears and that you have in your garden. That's a very valleys thing – like the monkey trees you saw throughout south Wales too, what the posh people would have in their gardens.

You paint mainly in this room at the front of the house?

Yes, I hope there is a sense of activity and movement. Painting for me is like moving about a place mentally, using memory as well as looking, it's all part of the same process of extracting from your subject matter. I think of all the gathered bits as activities, and not as views of things, so if there's a sense of movement and energy, as you say, then that's all right by me. I've moved round several rooms over the years, downstairs and upstairs. So the junk room, where I empty the stuff when it's finished, also moves around the house. All my paintings are in the front beneath us at the moment.

So for the last decade or so, following your retirement, you've been able to take stock and, without leaving this situation, to paint your valley. Were you

glad finally to have the time to concentrate on that task?
When I was in Newport the course was great and the idea of teaching adults art, but there was always a conflict about taking the time to work on your own stuff. It is a privilege to work with students and be able to do your own work as well – and it pays off in the sense that it keeps you alert and aware in a teaching situation. Though after a while you find that you can't go ahead with your work at the pace you want. You need to be on your own, isolated, for any deep consideration of what you are doing. I took early retirement at the age of fifty-seven in 1984. It's taken me from that time to this to get up some kind of intensity, to regain something. You work at the beginning, then there's this great interruption of a job, though everyone needs money and there are benefits to college anyway, then you have to get back a head of steam. It's the same for all people, I suppose.

But teaching is an important social function; you are putting something back into the system, doing some good. In Health and Education you are working for people, and that must be good.
Yes, and it keeps you on your toes too.

When I was driving up and down Penrhys hill trying to find your house, I met one person who thought I meant that I was looking for a painter and decorator and one person who knew you as the local artist. I wonder how many people walking past this house up the tortuous hill to the estate realise what's going on in this room? Do you want your valley to be one that they could recognise, or is this work an essentially personal vision?
The neighbours know I paint, but how far this extends, I have no idea. When you are working, you don't think of such things, but perhaps afterwards you hope for this recognition, that you have made some kind of contact – again, what concerns me is the work.

I use and rely on the subject matter around me, to the extent that for the present it is taken for granted, so what's next presents no problem; the subject matter is almost of no consequence. I get on with the painting. This subject matter has helped me in forming some kind of visual language, literally given shape to the work; as well, I have been deeply moved by it, energised, strengthened somehow. Even so, I think the greatest stimulation for a painter is other painting. Seeing great painting sets the blood going

In painting, I think of what I am doing as my work. Perhaps it is extraordinary work, I mean if I dug the garden, mended the fence, laid a pipe down, this would also be work, but I wouldn't have the excitement or exhilaration, or be touched with the magic that painting might give. It's something that occupies you entirely, it takes over. It's also strange, because however strongly you feel about painting, whatever the thoughts, theories or ideas you have, they are for the periods in between working times – it's all of no help when working. Then it's a different matter, you do things because you feel they are right, with no reason.

My hope in working is that I can reach what I am attempting, and the result can be shared with others. If it has any value, then that is for people to decide.

IWAN BALA

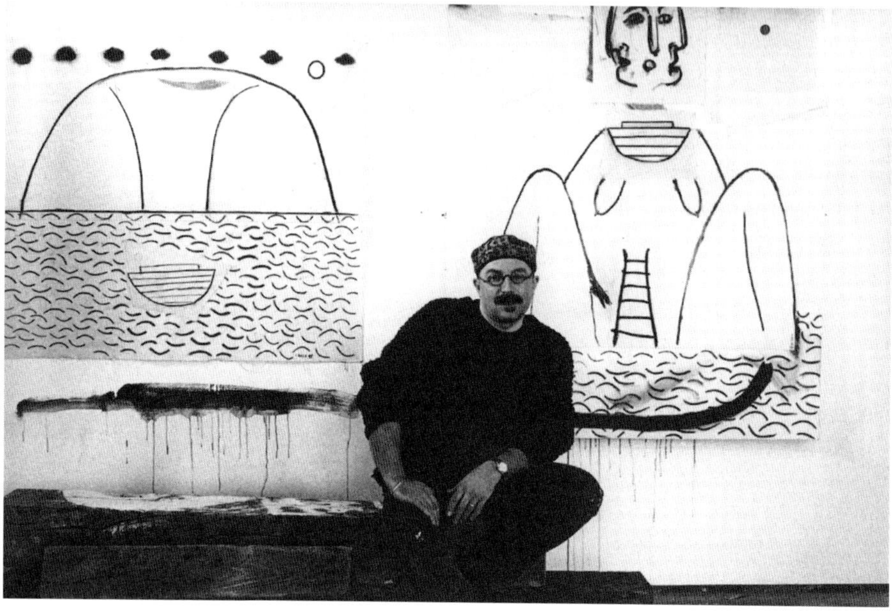

Iwan Bala's studio is a cold and windy space in an old laundry building in Canton, Cardiff. The cracked panes give out onto no distracting view and this rough space clearly encourages mess and experimentation, proving no constriction to the physical and expressive range of Iwan's painting in a variety of media. I met him initially in 1997 in his neat terraced house in the Riverside area of Cardiff and some weeks later we talked for hours at the studio, the interview punctuated by phone calls concerning his Artists' Project work. Further meetings and correspondence took place.

You've said to me previously that in a sense you were moving away from seeing yourself as a painter. What do you mean by that?
It's more to do with the definition between drawing and painting. When people talk of 'painters' I get this picture in my head of the artists being totally involved with paint – like Shani Rhys James, whereas I use paint, but I use paint more as a drawing method. I use it straight from the tube and what I do is not so much about painterly effects or tonalities, it's more about filling the narrative; it's mark making, almost in an abstract sense, but abstract marks can come together to make a figurative thing. I'm more interested in the drawing than the qualities of paint. These are oils that I've recently gone back to, I have a facility for it but I have abstained from it for the last three years – doing charcoal and pastel drawings – and maybe that's been a good thing because I can go back to oil painting having cleared up something; there's a space that's been opened up and the surfaces are not cluttered with paint. Also, I've done an MA course at Cardiff which finished in 1993. So I've dealt with the theory that "painting is dead" and the wider current critical theories. My work with the Artists' Project has meant too that I have been involved with a lot of installation artists and work which is site-specific. Those two experiences tended to push one away from painting; but I know that painting is my form, using paint on canvas, making marks and I've come back to it. Also, thinking about this book you're doing and thinking of myself as a 'Welsh painter'; then I have to have paintings as such for the Museum exhibition. Exterior things do affect what you're doing, and that is good.

This large canvas is for the *Borders* exhibition at the Museum of Modern Art in Zagreb and I need a large work there because most of the exhibiting artists will be doing installations. These canvases of mine do carry a message. This series is called 'Haunted by Ancient Gods', which I think started from my re-reading of John Cowper Powys's *Obstinate Cymric*. Powys is a romantic but if you read Gwyn Alf Williams and Raymond Williams you do get some of that repeated there – a special quality of the Welsh, an elusiveness, a quieter sort of survival that is still instinctively with us. I've used this Janus double-head which is inspired by a Romano-Celtic carving. One profile faces the past, the other faces the future. I thought that it would be right for Croatia, where ancient enmities surfaced again and they are haunted by ancient gods. It's an ambiguous thing, the complexities of national identity. The burden of history, haunts us still, Welsh, Croat, whatever.

That is a dilemma, isn't it? Because if you have been dealing with the matter of Wales in much of your work so far, then recent events in Europe have shown how dangerous nationalism can be. Communism served to paper over the cracks. An ideology that was subsuming all that energy into something bigger.

If it was. From what we are hearing now we gather that very few agreed with the Communist principles. It was forced on them. It was a suppression of people's individualism.

But in what was Yugoslavia they were massacring and raping their neighbours, bulldozing them into mass graves.

There's a problem now that nationalism has got a bad name. But there are different kinds of nationalism and it doesn't have to be that way. It's a bad example.

There's a confusion of identity when you get to the borders and the Marches of Wales, but you come from Bala where there is no risk of confusion.

Yes, this is what I say in my essay about formation and alignment in *Planet*. When I was living in Bala the language was very strong and cul-

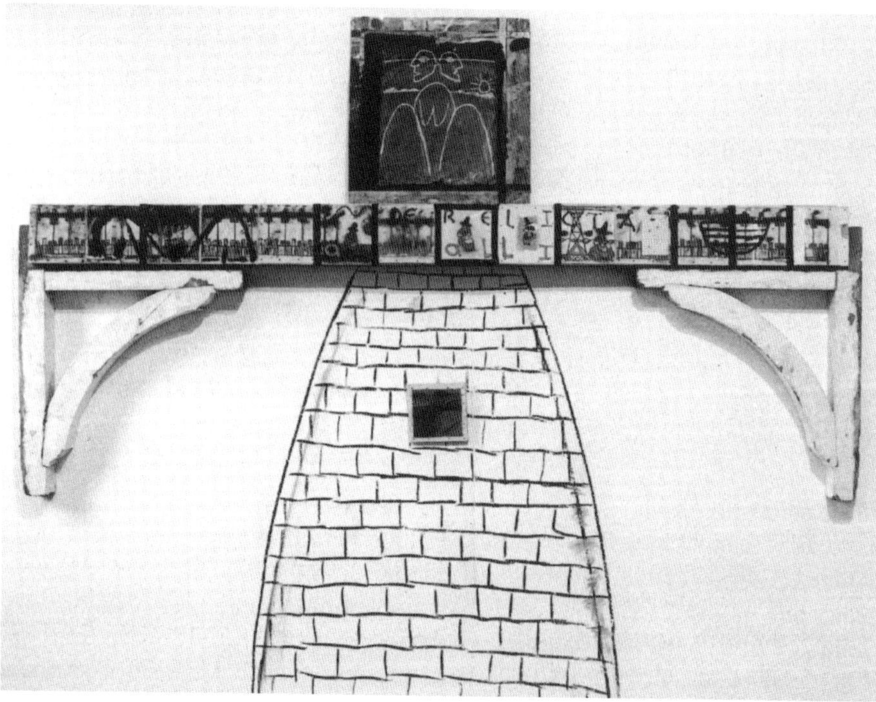

Truly Imagined: The Welsh Costume — pastel, paint, wood, slate, perspex, 156 x 220 cm, 1997, Installation, Museum of Modern Art, Zagreb

ture was all about Welsh language culture ("Y Pethe" to quote local writer Llwyd o'r Bryn), literature, *eisteddfodau*, farmers who wrote poetry. That background is still carried in my head, a particular kind of Welsh identity in a Wales of "many voices".

And you don't want to go back to it?
At the moment I don't think so. It wouldn't be the same as I remember, and I've moved into a different area of work which means that I have to be amongst different artists, on the edge of this international arena which we are beginning to feel in Cardiff.

The problem here is not Welsh nationalism, but the English nationalism that has obstructed the Welsh form; some sort of end of Empire thing where England is becoming more concerned to define its own identity. They are so fearful of being involved in Europe and of German power. I've just come back from Germany and though they are like us on the surface, underneath there's a huge difference – everything is cerebral and logical, there's a strange area of thinking, a totally intellectual will to manage things. The English, however, are over-sensitive and fearful of this.

Though it's led to wonderful things in both the arts and the sciences. Germany, like Italy is so new; it's really the Austro-Hungarian empire underneath. Break-ups of these empires inevitably lead to tragic events – Russia and Yugoslavia, of course. Perhaps larger national units can never accommodate properly the patchwork quilt of regions and sub-nation groups they invariably enclose. The USA is about as successful as it gets, where Swedes and Mexicans and the Scots and Welsh and so on agree to believe in the myth of America.
Yes, it's held together by myth – look at that film, *Independence Day*. It's the worst kind of clichéd, sentimental rubbish; it's forced and corny. America, White America, has to re-iterate its myth in the face of the Latino and African threat to cultural homogeneity.

It's interesting that the Americans still need to re-iterate that sort of thing. Is it just an end of the millennium phenomenon, or is it that the USSR is now clearly a rusty, clapped-out empire, a nuclear power we feared, which is now a country where they can't even get the carrots fresh into their cities?
But Wales, too, defines itself by England being there. We all define ourselves by not being someone else.

I thought that Fintan O'Toole's essay on national identity was very fine in the catalogue to your Hiraeth *collaborative exhibition with Ed Thomas. Whose idea was that?*
Well I thought of him because I'd come across his writing in Irish art magazines dealing with theatre and visual arts. Jeni Spencer Davies at Oriel knew him so she flew him over to work with Ed and myself, and he produced a piece of creative writing that I was very happy with. It

added another dimension to the exhibition. He also had the Irish experience to draw on.

When you grew up in Bala, were you completely secure in that Welsh context, growing up in that closed, Cymraeg community? Or did the streams of visitors act as a questioning of that identity and belonging?
We did have hippies moving in, but I didn't see that as a threat at the time; it was interesting. I became more aware of the issues at the end of the Sixties and the early Seventies with Cymdeithas yr Iaith Gymraeg, starting to get involved with painting the road signs; there was a local cell which was active. I played a minor part in some of that. Of course, when I go back, the influx of English settlers is more apparent.

Though that campaign worked, and later the threat of Gwynfor Evans to go on a hunger strike secured the establishment of the television channel S4C.
But I also think that it was a good way for the English to maintain control, because a lot of the active people from the Welsh protest movement went into the media and they became the establishment. I don't think it worked in the way Gwynfor Evans would have wished, there's less activity out in the community now.

When did you get politically involved, was it in the sixth form?
Politically aware, yes. There was the Tryweryn protest, too. I remember a boy in my class writing about that village where he'd lived, and that brought it home to me. It was a community that they drowned. I suppose that a sort of duality set in: being involved with that activity of protest, and at the same time buying David Bowie albums and doing what all other teenagers did. I remember coming down to art college in Cardiff as if I had totally come out of the bush, because most of the students came from English cities, no-one else came from rural Wales. I did find a problem in communicating. Over the years it has changed so that I can speak better about art in English than Cymraeg. I've lived over half my life in Cardiff. I had a good art teacher in Bala called Glyn Bains; and since I've gone on with art a number of others have gone from Bala to become artists.

You had a year in university in Aberystwyth though?
Well, my parents wanted me to get a degree and a profession. I went to study Geography, but we had to do six subjects, including Economics, and I didn't get on with it. So I left and did a foundation course in Chester and then came down to college in Cardiff where I was firstly in sculpture, which was a mistake. I didn't settle into the course and didn't finish it. Gradually I moved into paintings, 'self-taught' I suppose to a great degree, but influenced by other students and artists I admired.

When you were growing up in Bala did you see much art – Glyn Bains's work, for example?
No, Glyn was too busy teaching to do much, though he's now retired

and painting more. We did have trips to London; I remember a Munch exhibition vividly. As a family we visited interesting places when we went on holiday. Wherever we went in Wales my father would point out historical sites – mounds, castles – so the landscape has always had significance.

So landscape has always been an element in narrative and has carried a sense of identity.

Yes. I was very lucky to have that. And we would go over to see art in the Walker Art Gallery in Liverpool occasionally. I owe a lot to my parents' 'educational' excursions!

So you had expeditions to 'culture' in London and Liverpool.

Thinking back one of the first pictures I remember seeing as a child was a book cover of *Un Nos Ola Leuad* by Caradog Pritchard, and that was a cover by Kyffin Williams of a man wearing a flat cap looking up at the moon. I remember taking this book out and being really struck by it. It was different and expressive. It was years later that I actually read the novel. And I have used the poem that appears at the end of the novel in a picture. It is a novel about a child growing up just after the First World War. It ends with a body found in a lake. The poem says, "I am the Queen of the Dark Lake, rejected by the Fair One", and goes on to talk of her suffering and sorrow. It equated with the *Mabinogi* in the way that history relates to the lakes of Wales. And that reinforces the feeling that I had growing up among the mountains, which you love and fear. I mean, driving through the night back to Bangor from Bala they are just black forms, so forbidding and dark. The novel has an underlying darkness.

And the lakes are deep and dark and dangerous. You grew up next to Bala lake.

But Bala lake is open and clear; I mean those mountain lakes you come across suddenly when you didn't know they were there. There's Arenig above Bala; it's a lovely glacier lake like a horseshoe. They are everywhere in the mountains. When you went up to Arenig there was this spiritual awakening, it's got that mystery about it. Caradog Pritchard's novel creates that sense with the child not knowing it until the poem at the end. I saw Ed Thomas's film *House of America* recently in which I found that same awareness. I asked Ed about it, but he doesn't know the Pritchard novel. I find it more interesting that though he hasn't read that or the *Mabinogion* these mythic elements still come through. The mysterious father figure is embraced at the film in a kind of mythic American desert that almost becomes this Celtic other world.

Perhaps this generation's children are more aware of American myths than Welsh myths. Their touchstones are likely to be imported ones, themselves false and constructed myths like the West.

I think that Ed's film develops into a Welsh model through the American characters and myths. The 'gods' are the same, only the names have changed. Taliesin as Kerouac if you like!

When did you think you wanted to be a painter?

I think you drift into that decision because it's in you. It's a vocation. When I left college the first time I started working on showground construction as a job to make money. I worked on the Eisteddfod field and then I worked with the same company in the south of England. Some friends of mine from college did continue to paint and show things and I gradually began to do the same. Iwan 'Bala' was a nickname in college and I decided to use that when I began to exhibit. And it stuck. I got into the game of getting more and better exhibitions. It's a problem for my wife and family, of course, because it's so hard to make a living out of it, and I can't do anything else now, it seems.

You finished in Cardiff in 1978 and didn't do the usual thing of teaching; you didn't see yourself doing that?

Both my parents were teachers and I didn't want to do that. I was afraid of following the route via Art College to teaching training college and into full time school teaching. I was an idealist or fantasist perhaps, still am, who wanted only to be an artist. But my life hasn't developed through decision-making, things seem to have happened without a plan. I quite enjoyed the physical work of the marquee job. I worked long hours, but saved up enough to visit relatives in the States in 1980. Again, working on my uncle's farm in Iowa. First I flew to California. Then I travelled to Denver and Wyoming and Santa Fe and then to my uncle's farm. I called at art galleries often on the way. I went to Chicago and then took a train to New York. I saw a lot of naïve painters' work – settlers who'd moved to America and painted their farms, ordinary people – and that influenced me.

That work would have been celebrating the fact that they were making the land theirs.

Yes. And they were free from that European Academy inhibition of having to make 'proper art'. I started to paint more after that trip. Travel has always been important to me. Some ten years later, I went to Zimbabwe as an artist in residence in Harare. In the end it was seeing the art of the people there that reinforced this idea I had about Welsh art and what it should be about. About the matter of Wales, if you like. Zimbabwe stone sculptors use their own mythology, their own spirituality in their work. They wouldn't say that to the buyers, but would weave a story about the piece to suit the people who were buying. But you got to know the depth of where the sculptures were coming from. And amazingly this was a new thing, this carving only started in the late 1950s. Unlike west Africa where there was mask carving, there wasn't any tradition there, apart from the great Zimbabwe ruins which go back to the fifteenth century, there hadn't been anything since. It was introduced by Frank McEwen, first keeper of the museum there who suggested that the warders started carving the stones.

But if they didn't have any art, did they really exist as a people?

They existed through their tradition, their culture. They decorated utensils, baskets and so on, but there wasn't a sculptural tradition. The earlier, San inhabitants left rock paintings going back thousands of years. But the serpentine stone was naturally there and the Shona people didn't use it. It was interesting to me because there was a denial of this facility to make art, and in a way that was like Wales, because for a long time we were told that we had no facility to produce visual culture and we actually believed that ourselves.

I've come to believe in a particular people producing its own art, not some sort of Eurocentric high art. The other thing was that Zimbabwe artists were introduced to modern art, Henry Moore and Jacob Epstein. Work which African art had influenced was then going back to influence African artists.

That reminds me of the Inuit art that you buy in the big stores everywhere in Canada. It's very much a twentieth century phenomenon; they were intro-

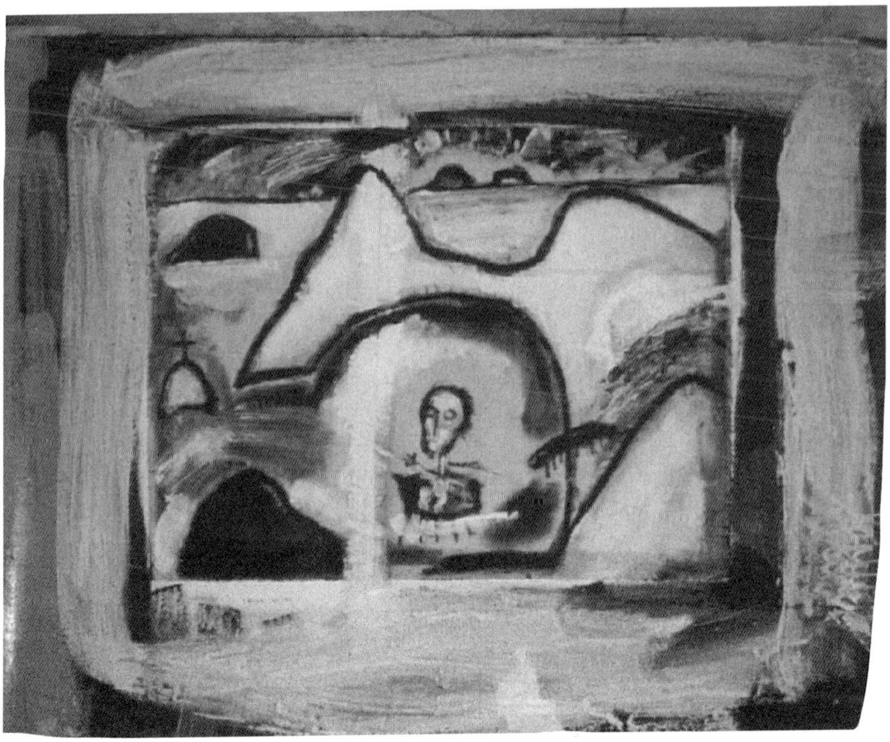

Study for Inner Landscape mixed media on canvas, 56 x 71 cm, 1990, coll: the artist

duced to the idea of using soapstone as a carving material and have excelled at it. I can see the dilemma of feeling that this is not indigenous and that it's been grafted on to them and their culture. But that's what education is; if people in Wales see you and others painting in and for Wales, then they will be encouraged to imitate that endeavour.

I've been told this by younger artists. Someone coming from Bala and going to art college; it wasn't a conventional route.

When you work, do you feel that the next generation is looking over your shoulder? If you're doing something new in Wales is there also that burden of responsibility?

Not a burden in that sense, but perhaps in trying to make the work maintain the content, the issues, and that I don't get seduced by the form of the work, pure painterly issues. I see that happen in modernism – the purely formal becoming a mannerist device. I'm interested in installation work, but even that can be mannered. When people said that painting was dead it was because it was so minimal that it was saying nothing, it had reached the end of what it could do. I think that Rothko committed suicide at the end because he felt there was nothing else he could do. There has been a time when we've had to regain painting and bring it back from that abstract level to the narrative. That's the general area of critical aesthetics which has affected me on a personal level. Working with installations and conceptual artists has given me a fresh idea of what I can do with paint.

So you haven't swayed from your commitment to being a maker of marks, rather than creating a space where things can be projected, but you have a sympathy for those artists who create a context in which many painters would be uneasy. Still, in the current work for the Croatian show, for example, you have begun working on a very big canvas because in that context you have to claim space for yourself.

I don't think that simply increasing the size has that effect; but art in the past has tended to move into larger areas. You are thinking about several things at the same time: you are thinking about the space for exhibiting, but the actual size of your studio affects the way you work. Working on the events in the Artists' Project in site-specific places – *Site-ations* – moving around the place you may pick up a piece of something and staple it onto the work and that may change it and lead into something else. And the original drawing gets covered up and changed totally by an accident. So you concentrate on the accident. As you become more experienced you learn which accidents to follow and which not to follow.

So it's like Pollock – anyone can drip paint, but it's knowing when to stop. Kyffin Williams works within the time restriction of the malleability of the paint and the process he employs, but do you know when to stop?

Well let me use the example of that canvas over there. There was an abstract painting on that which I did in 1994 – I had been thinking about myth and the haunted by ancient gods idea and I came into the studio after taking my child to school and in half an hour I had drawn over what was there and was much happier with it than with work that I had been thinking over for weeks before. The actual matter of what's already there makes a different sense because they underlie the drawing on top. They emphasize certain things; for example, there was a bit of red over there which suddenly to me began to look like a Union Jack. So the title of this became 'Haunted by Ancient Gods – Shooting Down the Union', and there is an aeroplane crashing down. It's great when that sort of thing happens, it surprises you.

Is there a sense in which you feel that the accidents were meant to happen, that there's a force which forms you from a pre-existing thing? That sounds very pretentious, but...

No, that's true in a way. When you move into a studio it's very difficult to get your work started. I've been here for four years now and it's as if the continuous thinking and forming of ideas leaves some sort of trace in the air, so that when I come in here it's like a charge or something which directs your thinking and serves an end. Picasso thought that art was a separate thing, a god-like thing, that he was a medium to and accommodating of. Throughout history there have been artists who have acted that role of being conduits to that creative force. The Zimbabwe sculptors see the stone in the quarry and they immediately know that the form is in the stone for them to release. They can recognise a stone that has a head in it, or a rhinoceros.

Of course, that's been suggested to them, taught them, so when does a practice become a tradition? It's been no more than thirty years for them apparently.

It's partly taught, partly intuitive. Zimbabwe's sculpture has two aspects: the airport art, the tourist art, and then there's great sculptors in whose work you feel a presence, a spirit they've brought out. This sculpture is now exported all over the world and is highly regarded. A younger generation is now developing new directions – this is what constitutes tradition.

That's instructive, isn't it, if, as you say, there isn't a great tradition, a great wealth of Welsh people visualising themselves as Welsh people and Wales as Wales. But if you can do it in Zimbabwe in a generation, then maybe you can do it in Wales. Are we already in that process? And is what they have in Zimbabwe ahead of us?

Yes, in the Shona people, and there are other people with other aesthetics: you can spot the Malawi or Botswana styles. Perhaps it's more difficult in Wales because we've had more centuries of influences from outside. We are very tied to the European concept of high art, so the situation is more complex. The Shona are a people very much bonded by a tribal similarity, which we don't have. It was important for me to see, so that I could put into perspective what I could be doing in Wales. I'm not suggesting that every artist in Wales should be doing this; it was a personal thing that I wanted to do. I can see artists elsewhere who share that – it is becoming more acceptable to the 'Art World' to embrace artists from minority cultures.

Another artist who influenced me was a Basque, Agustin Ibarrola. I went to the Basque country in 1989 and again in 1992 and visited him. He is not well known internationally, but in that country he has a position akin to Kyffin Williams in Wales – but is more progressive and political. He is aware of the needs and identity of his people and expresses their spirit in his work. It's what I've seen described by Fiona Folet, an Australian Aboriginal, whose art is not actually doing typical aboriginal things, as 'custodial aesthetics'. It's about the memory of her people and where they've lived, Fraser Island, from which they were evicted in the north of Australia. That's what I would like to do in my work about the matter of Wales. I was in a period where I was doing these pastel drawings, 'Headlands', landscapes with islands which were also the form of my wife who was pregnant. It was about the birth of

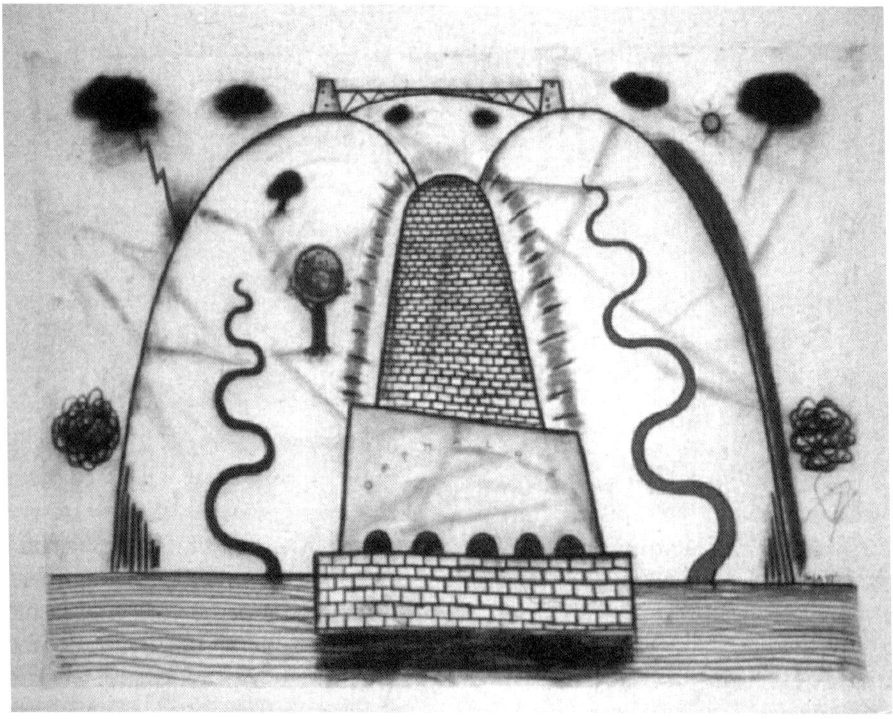

Omphalos pastel, charcoal on board-mounted canvas, 73.5 x 91.5 cm, 1997, coll: the artist

Elis, my son, and the fertility of this landscape woman, but also about the birth of Welsh consciousness, something like that. One evening I looked up in this directory of symbols about islands and there I read about the idea of 'Omphalos' the Greek word that now has universal meaning as island in a sea of chaos. Every sacred place is an omphalos, and suddenly it really made concrete the thinking that I was putting into these drawings. So I made this drawing called 'Omphalos' which incorporated obelisks. I saw an obelisk in Great Zimbabwe, like an upturned corn basket in form, a tower of stones, and had been using that in my work. I reintroduced it into my Welsh work to emphasize the idea of the navel of the world. The same evening I read a magazine on Third World perspectives on art and culture, and that is where I read about the 'custodial aesthetic' idea. Sometimes it isn't just the paintings that come to you, it's all the reading around that clicks to make sense of everything. The Aboriginal woman was using pastels, as I was at that time and there was something about the charcoal, a piece of burnt wood, anyone can get it, and yet it makes a mark which you can't erase. That became involved with the idea of the rock paintings of Zimbabwe which have lasted for thousands of years. So, in a way the tool the artist uses becomes important in itself as a way of getting the ideas across. Pastel and charcoal is impermanent and yet paradoxically it leaves traces, like the San's rock paintings, that last hundreds of years.

Yes, the article says that 'custodial aesthetics' is the way forward, rather than "the prevailing pseudo-existential obsession with death and nothingness". It backs up what you were saying about the abstract expressionists reaching a point where they are unable to say anything more. A blank canvas that you simply slash with a knife.

Painting will always come back. And the 'custodial aesthetic' idea is beginning to come into mainstream art. Art from Third World countries is making an impression. As we come to the end of the century people want to regain a spirituality, they don't want this formal stuff any more. They want something that can talk about what is behind our immediate perceptions, and the art colleges should be dealing with these other aspects of visual culture.

What was your art college experience like in the late Seventies? Was there a Welsh dimension, or could you have been anywhere?

Cardiff college could have been anywhere. At the time there was no awareness of a Welsh context. Paul Beauchamp was my tutor there, and is now Head of Fine Art. When he first came to Cardiff he said that he thought it would be doing missionary work, teaching modernism to the natives! Now he's far more aware of the Welsh dimension; for example, it was his suggestion that the Artists' Project (of which he is a director) should reflect that dimension more. Obviously, the Poles and the Croatians who have joined the project are affected by the political system from which they've come. There's an obvious awareness of the distinctiveness of the place, the particularity of experience. I think the colleges are beginning to see the wisdom of a more 'holistic' approach, but it is not a good time for art education generally. I am certain colleges could make more use of artists as visiting lecturers – and I don't mean artists from London!

Who initiated the Artists' Project?

It was Sean O'Reilly, who was born in Leeds of Irish descent. He came to Cardiff Art College and after that he set up these studios in Canton. Sean was invited to Poland to work at the Artists' Museum. They liked the installation piece which he did there and later I went over with him and we set up this relationship with the Artists' Museum, which was established at the time of Solidarity. An event under the title *Construction in Process* was created to encourage links with artists in other countries.

The title 'Museum' is a contradiction in terms, because the whole emphasis is on process rather than finished product, isn't it?

It's ironical, a deliberate questioning of the role of a museum. The work that was made was recorded and some of the pieces made were stored at the museum to be brought out again and recreated. It did establish this idea of artists coming from all over the world, phoning or faxing ahead to request certain materials; for example, when we hosted it here in 1994 an Israeli artist asked us for two tons of coal and we got that from Tower Colliery so that he could work on his piece. And there were a hundred artists coming to Cardiff, all with requests! Someone wanted to paint camouflage on a boat and sail it up the Taff. Another wanted cups and saucers to install in the harbour so that the tide filled them up as it rose. We had to liaise with the harbour master. These artists weren't paid to come, so we had to assist them in these ways. We were living and working together, using this building to live and eat and work from. It took up a lot of our time, with little funding from public or private sponsors. Now that we have constituted ourselves formally we can apply for funding more effectively.

This must have been energising for you, but you surely have to be careful that you don't get sucked fully into that business of organising and become an administrator.

So far we've managed to achieve that and continue to do our own work as well as dealing with everybody else. We do get invited to these other countries to concentrate on our own work; it's reciprocal. This Croatian venture will involve Welsh artists. Luckily David Alston at the National Museum was interested in helping, the first time that someone from that institution has been supportive. That's a real boost for us.

Again, it leads us back to considerations of the meaning of the word 'museum' and its role. One might put forward the argument that, as in Poland, it's been an ironical title for a warehouse that hasn't in the past paid enough attention to art in Wales. Ernie Zobole and Charles Burton coming down from the valleys after the war to college found that the Museum was so important to them as a place where they could see major painters. The Museum seems to have been fought against by practising artists in recent years.

It's been seen as a colonial institution run by English people from London as a career move; people have not been interested in Wales and its culture, apart from St Fagan's, a sort of authentic Welsh folk repository. It should pay attention to contemporary visual practice here if it really is to be 'national' in terms of Wales and not just in the sense of Great Britain.

Architecturally it seems like a branch of the Empire with its frieze and dragons.

I think there is a climate of change. I think that David Alston is changing things with the exhibition to accompany this book. Peter Lord has also made a great impression with his arguments against previous policies. And the Artists' Project offers something that David Alston spotted immediately as being part of his agenda. The Artists' Project also fits into the movement to devolve much of the Arts Council's responsibility. We are pushing the profile of Welsh art with our connections and exchanges internationally.

Wasn't that what the 56 Group Wales was aiming for forty years ago?

I'm a member of the Welsh Group which is doing a similar thing. I was involved with the Beca Group, named after the Rebecca toll-gate rising, which was started primarily by Peter Davies and included Paul Davies, Ivor Davies and others. That lost its impetus after Paul died. But the Artists' Project is not so much a group promoting the members' own work, but rather inviting other artists into the event. We have a constitution and a small board to make decisions, but we rely on contacts abroad who share our aims. It tends to be artists who are involved in installation work. I would like to see more painters involved: I would like to see Kyffin Williams working with us, for example. There are endless possibilities. It's different to the 56 Group who were gallery oriented. We don't have to be, we can use spaces of any kind, and what's exciting about it is the involvement of the artists themselves. We want to arrange artist contacts with other artists abroad, then they can set their own things up.

So you are circumventing the commercial gallery system?

Much of our work could not be sold; it's not a commodity. It's something you see and then it's gone. Commercial galleries serve a different purpose – mostly their own!

The problem is that if you want to change things in Wales and perceptions of ways in which Wales could be visualised there is something rather threatening about things being ephemeral. It's like performance art where one feels, thank god we can video it.

The thing itself may be ephemeral, but the thoughts that you have when you see it are not ephemeral. Particularly for the participating artists because the philosophy of the event makes you think differently. It's akin to a religious experience and you know that you are not alone any more in what you are doing. I like the idea that someone from Milan can send a fax through about collaborating while I may be working here in Cardiff on my own work, it's a fraternal thing. I think the effect which *Site-ations* 94 had on those who saw it was valuable and lasting – and it put us in Wales on the international map.

You talked about the wider world of politics, the deconstruction of empire, the attack on empire, but there are personal elements in your recent work. You are a new father, a new man. There's lots of imagery from sexuality and parenthood and childbirth here in this new work.

Art itself can be seen as a mistress which distracts you from family and responsibilities. There are tensions set up which maybe I am trying to deal with. In this painting I've shown my wife in the Greek profile – my wife is Greek – and also this Cymric god. Now it's changing from her appearance in the birthing form, the island form, and now she's present as a figure. She's creeping into the picture, which is still a Welsh landscape, but aeroplanes suggest movement and change. There may be a duality of intent about my work – on the one hand they are about the matter of Wales as I have said – but on the other, perhaps deeper level, they are about my own life.

And it seems impossible to escape to the quiet of rural Wales without being dive-bombed by the roar of those aeroplanes.

Also there are the boats, which go back to a series of paintings called 'Madog's Boats' which used the boat as a mythic thing – Arthur crossing to Avalon – and Madog's myth is important, as we know, to the Elizabethan claim to lands in America. What I've read is probably siphoning through into the work. By the use of these personal, universal and archetypal symbols people may understand not only the personal, but also the universal side of the work. I started doing oils in the mid Eighties and they were almost illustrative pictures from the *Mabinogi*. there was an audience, a buying public then for the work. Words were important for me. At that time I worked with Welsh language poets and then, a little later of course, with Ed Thomas whose work has been an important influence on mine. In *East from the Gantry* he was interested in an almost abstract use of language; memories of the characters would come in almost in an abstract way. Personal and universal myth making is one of the things he and I share as artists.

And that is very evident in this new large work in progress. Do you have a title for it yet? Can you put what you are doing into words?
Maybe a perfect title for this large canvas should come from the Caradog Pritchard novel *Un Nos Ola Leuad* which I mentioned earlier. Following the generic title 'Haunted by Ancient Gods' would come 'A'i hwn yw'r Llais tybed?' which comes at the start of the poetic piece that ends the novel. It seems to me that the character in the novel is seeking the 'voice' of the ancient landscape, its pre-Celtic soul. A voice so hidden under the layers of memory that it is almost inaudible. A voice that was still strong when the Romans came. He stands by the lake and asks, "Is this the Voice I wonder? Yes, this is it". and the Voice answers him, "I am the Queen of the Dark Lake, shunned by the Fair One; my territories are the sorrowful waters that lie beyond the ultimate sorrow, and whose bitterness sweetened the waters of Mara...". Having said that, I hope that this painting is about today. The trick is to redefine the past to serve a contemporary purpose.

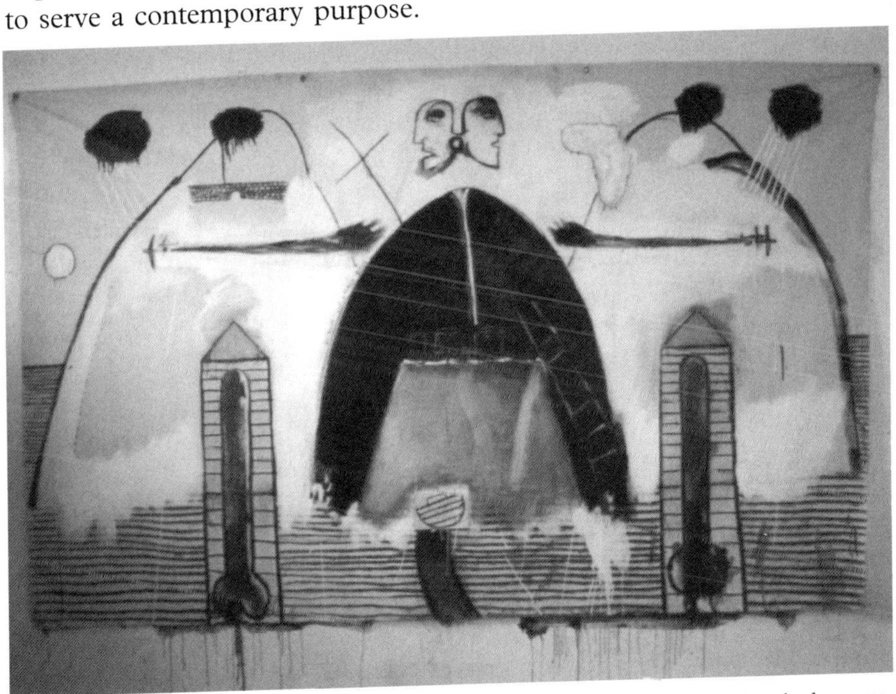

Haunted by ancient gods (is this the Voice?) mixed media on unstretched canvas, 183 x 274.5 cm, 1997, coll: the artist

How in control do you want to be? I suspect that even on the canvas you are setting up an occasion, a context, from which the viewer may well go off in another direction. Does that worry you?
Not really. The only control I have once the work is done is through the titles, which I think are really important. They are very literary, I like the use of language. They are not totally explanatory, there is ambiguity, but

they lead you into the paintings and show the way I am thinking. People can choose not to use the titles and see the work in a different way. I know what I want to say, but when I deliberately set out to say that often the painting doesn't say it at all and I have to go back to it when I've almost forgotten what I was trying to say. And then it comes through in a stronger way. It's that balance of getting close enough to say it without being literal. It's a feeling you get, rather than a didactic piece.

I very seldom do preparatory drawings; I do little doodles when I can't get to the studio, in the car or at home. But the drawing will not translate onto the canvas; it will change in the process of what the paint does. Sometimes you hang a canvas and like those Zimbabwe sculptors you see something in there that you couldn't have thought of doing otherwise, then you use the charcoal to bring that out, a crease or stain. The work that seems to succeed for me is the work that surprises me, it's as if I didn't do it, it just happened. It's fresh and alive, whereas with something that I've laboured at and tried to achieve, you get such a feeling of relief but after that you get nothing. It's a kind of accident that you choose to use.

I can see in this large, new work on loose canvas with the two heads and your wife, you've got a dribble of paint that seems like a vapour trail, and you've left that in.

Yes, that's what I mean by something just happening. I could have wiped that out before it dried, but it's that abstract mark-making I've talked about. I like the quality of that mark.

And in this other smaller painting of a similar theme in a framed canvas there's your wife who is almost dripping down the picture. Which is the finished piece? The framed work, or the unstretched canvas nailed to the wall?

Well, the framed canvas is finished but the loose canvas is also one I would consider putting in the National Museum exhibition for this book. It's the only way it could be exhibited. You see if it goes to Zagreb for the Croatian show, that's the only way it could travel – rolled up.

But won't it damage the paint if it's rolled?

Well, my initial idea was to keep the paint thin so that it could be rolled, but the painting itself took over; but it's been primed with PVA so it should be okay. It will show well in that form with the installation work of the show. In a way, I'd like to paint directly on to the wall of the gallery.

This piece also has the profile of Africa which you used centrally in the Hiraeth *show at Oriel in various angles and turning it through 180 degrees. It's genital too, isn't it?*

Well, the African experience was important to me. I had a relationship with an African woman while I was in Harare for four months. I was not sure whether to move out there or bring her back here to live. That created the whole scenario that I dealt with in the *Hiraeth* paintings where there is a gap between paint on the glass and paint behind it on the canvas. And they don't meet. Africa is not my place. Then I was helped by the MA course in Cardiff which led to a more rigorous criticism of work in progress. It also helped me to get through these feelings I had about Africa. I dealt with Africa in the paintings and I dealt with it in my life. That chapter is finished with. But I'm glad that Africa happened for me. On that canvas it was a stain that I noticed was Africa hovering between two ancient gods. I make a mark and then look at it for a while. I just drew it in to see what it looks like. It may not stay there; it's a decision I have yet to make. Does it all add to the meaning of the picture, or does it tip the meaning into something else. If it is redundant it has to go, even though I may like it as a shape.

There Africa is very much like a prick and balls in a tower, a repository.

I have been working on this for four or five months. It started as a female landscape and the male towers which are not totally about transgression, are threatening constructions fatally placed there. I was dealing with that issue of sexuality and building blocks of higher and higher skyscrapers and, before that, church steeples. Like in Chicago they had to build skyscrapers as an aesthetic act to create something in a flat land. They're all doing that in the East, for example Singapore, it's a male statement. Then I use rows of houses to show the population made small by the landscape and the ancient gods. These may be in the valleys, but I'm not using these as Ernie Zobole might. I know his work and in a way it is a logo for Welsh art. I'm using them in the sense of trying to depict an area, it's more of a symbol.

The valleys can be too easily seen by outsiders to represent the whole of Wales. Ernie Zobole talks about fighting against "the tyranny of perspective".

Yes, Ernie dealt with that when it was an issue, and so when I came along I didn't have to worry about that, I could push my things in another direction. I am always wanting to move on, informed by my reading and other cultural things. Ernie is more painstaking, following a prescribed route. Though thematically I can see a continuity in my work, formally it has gone through a lot of changes.

I started off as a sculptor, going off to Lavernock beach to search for driftwood logs and then to carve them back in college in Cardiff. This was the time of minimal sculpture. But I found them so beautiful that I didn't want to do anything with them. I should have left them on the beach and just taken a photograph of them. But even this dead end was valuable and still informs my later practice.

It's like Kettle's Yard in Cambridge where the pebbles Jim Ede found take their place next to the Henry Moores. If someone wanted to start an art collection they could go and look for such things on a Pembrokeshire beach or use the slate discarded by the quarries in north Wales. I think that objets trouvé *can easily become* objets d'art.

The setting is important – the case of Carl Andre's bricks in the Tate is the best example. A lot of that kind of art needs the white spaces to, as it were, 'frame' it.

Yes, and the artist or writer needs the gallery or publisher to reach the public and deliver that agenda about identity or empire.

True, but the further the art leads you on the further you are led away from what the public thinks art should be. You either decide to do things that the public likes and appreciates and you don't push the boundaries of your work, or you push your boundaries and hope that someone else is going to deal with that issue of the public. In Wales there aren't many of these intermediaries. Which is why I do a bit of writing about the work, albeit to a small public like that for poetry. Somebody has to do it. We all need to surround ourselves with people who understand what we are doing; it's a kind of ivory tower. The Artists' Museum was based in Constructivism from the Communist bloc which argued that everything you used, and where you lived, involved art. But the art that's coming from Poland now is about as far away from what the wider public understands as possible. Selling is one way of gauging public reaction. I do manage to sell works occasionally but there isn't a large public for my work, or there isn't much of a buying tradition in Wales.

At the recent Kyffin Williams exhibition at the Albany Gallery there was a rugby scrum of people pressing to buy his work. Everything was sold.

Everywhere needs such a painter. If there wasn't a Kyffin you'd have to invent him, there's a need for him.

Yes, and down here in the south too where we want that idealised, harsh, beautiful seductive myth of the rural north.

Yes, but we need another dimension that's been lost.

Your pre-Renaissance mark-making?

What really gave me a buzz was to see these rock-paintings in Zimbabwe, there are thousands of these, not like the Lascaux caves. You can find one of your own that no-one has seen for hundreds of years. This guy took me to a special place where you had to lie under rock on a ledge to see. And there was a rock hollowed out by all those who'd been there to look before; it must have been like going to the cinema. There was a frieze about half a metre in length of dancing figures with a shaman figure in the middle. It was incredible; you were transported back to that time when these things really meant something. This drawing still had that meaning. Which is totally different from seeing a Renaissance picture in a gallery. I had the same spiritual feeling in the Zimbabwe ruins. This huge building decorated with stone work that originally would have been painted as well; you felt that this was one of those places in the world where there is a natural force present, in the absence of people you felt the presence of all the people who had been there. That to me is the ultimate thing you can get from art.

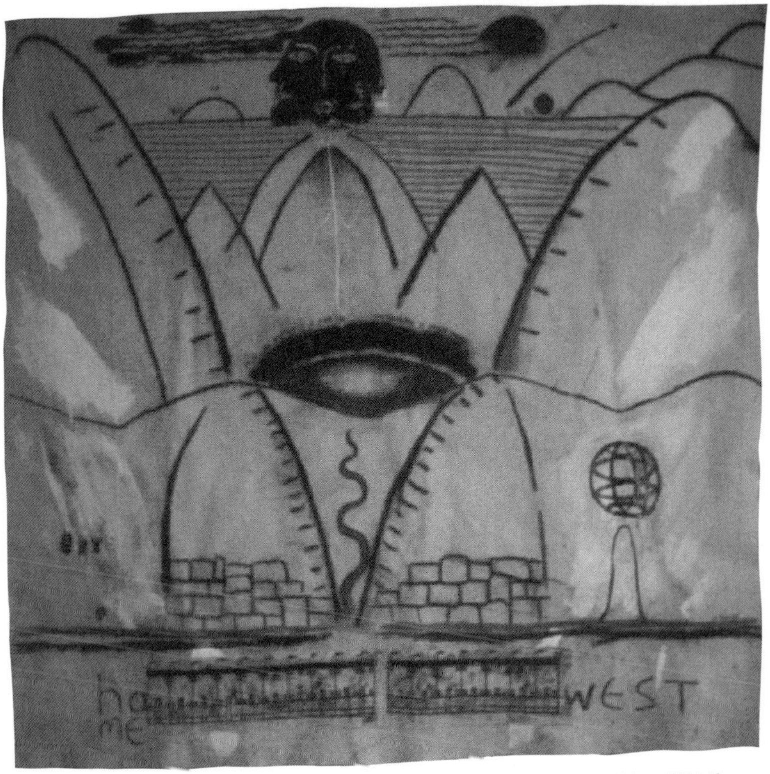

Home West mixed media on unstretched canvas, 183 x 274.5 cm
1997, coll: the artist

You can get that from the mountains in north Wales, or looking down at your Lake Arenig.

But especially when those places bear some human construction as well, showing that someone has noticed and given attention to that and built there, like on the Lleyn peninsula and the stone huts there. Incidentally, after doing these drawings of female figures as mountains I visited Lleyn again and saw them; they were more graphically women than in my drawings, they had mounds with nipples on top. They're called the Irishmen's Huts. They are rounded stone-age settlements. If you go from Pwllheli to Caernarfon you see them. I haven't drawn them as Kyffin Williams would do, yet I still remember and use that landscape and the names we give them. I wouldn't paint a landscape because it's a beautiful landscape; it has to have a story, an added meaning. Maybe I had to go away from Wales to come back and start using them like that. Going to Africa was a crucial experience for me.

Does religion inform your work?
No, but I was brought up to go to the Methodist chapel in Bala, so something of that tradition probably remains. There may be a sense of a crucifixion in that big canvas I'm currently working on. The way that ministers would go into a trance-like state was close to the ancient shamans. It was quite frightening to a young child. The preaching was quite educational and sociological. It was a wider community thing and it was part of our history. The Bible was translated just over the mountain from Bala, you know. I suppose you could say that I am delivering a sermon in my paintings, in the Methodist tradition. I take a text and enlarge on it.

And yet your recent influences have been pagan, it seems.
Well it's all interconnected, the ministers could have been Shamen. There's a whole gamut of influences you could draw on. Looking at Etruscan and Cretan heads on vases I see that they could be my wife Sophie. Ironically, two of my relatives from north Wales became Greek Orthodox priests. Father Barnabus, who had his own monastery in the mountains of mid Wales; and he taught another cousin on my father's side who is now running a church in Blaenau Ffestiniog. My mother told me that when Father Barnabus was a child he had a little church in the wash-house at the back, with icons and everything. All the other children would have to go there to play in his game, and he conducted the ceremony. My grandfather produced electricity in the village, and my mother had to go round and collect the fees from the people who used it. He had the first car, he was a builder, he was an undertaker. There were stories about witchcraft and people being cursed. This was in Pennal, near Machynlleth. It's as if it were in the last century when my mother grew up there before the war. It's not that far removed from stories from the African bush. Macabre stories around my father being an undertaker. Very recently, about fifteen years ago, the local minister was prosecuted for cutting off male genitalia from corpses before funerals and pickling them. The police found jars and jars of them, all labelled! It seems the pagan past isn't that far away from us.

Certainly you don't have to go back to Madog for your myths, there's a huge image hoard already available from recent history.
You know, it would be so easy to draw more fully on those early experiences. Someone who was bitchy once called me "that north Wales Chagall". But I don't want to do that parochial thing. The Madog myth however has been regenerated and can be regenerated again. I was influenced early on by Chagall, but I don't want to romanticise the past. I'm interested in that idea from Raymond Williams that I mentioned earlier – 'formation and alignment'. The artist must choose to be the bridge between core-identity and multiculturalism, between the archetypal imagination on the one hand and the world of electronic communication

on the other. We are not without responsibility. Tradition is a living thing and we make it as we go on. That's the artist's job. As the man said, we must "not go gentle into that good night".

Biographical Outlines

ARTHUR GIARDELLI

Born 1911, London

Training
Ruskin College, Oxford
Cedric Morris Art School, Suffolk

One Person Exhibitions (selected)

1960	Woodstock Gallery
1962	Bear Lane Gallery, Oxford
1965	Grosvenor Gallery, London
1973	University College, Swansea
	Dilwyn Gallery, Swansea
	Howard Roberts Gallery, Cardiff
	Stourbridge College of Art
1975	Oriel, WAC, Cardiff
1994	Oriel, Cardiff
1995	*Between Tides*, Aberystwyth Arts Centre

Group Exhibitions (selected)

c1940-50	Redfern Gallery, London
1949-57, 72	South Wales Group
1950, 52, 56, 66, 70	Royal National Eisteddfod
1951-52	Society for Education through Art
1951-52	Bear Lane Gallery, Oxford, Welsh Arts Council
1951-52	Gimpel Fils, London
1955-56	Grosvenor Gallery, London
1955-56	Haverfordwest Library
1955-56	Renaissance City, Chicago
1957-present	56 Group Wales annual exhibition
1958, 1963	Contemporary Art Society for Wales
1960	Galerie Greuze, Paris
1964	Manchester College of Art and Design (with Jeffrey Steele)
1965	Jefferson Gallery, Washington D.C.,
1966	Open Painting Exhibition, Belfast and Dublin
1968-9	*Art in Wales 1900-1956*, WAC, National Museum of Wales
1973	*Wales and the Modern Movements*, University College of Wales, Aberystwyth

Publications
'The Welshness of Welsh Painting' *Welsh Outlook*, No.3, June 1965
'Sut I Edrych Ar Orielau Lluniau', *Barn*, Tachwedd, 1964
Series of interviews with major Welsh Artists, *Spectrum*, BBC Wales
Between Tides Aberystwyth Arts Centre, 1996

Awards

1970	Royal National Eisteddfod prizewinner
1973	MBE for services to art in Wales

Collections
Tate Gallery; National Museums and Galleries of Wales; National Library of Wales; Contemporary Art Society for Wales; Arts Council of Wales; Arts Council of Great Britain; Municipal Gallery of Modern Art, Dublin; Musee de Beaux Arts, Nantes;

Saidenberg Gallery, New York; St Woolos Cathedral, Newport; National Gallery, Bratislava; National Gallery, Prague; The Grosvenor Gallery, London; University College, Swansea; University of Warwick; Keble College, Oxford.

Studio
Warren, Pembrokeshire

CHARLES BURTON

Born 1929, Treherbert, Rhondda.

Training

1947-51	Cardiff College of Art
1953-56	Royal College of Art, London

One Person Exhibitions (selected)
Prospect Gallery, London.
Lane Gallery, Bradford.
College of Education, Barry
St. Donats Art Centre, Wales
British Council, Brussels
Oriel , Cardiff

Awards

1956	Gold Medal, Royal National Eisteddfod
1964	Calouste Gulbenkian Foundation, travelling scholarship to Europe
1967	Liverpool Council of Education travelling scholarship to Crete

Collections
Welsh Committee of the Arts Council; Contemporary Art Society for Wales; Glynn Vivian Gallery, Swansea; University of Oxford; University of Cambridge; University of Liverpool; Department of the Environment; Educational Authorities and industrial organisations

Studio
Penarth

FELICITY CHARLTON

Born 1913, Bristol

Training
1932-37 West of England College

One Person Exhibitions (selected)

1973	Welsh Gallery, Abergavenny (with Evan Charlton)
1993	*Retrospective*, Newport Museum & Art Gallery

Group Exhibitions (selected)

1940s	Royal West of England Academy
1947-54	South Wales Art Society
1949-50, 52, 54, 59	South Wales Group
1949-57	Howard Roberts Gallery, Cardiff
1950	Royal National Eisteddfod
1952	*The Artist in Wales*, Welsh Arts Council/National Library of Wales

1955-56	Royal National Eisteddfod
1969	*Recording Wales – Chapels*, Welsh Arts Council
1974	*Some Recent Acquisitions*, Oriel
1977	*Prints for the Eisteddfod Proclamation*, Oriel
1981	*Evan & Felicity Charlton: Paintings 1937-81*, Newport Museum & Art Gallery

Collections
National Museums & Galleries of Wales; Arts Council of Wales

Studio
Porthkerry, near Barry

SALLY MOORE

Born 1962, Cardiff

Training

1980-81	Foundation Studies, South Glamorgan Institute, Cardiff
1981-84	Ruskin School of Drawing and Fine Art, Oxford University
1984-86	Worked at the Association of Artists & Designers in Wales, Cardiff
1986-87	MA Fine Art, City of Birmingham Polytechnic

One Person Exhibitions (selected)

1982-83	Somerville College, Oxford
1986	Viriamu Jones Gallery, University College Cardiff
1988	The Bridge Gallery, Polytechnic of Wales, Pontypridd
1991	Long & Ryle Art International, London
1995	Martin Tinney Gallery, Cardiff

Group Exhibitions (selected)

1983	Cardiff University Centenary Exhibition
1984	*Young Welsh Artists*, National Museum and Galleries of Wales
1983, 84, 86	Welsh Group, Travelling Exhibitions
1986	*Direct Contact*, Stuttgart/Cardiff Exchange, Kunstlerhaus Stuttgart and Chapter Arts Centre, Cardiff
1988	Delfina Studios Inaugural Exhibition, London
1989	*Inner Language*, Ikon Gallery travelling exhibition
	Christies' New Contemporaries, Royal College of Art, London
1990	*New British Painting*, Long & Ryle Art International, London
	Group Show, Thumb Gallery, London
	The London Group, Royal College of Art, London
	West Wales Arts, Cardiff Art Fair
1991	The Welsh Group, Glynn Vivian Gallery, Swansea
	Three Women Artists, Vera Grodzinski Modern and Contemporary Art, London
1992	Group Show, Wales/Philadelphia Visual Exchange, Philadelphia
	The Inner Landscape, Turnpike Gallery, Wigan
1993	10th Anniversary Exhibition, St David's Hall, Cardiff
	Prints and Paintings, British School at Rome, Italy
1994	Manchester Art Fair, Martin Tinney Gallery
	Summer Exhibition, Martin Tinney Gallery
1994	Winter Exhibition, Martin Tinney Gallery

Awards

1983	Travelling Scholarship, Somerville College, Oxford
1987	Emma Jessie Phipps Award, City of Birmingham Polytechnic

1988	2nd Prizewinner, Mid Art 88
	Lucy Morrison Memorial Prizewinner, Royal Overseas League
	Residency at Delfina Studios Trust for two years
1992-93	Abbey Memorial Scholarship, to the British School in Rome
1994	Prize Winner, National Eisteddfod of Wales Exhibition

Publications (Reviews)
Arts Review, Charles Hall, 1990
The Sunday Times, Alison Beckett, 1990
Arts Review, Edward Phelps, 1991
World of Interiors, Lesley Geddes, 1991

Collections
Contemporary Art Society; Sunderland Art Gallery; South East Wales Arts Association; St. John's College, Oxford. Also private collections in Germany, Australia, Italy and Britain.

Studio
Stratford East, London

KYFFIN WILLIAMS

Born 1918, Tan-y-Graig, Llangefni

Training

1931-36	Shrewsbury School
1941-44	Slade School of Fine Art, London

One Person Exhibitions (selected)
Leicester Galleries
Thackeray Gallery, London
Colnaghi Galleries, London
Glynn Vivian Gallery, Swansea
Tegfryn Gallery
Albany Gallery, Cardiff

Awards

1944	Slade School of Fine Art, Robert Ross Leaving Scholarship
1970	Elected Associate Royal Academy
1974	Royal Academician
1978	Honorary MA, University of Wales
1989	Honorary Fellow, University College of Wales, Swansea
1991	Honorary Fellow, University College of Wales, Aberystwyth

Publications
Across the Straits Duckworth, 1973
A Wider Sky Gomer, 1991
Portraits Gomer, 1996

Collections
Arts Council of England; the Contemporary Arts Societyfor Wales; The National Museums & Galleries of Wales; The National Library of Wales

Studio
Llanfairpwllgwyngyll, Anglesey

WILL ROBERTS

Born 1910, Ruabon, Clwyd, Wales

Training

1928-32	Part time Scholarship, Swansea School of Art
1946	Began painting, studied with Josef Herman

One Person Exhibitions (selected)

1954	Roland, Browse and Delbanco, London
1958	AIA Gallery, London
1964	Dilwyn Gallery, Swansea
	Arnolfini Gallery, Bristol
1968	Howard Roberts Gallery, Cardiff
1968-72	Adelina Patti Memorial Theatre, Graig-y-nos, Powys, Wales
1972	West Wales Arts Association, Carmarthen
1973	Llandaff Festival, Cardiff
	Northern Artists Gallery, Leeds
	University College, Swansea
1974	Department of Music, University College, Cardiff
1981	*Stations of the Cross*, University College Swansea
1988	Albany Gallery, Cardiff
	Attic Gallery, Swansea
1993	Oriel Mostyn, Llandudno and touring exhibition

Group Exhibitions (selected)

1949, 51, 54, 61	South Wales Group
1949-65	Welsh Arts Council
1952	*The Artist in Wales*, NLW/WAC
1953	*Twentieth Century British Romantic Painting*, WAC
1954	*Expressionist, Fauve and Cubist Painting*, Roland, Browse & Delbanco, London
1955	Artists International Association
1956, 58, 61, 64	Society for Education through Art
1956-69	Howard Roberts Gallery, Cardiff
c.1955-65	London Group
1958	Partisan Club, London
1950, 52, 54, 60, 64, 66	Royal National Eisteddfod
1956, 60, 61 63, 67	Contemporary Art Society for Wales
1962	Royal College of Art
	Two Artists of West Wales (with Alfred Janes), WAC, tour
1963	*Drawings*, WAC and Clare College, Cambridge
1964	*Face of Wales*, WAC
	56 Group Exhibition, Arnolfini Gallery, Bristol
1965	Two man show (with Charles White), Atlantic College, St. Donats
1968	*Art in Wales 1900-1956*, WAC
1969	*Recording Wales – Chapels*, WAC
1971	RCA, Conway (with Howard Roberts, Tom Nash)
1977-91	tRoyal Academy, occasionally with New English Art Club
1986	Centenary Exhibition, New English Art Club, London

Awards

1961	Contemporary Art Society for Wales, Byng-Stamper Award

Collections

National Library of Wales; Academy of Music, Art & Drama Czechoslovakia; University

College of North Wales, Bangor; National Museums & Galleries of Wales; Arts Council of Wales; Glynn Vivian Art Gallery & Museum; Contemporary Art Society Wales; City of Coventry Art Gallery & Museum; City of Hereford Art Gallery; University College, Swansea; Neath Borough Council; HRH Prince of Wales and private collections throughout the world.

Studio
Neath

PETER PRENDERGAST

Born 1946, Abertridwr, near Caerphilly, Wales

Training
1962-64 Cardiff College of Art
1964-67 Slade School of Fine Art
1969-70 Reading University

One Person Exhibitions (selected)
1973 Bluecoat Gallery, Liverpool
1979/80 UCNW Bangor Art Gallery, North Wales
1975 Oriel, the Welsh Arts Council Gallery, Cardiff
1983 Mostyn Art Gallery, Llandudno
Camden Arts Centre, London
1987 Heartland, Artsite, Bath
1987-88 Andrew Knight Gallery, Cardiff
1993 Agnews, London and Turner Hous, Penarth, touring exhibition

Group Exhibitions (selected)
1974 John Moores Liverpool Exhibition 9. Walker Art Gallery
1975 *Earth, Air and Water*, Royal National Eisteddfod
What's New, Welsh Arts Council touring exhibition
1977, 79-81, 97 Summer Exhibition, Royal Academy of Arts
1979 *Recent Purchases*, Contemporary Art Society for Wales, National Museum of Wales
1979 *The Native Land*, Mostyn Art Gallery
1979 *The Probity of Art*, Welsh Arts Council touring exhibition
1980 *Fragments Against Ruin*, Arts Council of Great Britain, tour
1981 *The Dark Hills, The Heavy Clouds*, Welsh Arts Council, tour
1982 New Members' Exhibition, 56 Group Wales, Cardiff..
The Natural Parallel, Riverside Studios, Moria Kelly Fine Art
1983 *Recent Purchases*, Glynn Vivian Gallery, Swansea
1984 *The Hard-Won Image*, Tate Gallery, London
1985 *Landscapes from Britain*, Perth Arts Festival, Australia
1986 *Recent Acquisitions*, Tate Gallery
1986-87 *Rocks and Flesh*, Norwich School of Art touring exhibition
1986 *British Sea Painting*, Laing Art Gallery, Newcastle-upon-Tyne
1987 *50 Years of CASW*, National Museum of Wales
1988 The *Self Portrait: A Modern View*, Artsite Gallery, Bath and tour
1989 *The Natural Element*, Welsh Arts Council, Oriel, Cardiff
1990 *Artists in National Parks*, Victoria and Albert Museum tour in UK and USA
1991-92 *From the Land and Sea*, Scarborough City Art Gallery and Glynn Vivian Gallery (with Len Tabner)
1991 *Modern British Drawings*, Agnew's London
1993 *Hortus Cambrensis: Gardens of Wales*, the National Trust
1994 *Artists from Wales*, Martin Tinney Gallery and Eleanore Austerer

Gallery, San Francisco
Disclosure(s), Mostyn Art Gallery, Llandudno and Welsh tour, and Caixa de Terrassa, Barcelona

Publications

Eric Rowan, *Welsh Art 1890-1980*, University of Wales Press, 1982
David Cole, *The New Wales*, University of Wales Press, 1986
Edward Lucie-Smith, *Self Portrait*, Sarima Press, 1987
Brian Redhead, *Inspiration of Landscape*, Phaidon, 1990
Hortus Cambrensis, catalogue, 1991
Catalogue, Agnew's exhibtion, 1993

Awards

1961	Glamorgan County Art Scholarship

Collections

Tate Gallery; British Museum; Contemporary Art Society for Wales; Arts Council of Wales; National Museums & Galleries of Wales; Glynn Vivian Gallery, Swansea; North West Arts Association, Manchester; National Gallery of Czechoslovakia; National Trust; Carmarthen County Council; Baring Asset Management, London.

Studio

Deiniolen, Gwynedd

KEVIN SINNOTT

Born 1947, Maesteg, Wales

Training

1967-68	Cardiff College of Art and Design
1968-71	Gloucestershire College of Art and Design
1971-74	Royal College of Art, London

One Person Exhibitions

1980	House Gallery, London
	Ikon Gallery, Birmingham
1981	Riverside Studios, London
	Gallery Gwyn Hodges, Oxford
	St Pauls Gallery, Leeds
1982	Blond Fine Art, London
1983	House Gallery, London
1984	Chapter Art Centre, Cardiff
	Blond Fine Art, London
1986	Bernard Jacobson Gallery, London
1987	Jan Turner Gallery, Los Angeles
	Bernard Jacobson Gallery, London and New York
1988	Roger Ramsay Gallery, Chicago
	Bernard Jacobson Gallery, New York
1990	Anne Berthoud Gallery, London
	Bernard Jacobson Gallery, London
1992	Flowers East, London
1993	*Recollections* Flowers Graphics, London
1994	Flowers East, London
1996	Martin Tinney Gallery, Cardiff
	Galeri Henrik Kampmann, Copenhagen
	Flowers East, London

BIOGRAPHICAL OUTLINES

Group Exhibitions

1978	Whitechapel Open, London
	John Moores, Liverpool
1979	Open Studio Show, Berry Street, London
1980	Whitechapel Open, London
	John Moores, Liverpool (Prize Winner))
1981	Ruskin School of Art, Oxford
1982	St. Martin's Painters
	Second International Drawing Triennial, Nuremberg
1982-85	Blond Fine Art, London
1986	L.A. Louver Gallery, Los Angeles, U.S.A
	Bernard Jacobson Gallery, London
1987	Koplin Gallery, Los Angeles, U.S.A
	Bernard Jacobson Gallery, New York, U.S.A
	British Figurative Painting, Pamela Auchincloss, New York, tour
	The Self Portrait: A Modern View, Artsite Gallery, Bath and tour
1988	*The New British Painting*, The Contemporary Art Centre, Cincinnati
	Mother and Child, Lefevre Gallery, London
1989	Bernard Jacobson Gallery, London
1990	*Contemporary Vision*, Contemporary Art Centre, Cincinnati
1991	*Friends of John Jones*, John Jones, London
	Nudes, Watermans Arts Centre, London
	The Downeen Collection, Angela Flowers (Ireland) Inc, County Cork
	Seven City Artists, Tobacco Dock, London
1992	*Artists' Choice*, Flowers East, London
	Print Show, John Jones Gallery, London
	Print Show, Purdy Hicks Gallery, London
	Art LA, Los Angeles, U.S.A
1993	*Modern Graphic Art in Britain*, British Museum, London
	Contemporary Art at the Courtauld Institute, London
1994	Flowers East, London
	Martin Tinney Gallery, Cardiff
	Art New York International, U.S.A
	Art Miami, U.S.A
	Art Cologne, Germany
	Lineart, Ghent, Belgium
1995	Flowers East, London
	Martin Tinney Gallery, Cardiff
	FIAC, Paris, France
	Art 95, London
	Art Frankfurt, Germany
	Art Chicago, U.S.A
	An American Passion, The Susan Kasen Summer and Robert D. Summer Collection of Contemporary British Art, Glasgow Museum of Art and Royal College of Art, London
1996	Flowers East, London
	Martin Tinney Gallery, Cardiff
	Art Frankfurt, Germany
	Art Chicago, U.S.A

Collections

Arts Council of Great Britain; British Council; British Museum; Contemporary Art Society for Wales; Isle of Man Arts Council; Metropolitan Museum of Art, New York; National Museums & Galleries of Wales; Royal College of Art, London; Whitworth Art Gallery, Manchester; Wolverhampton City Art Gallery.

Studio

Pontrhyl, Maesteg

SHANI RHYS JAMES

Born 1953, Melbourne, Australia

Training

1972-73	Loughborough College of Art, Foundation Course
1973-76	St. Martin's School of Art, London,

One Person Exhibitions

1992	Beaux Arts, Bath
1993	Martin Tinney Gallery, Cardiff
	Blood Ties Wrexham Library Arts Centre and touring
1994	Glynn Vivian Art Gallery, Swansea
	Midlands Art Centre, Birmingham
	Newport Museum and Art Gallery
	Carmarthen Art Gallery
1995	Martin Tinney Gallery, Cardiff
1996	*Re-Visions, Fettered Past*, Midlands Art Centre, Birmingham
1997	Mostyn Art Gallery, Llandudno and touring

Group Exhibitions

1974	Royal Court Theatre, in conjunction with *The Life Class*
	New Contemporaries, touring
1976	New Contemporaries,touring
	I.L.E.A. Travelling Exhibition to South Korea
1982	Royal Academy Summer Exhibition
	Tower Hamlets Picture Loan Exhibition
	Whitechapel Open Show, Whitechapel Art Gallery, London
1984	Royal Academy Summer Exhibition
1988	*Images of Childhood.* Workshop Gallery, Chepstow.
1989	*Wales Open,* Aberystwyth Arts Centre
1990	Two Person Show, Oriel Theatr Clwyd
	Child's Play, Piece Hall Art Gallery, Halifax
	Wales Open, Aberystwyth Arts Centre
	Kivert Gallery, Clyro
	Probity of Virtue, Mostyn Art Gallery, Llandudno
1991	*Under the Eye of Saturn*, Mostyn Art Gallery
1992	Hunting / *Observer* Art Prize Exhibition, Mall Galleries, London, tour
	Two Person Show, Aberystwyth Arts Centre
	Beaux Arts, Bath
	Royal National Eisteddfod, Ceredigion
	Martin Tinney Gallery, Cardiff
1993	Hunting / *Observer* Art Prize Exhibition, Mall Galleries, London and City Art Gallery, Bath
	Exhibition of Welsh Artists in San Francisco
	Hay-on-Wye Festival of Literature
	Royal National Eisteddfod, Powys
	Reclaiming the Madonna, Artists as Mothers, Usher Gallery, Lincoln, tour
1994	Martin Tinney Gallery, Cardiff and at Islington Art Fair
	Hunting / *Observer* Winners Exhibition, Royal College of Art
	Artists at Work Exhibition, Walker Art Gallery, Liverpool
	Disclosure(s), Mostyn Art Gallery, Llandudno, Welsh tour and Caixa de Terrassa, Barcelona
	Members Touring Exhibition, RCA Conwy, National Museum of Wales
	56 Group, Libramont, Belgium
1995	*Art 95,* Islington Art Fair with Martin Tinney Gallery
	Intimate Portraits, Glyn Vivian Art Gallery, Swansea and tour
	56 Group, Moscow and Old Library, Cardiff

	Visions, R.C.A. touring exhibition
	Museum of Modern Art, Machynlleth
	Ghent Art Fair, Belgium with Martin Tinney Gallery
1996	Hunting Art Prizes, Winners Exhibition, Royal College of Art
	Art 96 Islington Art Fair with Martin Tinney Gallery
	Connaught Brown Gallery, London
	Carlow Art Festival, Ireland
	The Art of the Possible, Viramu Jones Gallery, Cardiff and tour
	Harlech Biennale
	56 in 96, Turner House Gallery, Cardiff
1997	*In the Looking Glass*, Usher Gallery, Lincoln and tour

Publications (selected)
'A Day in the Life of' Shani Rhys James. *Art News*, 1992
Reclaiming the Madonna. Susan Wilson. Lincolnshire Co. Co. Exhibition Catalogue. 1993
Blood Ties. Edward Lucie-Smith. Wrexham Arts Centre Catalogue, 1993, illus.
Art Today. Edward Lucie-Smith. Phaidon, 1995, illus.
Shani Rhys James. Sister Wendy Beckett. *Modern Painters*, Autumn 1995, illus.
In the Looking Glass, Usher Gallery Catalogue, Lincoln. Text by Judith Collins, illus. 1996

Awards

1985	Welsh Arts Council setting up grant
1989	First Prize, Wales Open, Aberystwyth Arts Centre
1990	Second Prize, Wales Open, Aberystwyth Arts Centre
1991	First Prize, Mostyn Open, Oriel Mostyn, Llandudno
1992	Gold Medal for Fine Art, Royal National Eisteddfod
1992-93	Welsh Arts Council Travel Award to Tuscany and Umbria
1993	First Prize, Hunting / *Observer* Art Awards
1994	Second Prize, BP National Portrait Award
	Winner of the BBC Wales Visual Artist of the Year Award

Collections
National Museums & Galleries of Wales, Cardiff; Glyn Vivian Gallery, Swansea; Newport Museum & Art Gallery; Contemporary Art Society for Wales; Usher Gallery, Lincoln; London Borough of Tower Hamlets; BBC Wales and private collections throughout the world.

Studio
Dolpebyll, Llangadfan, Powys

JOHN KNAPP-FISHER

Born 1931, London

Training
Graphic Design, Maidstone College of Art

One Person Exhibitions (selected)

1960	Archer Gallery, London
1963, 64, 66	Aldeburgh Festival Gallery
1965	The Minories, Colchester
1966-onwards	David Griffiths Gallery, Cardiff (later the Albany Gallery)
1974	Haverfordwest Museum
1976	The Pavilion - Cheyne Walk, London
1980	Workshop Wales, Fishguard
1980, 81	Century Gallery, Henley-on-Thames

1982	Queen Elizabeth Medical Centre, Birmingham
1983	Aldeburgh Cinema Gallery
1984	Falcon House Gallery, Suffolk
	Sessions House Gallery. Newport Pembrokeshire
1988	Century Gallery, Henley-on-Thames
1989	*A Retrospective* Carmarthen College of Art
1992	*25th Anniversary Exhibition* Trevigan Cottage Gallery
1995	Senecio Press, Charlbury, Oxford

Group Exhibitions (selected)

1960-61	Kensington Art Gallery, London
1961	Ashgate Gallery, Farnham
1960, 61, 63, 82, 83	Summer Exhibitions, Royal Academy of Arts, London
1966 onwards	David Griffiths Gallery, Cardiff
1967	*English Landscape* Upper Grosvenor Galleries, London
1968, 69, 71, 72	-Attic Gallery, Swansea
1969	*200 years of English Watercolours* Margorie Parr Gallery, London
	Summer Exhibition Royal West of England Academy
1971	*Dylan Thomas Country* Upper Grosvenor Galleries, London
1978, 79, 80, 81	Business Art Galleries, Royal Academy, London
1980	Fry Gallery, London
1981	*Shadow Of My Hand* Oriel, Cardiff
1982	Phoenix Gallery, Lavenham
	National Eisteddfod, Swansea
1983	Bankside Gallery, London
	Alpine Gallery, London
1984	*Pembrokeshire Artists* Dyfed Museums
	Hill Court Gallery, Abergavenny
1988	Ayling Porteaus Gallery, Chester
1990	New Gallery, Mumbles
1992, 93, 97	Royal Cambrian Academy, Conwy
1993, 95, 96	Martin Tinney Gallery, Cardiff
1993, 95, 96	Riverside Gallery, Crickhowell
1994	National Museums & Galleries of Wales, Royal Cambrian tour
1995	Bank Street Gallery, Sevenoaks

Publications

A History of Firearms, written and illustrated. Maidstone College of Art 1957
Churches of Pembrokeshire, M. Fitzgerald. Rosedale Publications, 1989.
John Knapp-Fisher's Pembrokeshire, written and illustratedt. Senecio Press, 1995

Collections

Private and public collections throughout the world.

Studio

Trevigan, Pembrokeshire

ERNEST ZOBOLE

Born 1927, Rhondda, Wales

Training

1948-53	Cardiff College of Art

One Person Exhibitions (selected)

1964	Piccadilly Gallery, London
1967	Piccadilly Gallery, London

1968	Summer Arts Festival, Dynevor Castle, Dyfed
1978	Oriel, Cardiff
	North Gwent Arts Festival
1981	St Donat's Art Centre, Wales
1984	Bridge Gallery, Polytechnic of Wales
1986	Newport Art Gallery, Gwent, Wales
1988	St, David's Hall, Cardiff
1989	Ceri Richard's Gallery, University of Swansea
1990	Alcuin College, University of York
1991	Circle Gallery, Pontypridd, Wales
1992	Rhondda Heritage Park, Wales
1994	Martin Tinney Gallery, Cardiff
1997	Martin Tinney Gallery, Cardiff

Group Exhibitions (selected)

1962	9th Annual Exhibition of Welsh Painting and Sculpture WAC, tour
1963	10th Annual Exhibition of Welsh Painting and Sculpture
1965	*11 Welsh Painters,* Jefferson Place Gallery, Washington
1969	*Wales Now*, Welsh Arts Council
	Today, 56 Group
1971	*Art Spectrum Wales*, UK Art Exhibition
1973	*Wales and the Modern Movements* Aberstywyth University
1976	*20th Anniversary Exhibition* Group 56
1979	The Cleveland International Drawing Biennial
1980	*The Probity of Art* Welsh Arts Council
1981	*The Dark Hills, The Heavy Clouds* WAC touring exhibition
1985	*Focus on Landscape*, Western Australia,
1987	*Celtic Vision, artists from Spain, Scotland, Ireland and Wales*
	50th Anniversary Exhibition Contemporary Art Society for Wales
	25 Years Anniversary Exhibition, Attic Gallery, Swansea
1988	*Celtic Vision Invitation Exhibition* Dublin
1992	*30 Years Past and Present* Attic Gallery, Swansea
1997	Exhibited with the Welsh Group in Glasgow
	The Welsh Group, European Parliament, Strasbourg

Publications

Arthur Giardelli: An Evening with Ernest Zobole, *Anglo-Welsh Review*, Vol.13, No.32

Awards

1965	Welsh Arts Council bursary

Collections

National Museums & Galleries of Wales; Welsh Arts Council; University College, Aberstwyth; University College, Swansea; University College, Bangor; Contemporary Art Society for Wales; Contemporary Art Society; St. David's Centre, Cardiff; South Glamorgan Education Authority; Clare College, Cambridge; Newport Museum & Art Gallery and private collections worldwide.

Studio

Penrhys, the Rhondda.

IWAN BALA

Born 1956, Sarnau near Bala

Training

1974	University of Wales, Aberystwyth

1975-76	Chester College of Art
1976-78	Cardiff College of Art

One Person Exhibitions (selected)

1985	Sherman Theatre, Cardiff
1987	The Old Hall Gallery, Cardiff
1988	Theatre y Dolman, Newport
1989	*Reflections from the Western Shore*, Oriel Bangor, North Wales
1990	National Gallery of Zimbabwe, Zimbabwe
1991	*Lost Landscapes*, Oriel y Bont
1992	*Codi, Cario, Creu*, Y Bala, North Wales
1993	*Hiraeth* Oriel, Cardiff
1994	*Hiraeth* Wrexham Library Arts Centre
1995	*Edge of Land/Min Y Tir* Cardiff Bay Arts Trust
1996	*Panorama* Studio 8, Wrexham College of Art, North Wales

Group Exhibitions

1983	Llanover Hall Arts Centre
1984	Caernarfon Library and Oriel Mon, Llangrfni, North Wales
1985	*Furniment* Woodwharf Gallery, Greenwich, London
1986	Three Artists, Plas Glyn-y-Weddw, North Wales
1987	National Eisteddfod of Wales, Porthmadog
	Four Artists, Cafe Gallery, London
1988	*The State of Wales,* Cwmbran, Wales
	National Eisteddfod of Wales, Newport
1989	*Gweled Artists* Gregynog, Powys
	Armed of Dreams, West Wharf Gallery, Cardiff
	National Eisteddfod of Wales, Llanrwst
1990	Gallery Delta, Zimbabwe
	National Eisteddfod of Wales, Rhymni Valley
1991	*A View of Wales* Swansea Arts Workshop
	National Eisteddfod of Wales, Mold
	Trosi/Trasnu, Bank of Ireland Exhibition Centre, Cork, Dublin, Swansea Arts Workshop
1992	Chapter Arts Centre, Cardiff
1993	The Welsh Group, Newport Museum and Art Gallery
1994	*Site-Ations* the Artist Project, Cardiff
1995	*Intimate Portraits* Glynn Vivian Gallery, Swansea
	Standpoints Wrexham Library Arts Centre
1996	*Site-Ations 96* the Artists Project, Cardiff
	National Eisteddfod of Wales, Neath
1996	*Trans-Formations* The Artists Museum, Poland
	6X6, Gallerie Die Queeste, Belgium
1997	The Rotunda Gallery, Hong Kong
	Borders The Museum of Modern Art, Croatia
	The Welsh Group, European Parliament, Strasbourg

Awards

1988, 89, 93	Prizewinner, Royal National Eisteddfod
1990	Welsh Arts Council travel grant to Zimbabwe
1997	Gold Medal for Fine Art, Royal National Eisteddfod

Collections

The Welsh Museum of Modern Art, Mid Wales; S4C and Ffilm Cymru; National Gallery of Zimbabwe; The Welsh Language Board; private collections worldwide.

Studio

Canton, Cardiff

INDEX

INDEX